The Biology of Religious Behavior

The Evolutionary Origins of Faith and Religion

Edited by Jay R. Feierman

PRAEGER

An Imprint of ABC-CLIO, LLC

A B C · C L I O

Santa Barbara, California • Denver, Colorado • Oxford, England

Library of Congress Cataloging-in-Publication Data

The biology of religious behavior : the evolutionary origins of faith and religion / edited by Jay R. Feierman.
    p. cm.
    Proceedings of a symposium held in July 2008 at the University of Bologna, Italy.
    Includes bibliographical references and index.
    ISBN 978–0–313–36430–3 (hard copy : alk. paper) — ISBN 978–0–313–36431–0 (ebook)
1. Psychology, Religious—Congresses. 2. Human evolution—Religious aspects—Congresses. I. Feierman, Jay R.
BL53.B4655 2009
200.1'9—dc22   2009010608

13 12 11 10 9   1 2 3 4 5

This book is also available on the World Wide Web as an eBook.
Visit www.abc-clio.com for details.

ABC-CLIO, LLC
130 Cremona Drive, P.O. Box 1911
Santa Barbara, California 93116-1911

This book is printed on acid-free paper ∞

Manufactured in the United States of America

*To all whose lives
have been
affected by religion.*

Contents

Preface

The firstborn child of two young parents is born prematurely. The pediatrician tells her parents that she has a 50:50 chance of surviving. Her father, who previously had not considered himself a religious man, looks upward with tears in his eyes and says, "Please God. Don't let her die." A middle-aged man dressed in a dark business suit sits in the first row at the funeral parlor staring ahead at the mahogany casket containing the remains of his mother. His wife sits next to him with her arm around his shoulder trying to comfort him. His sorrow is consoled by the minister saying that his mother is now in heaven with her maker.

An old orthodox Jewish rabbi, who as a young man was liberated from Mauthausen concentration camp, explains that during that terrible time in his life when everything else in the world had been taken from him, all he had was God. A thirty-some–year-old Navajo Indian woman, who outwardly seems quite acculturated, is told by the Indian Health Service doctor that she has cervical cancer and needs surgery. She asks if the surgery could be postponed for a week so that she can have a traditional Navajo healing ceremony first.

A young Balinese Hindu man walks toward the grave of his father who, six months earlier, was buried in a temporary-grave area near the cremation grounds because the family did not have enough money for a cremation ceremony. On the way he buys a cup of hot coffee at a small roadside stand. He takes the Styrofoam cup with the hot coffee to his father's grave, carefully stirring in the milk and sugar as he walks. He stops and lights a cigarette. He kneels and then places the steaming hot coffee and the lit cigarette on the ground at the head of his father's grave. He bows his head and softly says something in the ancient Balinese language. A short silence follows. When asked what he just said, he responds in English, "For you papa."

All of these vignettes[1] show just how good, helpful, and comforting religion can be to human beings.

Yet, there is another less uplifting aspect of religion that also has to be addressed. It is that "the identification with values of a community, be they religious, party-political or ethno-nationalistic . . . have led to the most atrocious bloodshed in our history."[2] During the ten years since these words were written, the three types of community values referred to in the quote—religious, party-political, and ethno-nationalistic—seem to have undergone a change in relative importance. Party-political and ethno-nationalistic community values, which had been the main forces dividing the world in the twentieth century—as evidenced by two world wars plus the Cold War— have been partly overshadowed by community values associated with religion.

Religious communities, like all communities, have shared systems of beliefs, values, and behaviors that act as "in-group markers." Like most in-group markers familiar to anthropologists, they separate humanity into "we and others." If that is correct, then the often-quoted statement of John Cardinal Newman (1801–1890), "Oh, how we hate one another for the love of God,"[3] is somewhat of a misnomer. "We" do not hate ourselves! It is "other" in "an-*other*" to whom that famous statement really refers. The out-group "other" has the potential to become the object of the in-group's hate. "Oh, how we hate *others* for the love of God" has much more historical resonance.

We will show in this book how religion binds together and creates the "we" of a single religious community. It is the inevitable religious differences that create the "others," which are different religious communities. These differences have in the twenty-first century become associated with the number one national security concern for all of us, irrespective of what nation we call our home. But we must take first things first. To understand religious differences, we first must better understand religion, which is the primary objective of this book.

All of the book's contributors share the belief that the world is dangerously divided on the basis of religious differences and that neither religion nor science is going to bridge this divide alone. The contributors hope that the collaborative effort between the biobehavioral sciences and religion in this book will make at least a small contribution toward bridging the religious divide.

At the broad level of the biobehavioral sciences, what divides the major religions of the world is far smaller than what unites them. However, this similarity is a "double edged sword" because it also fosters competition. In many parts of the world people of the same religion who pray together tend to lay together. They then have children together. They become an in-group "breeding population," which then competes with other in-group breeding populations for the same limited resources. An awareness of some of these issues having to do with in-group/out-group and cooperation/competition, which we cover in the book, may be at least one small step toward understanding some of the religious-based differences dividing us.[4]

The realization of the need to better understand religion for all of our lives is what led most of the contributors of this book to come together for a symposium on the biology of religious behavior at the University of Bologna, Italy, in July 2008, as part of a larger international conference on human behavioral biology. That symposium provided the inspiration for this book.

We wish to thank a number of people whose work and help made this book possible: the organizers[5] and scientific and program committee[6] of the human behavioral biology conference[7] at the University of Bologna; numerous reviewers of earlier drafts of the book; Irenäus Eibl-Eibesfeldt, the "father of human ethology," who pioneered the application of behavioral biology to humans and whose eightieth birthday we celebrated in Bologna.[8] We especially want to thank Praeger Senior Acquisitions Editor Suzanne Staszak-Silva, who believed in the value of our project, and Kathy Breit, who helped to turn it into this book.

NOTES

1. None of these vignettes are fictional. They have all been experienced by the editor; one was experienced personally and the others were experienced as an observer.

2. Eibl-Eibesfeldt, I., & Salter, F. K. (1998). "Introduction." In I. Eibl-Eibesfeldt & F. K. Salter (Eds.), *Ethnic conflict and indoctrination: Altruism and identity in evolutionary perspective* (p. 1). New York: Berghahn Books. See also MacNeill, A. D. (2006). The capacity for religious experience is an evolutionary adaptation to warfare. In M. Fitzduff & C. Stout (Eds.), *The psychology of resolving global conflicts: From war to peace. Volume 1* (pp. 257–284). Westport, CT: Praeger Security International.

3. John Cardinal Newman, XIX Century.

4. Eibesfeldt, I. (1998). Us and others: The familiar roots of ethnona-tionalism. In I. Eibesfeldt & F. K. Salter (Eds.), *Ethnic conflict and indoctrina-tion: Altruism and identity in evolutionary perspective* (pp. 21–53). New York: Berghahn Books.

5. Marco Costa, Pio Enrico Ricci Bitti, and Luca Tommasi.

6. Wulf Schiefenhövel, Martin Brüne, and Astrid Juette.

7. The XIX Biennial Conference of the International Society for Human Ethology (ISHE).

8. Eibl-Eibesfeldt, I. (1989). *Human ethology*. New York: Aldine de Gruyter.

Introduction

The study of religion has traditionally been carried out by the disciplines of theology, religious studies, psychology, sociology, and cultural anthropology.[1] However, over the past several decades, new disciplines such as evolutionary psychology, cognitive science, cognitive anthropology, and philosophy of mind also have begun studying religion with interesting and informative results.[2] All of these new disciplines have approached the study of religion by using the Theory of Evolution by natural selection of Charles Darwin (1809–1882)[3] to try to understand religion itself. They have done this by exploring whether religion might aid in survival, if religion utilizes evolved cognitive mechanisms, and if religious teachings might themselves have evolved culturally within a society. This application of Darwinism to religion has been very timely, as it is being done at the same time as the world is preparing to mark the 200th anniversary of Darwin's birth with numerous international commemorative lectures, conferences, and celebrations. By coincidence, this birth anniversary falls quite close to the 150th anniversary of the publication of Darwin's greatest work, *On the Origin of Species* (1859).[4]

To those readers who view Darwinism and religion as mutually incompatible, studying religion from a Darwinian perspective may seem odd, even perverse. The popular media often portray Darwinism and religion as adversaries locked in battle with one another for the hearts and minds of school-age children. In actuality and with a few notable exceptions,[5] the community of scholars who bring Darwinian concepts to bear in studying religion[6] see no such adversarial relationship; and, none is seen either by some influential ordained ministers who are trying to reconcile evolution and religion from the pulpit.[7]

Using Darwinian Theory to understand religion is finally becoming acceptable in both scientific and religious circles.[8]

Such reconciling trends are evident within this book in which a number of contributors present intriguing, nonadversarial aspects of the interface between religion and Darwinism. It is hoped that this approach will be acceptable even to readers who hold religious beliefs that are in conflict with other aspects of Darwinian Theory. These chapters are not so much about the current debate between religious creationists and Darwinists over the origins of life on earth. Rather, Darwin's ideas are used as a general theoretical framework for understanding some aspects of religion itself. This is not to say that all of religion can be understood through the Darwinian lens, as one of the book's contributors, a respected theologian, argues cogently; but it is to see Darwinism as a valuable tool, among others. Hopefully, readers will appreciate that the approach taken in the book is part of an ongoing and fruitful dialog between science and religion.[9]

The contributors to *The Biology of Religious Behavior* are, as the title suggests, endeavoring to understand one important aspect of religion, religious behavior.[10] Religious behavior lends itself well to scientific study because it is readily observable. Religious behavior also lends itself to understanding important nonbehavioral aspects of religious experience, for when one starts with behavior, other aspects of faith and religion—including beliefs, values, moods, and feelings—often come into sharp focus. Studying religious behavior can thus serve as an empirical starting point for exploring the phenomenon of religion itself.

The book takes a broad perspective on religion—looking at religion across time, cultures, and even species. This perspective is quite different from that of most individuals, who understandably view religion "close up," with heavy emphasis on their own particular religion. Yet, as the contributors hope to show, much of what is seen at the level of a particular religion can also be understood from a broader perspective, because particular religions often demonstrate variation on a common theme. The existence of common themes, which we attempt to elucidate in this book, allows one to make generalities across religions that can only be recognized from such a broad perspective. As some of these common themes emerge, they are used as ways to try to understand all religions. This is a daunting task, as there are always exceptions. The exceptions are noted where known, but some most certainly have been overlooked.

The overall perspective in the book has been influenced by the discipline of *ethology*, which means "the biology of behavior."[11] The organization of the book and some of the methods used in the book follow the approach of Nobel Laureate ethologist Niko Tinbergen (1907–1988).[12] His method always began by observing and describing behavior, and then asking four specific questions: What is the behavior's evolutionary history? When and how does the behavior develop during the life of the individual? What are the behavior's immediate, mechanistic causes? What are the adaptive (reproductive and survival) values of the behavior, or can the behavior have adaptiveness?

In line with Tinbergen's approach, this book opens in Part One with a description of religious behavior, with the next four parts addressing the four key questions. The last part of the book contains a concluding chapter that explores several biobehavioral aspects of religious behavior that were not covered fully in earlier sections. The conclusion also emphasizes key points, tries to encourage interested readers to pursue some of the suggestions for further study, and outlines what needs to be done in the future and how it might be done. As for the types of material covered, the book contains reviews of some of the existing literature on aspects of religion, as well as original research material not previously published. To make the book more readable and interesting, emphasis is placed on religions that are most familiar to English-speaking readers.

What is presented in this book is clearly only an introduction to the biology of religious behavior. And religious behavior—though a starting point for broad study—is only one component of religion. We hope that by keeping a relatively tight focus on religious behavior we have complemented studies of religion from other perspectives. The contributors sincerely hope that all who read this book will be informed, that some will be inspired, and that at least a few will be motivated to undertake their own explorations of religion, including from the perspective of behavioral biology.

NOTES

1. As examples of classical works from traditional disciplines: Aquinas, T. (1948). *Summa theologiae* (5 vols.). Notre Dame, IN: Ave Maria Press. [Translation of the first complete edition from 1485]; Hinnells, J. R. (Ed.). (1998). *The new Penguin handbook of living religions*. London: Penguin Books; James, W. (1902). *The varieties of religious experience: A study in human nature.*

New York: Modern Library; Stark, R., & Bainbridge, W. S. (1987). *A theory of religion*. Bern and New York: Peter Lang; Banton, M. (Ed.). (1966). *Anthropological approaches to the study of religion*. London: Tavistock.

2. As examples of works from newer disciplines: Kirkpatrick, L. (2004). *Attachment, evolution, and the psychology of religion*. New York: Guilford Press; Boyer, P. (2001). *Religion explained: The evolutionary origins of religious thought*. New York: Basic Books; Atran, S. (2002). *In gods we trust: The evolutionary landscape of religion*. New York: Oxford University Press; Dennett, D. C. (2006). *Breaking the spell: Religion as a Natural phenomenon*. New York: Viking. See also Wenegrat, B. (1990). *The divine archetype: The sociobiology and psychology of religion*. Lexington, MA: Lexington Books.

3. For those readers not familiar with the evolutionary literature, the sequence by which Darwinian natural selection changes the frequency of genes in a population over time and by which populations evolve is as follows: random genetic mutation, structural variation, and selection of the fittest in a specific environment. This is not a completely random process, as survival of the fittest is not random. Any modern textbook of biology will contain more details about this sequence.

4. Darwin, C. (1859). *On the origin of species by means of natural selection*. London: John Murray.

5. Probably the most cited is Dawkins, R. (2006). *The God delusion*. New York: Houghton Mifflin Co. For a rebuttal of Dawkins, see McGrath, A. (2005). *Dawkin's god: Genes, memes, and the meaning of life*. Malden, MA: Blackwell Publishing.

6. Bulbia, J., Sosis, R., Harris, E., Genet, R., Genet, C., & Wyman, K. (2008). *The evolution of religion: Studies, theories, & critiques*. Santa Margarita, CA: Collins Foundation Press; Voland, E., & Schiefenhövel, W. (2009). *The biological evolution of religious mind and behavior*. New York: Springer-Verlag.

7. Dowd, M. (2007). *Thank God for evolution: How the marriage of science and religion will transform your life and our world*. New York: Viking/Plume.

8. There is a long tradition of cooperation and interaction between science and religion, as is evidenced by the Society for Scientific Study of Religion (SSSR) that was founded in 1949. Most of the research papers represented at the annual meetings of this society are from individuals in the more traditional disciplines that study religion, especially sociology. However, over the past few years there has been a small number of papers presented from individuals representing some of the newer disciplines using a Darwinian approach.

9. McNammare, P. (Ed.). (2006). *Where God and science meet: How Brain and evolutionary studies alter our understanding of religion* (3 vols.). Westport, CT: Praeger.

10. The word "behavior" has been used in various ways by both scholars and lay speakers. Contributors to this book were not required to use any

particular definition in their chapters. Some of the authors indicate a preferred definition either explicitly or implicitly; others do not; but in all cases,
the word "behavior" is used in ways that conform more or less to the
common meaning of the term. Some of the more authoritative definitions
and descriptions of behavior that are used in the biobehavioral sciences follow in chronological order:

Watson, J. B. (1924). *Behaviorism*. Chicago: The University of Chicago
Press. "what the organism does or says" (p. 6).

Skinner, B. F. (1938). *The behavior of organisms: An experimental analysis*.
New York: Appleton-Crofts, Inc. "what an organism is doing—or more
accurately what it is observed by another organism to be doing ... the
movement of an organism or of its parts in a frame of reference provided by the organism itself or by various external objects or fields of
force" (p. 6).

Tinbergen, N. (1951). *The study of instinct*. New York: Oxford University
Press. "the total of movements made by the intact animal" (p. 2).

Martin, P., & Bateson, P. (1986). *Measuring behavior: An introductory guide*.
Cambridge, U.K.: Cambridge University Press. "the actions and reactions of whole organisms" (p. 2).

Immelmann, K., & Beer, C. (1989). *A dictionary of ethology*. Cambridge,
MA: Harvard University Press. "What ethologists study in animals ...
change of position of parts of the body relative to other parts and to
environmental coordinates ... [or] ... in terms of consequences or the
outcome aimed at" (p. 27).

11. See Eibl-Eibesfeldt, I. (1975). *Ethology: The biology of behavior*, 2nd
ed. New York: Holt, Rinehart & Winston.
12. Tinbergen, N. (1951). *The study of instinct*. New York: Oxford University Press.

PART ONE

Description of Religious Behavior

In *ethology* (behavioral biology) the first step in understanding behavior is to observe and characterize (describe and define) it. Like almost everything biological, behavior can be characterized by its form or by its function. Once it has been so characterized, four questions follow: what is its evolutionary history, what is its development during the life span of the individual, what are the proximate (near) causes, and does the behavior have adaptiveness or survival value? In Part One, Chapter 1 describes religious behavior in societies of different socioecological and cultural complexity. Chapter 2 addresses the question of how we characterize a behavior as religious behavior. Chapter 3 addresses a little-studied aspect of religious behavior—the eyes. It addresses the question of why most Westerners close their eyes when they pray. Chapter 4 characterizes the control and development of religious behavior and shows what sacred narratives, such as the Holy Bible, and DNA molecules in biological cells may have in common.

CHAPTER 1

The Evolution of Religious Behavior in Its Socioecological Contexts

Stephen K. Sanderson

Despite the enormous amount of attention that has been devoted to the long-term evolution of human societies, especially their demographic, technological, economic, and political features, the evolution of religion has been little studied. Early anthropologists and sociologists, such as Sir Edward Burnett Tylor (1832–1917)[1] and Herbert Spencer (1820–1903),[2] were interested in the evolution of religion, but interest was sporadic after their time due to the critique of social evolutionism by the anthropologist Franz Boas and his school and the coming dominance of the functionalist anthropology of Bronislaw Malinowski and A. R. Radcliffe-Brown. There was a revival of interest in the 1960s, but this was barely followed up at all. Therefore, the only recent schemes of religious evolution remain those of Robert Bellah[3] and Anthony Wallace.[4]

Bellah distinguished five stages in his evolutionary scheme: *primitive religions*, which are found in preliterate bands, tribes, and chiefdoms; *archaic religions*, such as the early polytheistic religions of the Old and New Worlds; *historic religions*, which are the monotheistic world salvation religions; *early modern religion*, which was constituted by the Protestant Reformation and its aftermath; and *modern religion*, which is the religions of the twentieth century.

This typology is a useful one, but to my mind a somewhat more useful typology is that formulated by Wallace. According to Wallace, the religion of a society is made up of what he calls *cult institutions*. A cult institution is "a set of rituals all having the same general goal, all explicitly rationalized by a set of similar or related beliefs, and all supported by the same social group."[5] Wallace delineated four types of cult institutions: individualistic, in which individual persons perform their own private rituals; shamanic, in which a part-time religious practitioner (a shaman) performs special rites for others; communal, in which bodies of laypersons collectively perform calendrical and other religious rites (such as rites designed to ensure good harvests); and ecclesiastical, in which there are full-time priests who monopolize religious knowledge and perform highly specialized rituals before audiences of laypersons. Combinations of cult institutions yield four major stages in the evolution of religion: shamanic, communal, Olympian, and monotheistic. *Shamanic religions* contain only individualistic and shamanic cult institutions; religious practice beyond the level of the individual focuses solely on the conduct of a shaman and there are no calendrical rites. *Communal religions* contain individualistic, shamanic, and communal cult institutions, and religious practice focuses primarily on the conduct of laypersons engaged in collective calendrical rites, although shamanic rituals still exist and remain important. *Olympian religions* contain all four cult institutions, especially specialized priesthoods; numerous gods, usually organized in a hierarchical pantheon, are worshiped and worship is led by full-time priests. *Monotheistic religions* are like Olympian religions, except that worship focuses on a single god rather than a pantheon of specialized gods.

SHAMANIC RELIGIONS

Shamanic religions have individualistic and shamanic cult institutions, but nothing more. The shaman is usually the *only* religious practitioner. These religions occur primarily in hunter-gatherer societies that are organized into simple bands or tribes. In the *Standard Cross-Cultural Sample* (*SCCS*) of Murdock and White,[6] 63 percent of shamanic religions are found in hunter-gatherer societies and 83 percent in bands or tribes. Shamanic religions have been found in every major region of the world, and shamans continue to be found in societies at more advanced evolutionary stages.[7] It is this type of religion that would have characterized the vast majority of societies in the human ancestral environment. Shamanic religions thus constitute the primordial religion, and shamans the primordial religious specialists.

The Inuit provide a good example of a shamanic religion. They believe in a host of human and animal souls, local spirits, trolls, and a few higher gods, mainly Sedna the Keeper of the Sea Animals, the Sun, the Moon, and the Spirit of the Air. They have at least two individualistic cults, the Spirit Helper Cult (an individual's own guardian spirit) and the Game Animal Cult, both of which involve individual observances of taboos designed to avoid offending game animals. There is also a Shamanic Cult. Shamans make an annual trip to the bottom of the sea to get Sedna to release the game from her domain so the Inuit can live through the coming year. Shamans also are called upon to diagnose illness and to try to cure it by supernatural means.[8] The Lapps also have a shamanic religion. They believe in the existence of various spirits and recognize cosmological forces associated with animals, the weather, and space and time. There are shamans of both sexes who engage in healing practices and sorcery. Their most elaborate ritual is associated with the bear hunt.[9]

Shamans perform a variety of activities: healing and curing of illness, divination, protecting and finding game animals, communicating with the dead, recovering lost souls, and protecting people from evil spirits and the practitioners of malevolent magic. Shamans also go on "soul flights" and "vision quests." Shamanic rituals typically involve a great deal of rhythmic repetition, especially drumming and dancing, singing, and chanting, activities that are thought to induce altered states of consciousness and "anomalous experiences."[10] Considerable research indicates the existence of a so-called "shamanic syndrome" "characterized by hypnotizability, dissociative ability, propensity for anomalous experience . . . and fantasy proneness."[11] There are striking similarities among shamanistic practices all over the world.[12] These similarities suggest a common psychobiological basis to shamanic traditions, and thus that they are the result of independent invention rather than cultural diffusion.

There seems to be widespread agreement that the key shamanic ritual is the curing ceremony,[13] an event that anthropologist Michael Winkelman describes as of "unparalleled importance in hunter-gatherer societies."[14] In this ceremony the shaman incorporates the local community in activities imbued with a variety of emotional experiences, especially fear and awe. Shamans enact struggles of animals and spirits and summon their spirit allies who accompany them on their vision quests. They typically chant, sing, beat drums, and dance in violent and excited ways. After they collapse from exhaustion, they begin their magical flight into the spirit world, which involves ascending to the upper world and descending to the lower one in order to communicate with spirits and seek to obtain their co-operation in earthly matters.

Shamans claim to be able to control spirits, and their communities agree that they can. Shamanic curing assumes that illness is the result of people having lost their souls or that they are under the influence of ghosts, spirits, witches, or malevolent acts performed by other sha-mans. The altered states of consciousness that shamans undergo are trance-induced by means of hallucinogens or opiates and other drugs; through hunger, thirst, the loss of sleep, or other forms of sensory deprivation; or by extreme forms of sensory stimulation.

COMMUNAL RELIGIONS

Shamans do not disappear with the transition to agricultural soci-eties. They persist, at least in the slightly altered forms that Winkel-man[15] calls shaman/healers, healers, sorcerer/witches, and mediums. These new types of practitioners are not all that different, however; they engage in many of the same activities as the shaman, the most crucial of which is healing. Such practitioners continue to be found even in societies where ecclesiastical religions with formal religious doctrines and full-time priesthoods have developed. Indeed, even in affluent industrial societies a religious practitioner strikingly reminis-cent of the ancient shaman is found in the form of the "faith healer." However, communal religions add other kinds of ritual activities to shamanic rituals.

Communal religions are most common in the societies of the *SCCS* that practice extensive agriculture, with 52 percent of communal reli-gions found in societies with this mode of subsistence. Communal religions are most likely to be found in bands or tribes, although about a third of these religions are found in small chiefdoms. In communal religions we find individualistic and shamanic cult institutions operat-ing, but also communal cult institutions, which involve segments of a community coming together to engage in certain collective rituals. A good example is the Trobriand Islanders of Melanesia,[16] one of the best-known ethnographic cases of all time. The major communal cult institution is the Technological Magic Cult. Here persons carry out collective rituals presided over by a garden magician, who is likely to be the village chief, a canoe magician, and a fishing magician. The Trobrianders also have a Cult of the Spirits of the Dead, which carries out funerary services. There are also professional sorcerers, who can cause or cure illness, and individuals have their own personal use of magic to help them in matters of love and to protect them against malevolent spirits, flying witches, and other evil spirits.

The Mbuti of the Ituri rain forest of Africa, though hunter-gatherers, also have a communal religion. The Mbuti believe in a spirit who created the world, but who then withdrew from it and gave it no further attention. They also believe in a powerful forest spirit that has an influence on the souls of the dead. The Mbuti have shamans who are healers, and most Mbuti bands associate great hunting skill with supernatural abilities. Great hunters are thought to communicate with the supernatural and even make themselves invisible. The most important rituals are those associated with hunting, honey collection, and death. The frequency and intensity of hunting rituals relate to the uncertainty, danger, and difficulty of the hunt. The gathering of the first honey of the season leads to collective rituals involving music and dancing. Rituals performed after someone has died involve the participation of the forest spirit.[17]

Another major dimension of most communal religions is *ancestor worship*. Indeed, the spirits of the dead ancestors are often the key supernatural entities in such religions. Ancestor worship is likely to become of increased importance in communal religions because the societies in which such religions are most commonly found are usually organized into elaborate unilineal descent groups identified with a putative founding ancestor. Such groups require respect for ancestors, both living and dead. As authority figures, living ancestors are the sources of both rewards and punishments. It is not good form to offend them when they are living or when they pass into the realm of the dead.

POLYTHEISTIC RELIGIONS

The majority (50 percent) of Olympian (polytheistic) religions in the *SCCS* are found in societies that practice intensive agriculture, although almost as many (42 percent) are found in societies with extensive agriculture. Polytheistic religions may be found in bands or tribes (33 percent) or chiefdoms (25 percent), but more likely they are found in states (42 percent). Polytheistic religions have a pantheon of highly specialized gods and professional priesthoods who monopolize religious knowledge and lead elaborate rituals for a lay audience.

The gods of polytheistic religions are almost invariably very much like humans in their nature. Some are considered good, others evil; some are highly competent at what they do, whereas others are considered fools; the gods usually eat and drink and often have great banquets; they usually like sex and often have orgies; they also fight and go to war. Like humans, polytheistic gods are finite and mortal; they can be killed and even eaten.

Another feature of polytheistic religions is their ritualistic use of animal sacrifice. Indeed, this has been claimed as a universal feature of such religions.[18] Anthropologist Marvin Harris (1927–2001) commented that "Persians, Vedic Brahmans, Chinese, and Japanese all at one time or another ritually sacrificed domesticated animals. In fact, it would be difficult to find a single society in a belt across Eurasia and North Africa in which domesticated animal sacrifice was not part of state-supported cults." [19] The animals sacrificed are almost always highly valued domesticated animals, wild animals rarely if ever being objects of sacrifice because they are a free gift of nature.[20] In Arabia and much of North Africa, for example, camels were commonly sacrificed; bulls were important objects of sacrifice throughout the Mediterranean world, and pastoralists in Central Asia were noted for sacrificing horses.[21] Human blood has also been widely used in sacrifices[22] and, indeed, sometimes the animal being sacrificed is the human animal.

Perhaps the most famous polytheistic religions were those of the ancient Sumerians and Egyptians, the ancient Greeks (from whom Wallace derives the name Olympian), the ancient Romans, the Maya, the Aztecs, and the Incas. There seem to be two evolutionarily different types of polytheistic religion. Many polytheistic religions are found among extensive agriculturalists who are politically organized into tribes, chiefdoms, or small states. For example, the Ashanti of West Africa were organized politically at the state level. They worshiped a supreme being known as Nyame, the Sky God, who was regarded as aloof and thus as having little direct role in human destiny. There was a series of lesser gods who were thought to have been delegated their power by Nyame. There was also an Earth God, but he was less well known than Nyame. In addition to medicine men and witch doctors, the Ashanti recognized a special class of priests, who performed all ceremonies. The Ashanti constructed temples and shrines dedicated to Nyame, but there were no temples dedicated to the Earth God. The Inca of ancient Peru worshiped a creator god known as Viracocha, who was thought to have created the other supernatural beings. These included the Sun, the Weather God, and the moon, stars, earth, and sea. The highest priest was also a governmental official and a close relative of the emperor. The Incas built great temples and shrines and only priests were allowed to enter the holy temples. Sacrifice was an important part of all rituals.[23]

Then there are more "advanced" polytheistic religions found among intensive agriculturalists with more complex states. Here we find the religions of Eurasian antiquity. In East Eurasia, the Aryans who invaded India prior to the establishment of Hinduism believed in many gods, but four stood out in particular: Indra, the god of war and the weather; Varuna, who maintained morality and social order; Agni, the god of fire who had a close association with the priests who performed rituals using fire; and Soma, a plant god associated with a drink made from the soma plant and who was an integral part of another sacrificial cult.[24]

In West Eurasia at about the same time there were complex states with polytheistic religions. The Egyptians believed in a supreme power, or *neter*, who created the universe and a number of lesser gods, or *neteru*.[25] These included Horus, the falcon god; Re, the sun god; and Osiris, the god of vegetation.[26] Egyptian religion was actually a confusing and somewhat disorderly mixture of gods, each with its own priesthood.[27] The ancient Greeks worshiped a pantheon that included Zeus at the top; Phoebus, the god of light; Poseidon, the sea god; Aphrodite, the goddess of love; and Dionysus, the god of vegetation.[28] Polytheism among both the Egyptians and the Greeks was organized such that each city or city-state tended to focus its religious activity around one particular god. Thus, the Egyptian god Amon was the god of Thebes in Upper Egypt, and the Greek goddess Athena was the patron god of Athens.

In polytheistic societies that are highly stratified and organized politically into chiefdoms or states there is an important distinction between the religious practices of elites and those of the rest of society. This is a distinction between official and popular religion.[29] Non-elites may worship some of the same gods as elites, but their religious practices are separate and focused on their own spirits and deities. Families generally have their own shrines that are the focal point of ritual. In ancient Mesopotamia, for example, family religion combined ancestor worship with veneration of a family deity.[30] The noted British archaeologist Sir Charles Leonard Woolley (1880–1960) indicated that the "chapels in the private houses and the little clay figurines . . . which we find in the ruins of the houses and in the graves may simply mean more magic brought into the home, but equally they may bear witness to a faith more intimate, more simple, and more genuine than that contained in the elaborate sacrifices and set liturgies of the church."[31]

MONOTHEISTIC RELIGIONS

Historically, the major monotheistic religions all emerged during the period known as the Axial Age, which can be dated from about 600 BCE to 1 CE. It is at this time that Judaism shifted to the mono-theism focused on the One True God Yahweh and that we see the emergence of Hinduism and the Buddha in India and Confucius in China. Slightly later we see the emergence of Laozi and Taoism in China. Several hundred years later, of course, Christianity emerges out of Judaism, the result of messianic movements that had been occurring within Judaism for some two centuries. Islam is the last of the great monotheistic religions, but it is a bit of an outlier since it occurs so much later than the others, and to a large extent it was formed mainly as a sect of Christianity. Although converts to Christianity in its first centuries were mostly people living in urban areas, the West Eurasian peoples who developed Judaism, Christianity, and Islam were all intensive agriculturalists or pastoralists or practiced some combination of the two. The same is true for the East Eurasian peoples who developed Hinduism, Buddhism, Confucianism, and Taoism. (Actually, the first monotheistic religion was probably Zoro-astrianism, which is now dated to about 1200 BCE. It had a significant effect on both Judaism and Christianity. It is now a minor religion practiced only by a few million people in Iran.)

What was new in the major world religions that evolved and spread during the Axial Age? There were many important novelties, but the following seem most important:

1. In the polytheistic religions, the various gods were conceived as having human characteristics and desires, but the God of the monotheisms was a *transcendent* god that was little like humans. He was also omnipresent, omniscient, and omnipotent.

2. The monotheistic religions emphasized salvation from this world and God's love and mercy.

3. Although pre-Axial Age religions could sometimes have some very punitive elements, with the new monotheisms there was a

    dramatic increase in the controlling, demanding, and potential punitiveness of God.

4. Religious doctrines became much more elaborate.

5. There was a sharp decline in animal sacrifice.

6. Even though polytheistic priesthoods, such as existed in ancient Egypt, could be very powerful, in the monotheistic religions priests intensified their control over religious ritual and became much more powerful religious functionaries than in most of the polytheistic state religions.

As in the case of polytheistic religions, monotheistic religions have contained official and popular versions.[32] In preindustrial societies with monotheistic religions, the vast majority of the population are uneducated city dwellers or peasants. According to the influential German sociologist Max Weber (1864–1920), the peasantry is never a carrier of a major world religion.[33] For Weber, peasants remained bogged down in magic and animistic beliefs. In late medieval England, for example, many common people eschewed official Christianity in favor of magical healing, witchcraft, divination, astrology, and ghosts and fairies.[34]

THE SOCIOECOLOGICAL CONTEXT OF RELIGIOUS EVOLUTION

Stephen Sanderson and Wesley Roberts have carried out a study of the main predictors of religious evolution using an operationalized version of Wallace's typology and the *SCCS*.[35] The two best predictors were the mode of subsistence technology—how people go about the process of getting a living—and the presence or absence of writing and records. Together, just these two variables explained 65 percent of the variance in stages of religious evolution. Sanderson and Roberts regarded these variables as important social prerequisites of religious evolution. Ecclesiastical religions with professional priesthoods are not really possible until a society has developed a fairly intensive form of agriculture because large economic surpluses are needed to support specialized religious functionaries. Sanderson and Roberts found that many polytheistic religions are located in societies without writing, but the vast majority of monotheistic religions are found in societies with true writing. Priests are religious literati who form themselves into guilds and who monopolize religious knowledge and ritual.

However, Sanderson and Roberts regard their study as identifying only the *social prerequisites* of more advanced religions. We still need to understand in more specific terms why communal religions generally follow shamanic ones, why polytheistic religions come later in social evolution, and why polytheism eventually gave way to monotheism (although, of course, with a certain number of retrogressions back to polytheism here and there).

Communal religions are sometimes found among hunter-gatherers, but they become much more common with the shift to agriculture. How does this shift bring about the transition from shamanic to communal religions? Some of the most important rituals in communal religions are collective agricultural rites. In agricultural societies the rhythm of the seasons is of great importance and is thus given religious significance. According to the famed historian of religion Mircea Eliade (1907–1986), agricultural rites are "intended to assist the growth of cereals and hallow the work of the farmer."[36] Eliade adds that

> we can perceive that the endless variety of agricultural rites and beliefs all involve the recognition of a *force manifested in the harvest*. This "force" may be conceived as impersonal, like the "power" of so many things and actions, again it may be represented in mythical forms, or concentrated in certain animals or certain human beings. The rituals, whether simple or elaborated into complicated dramas, are intended to establish favourable relations between man and these "powers," and to ensure that the powers will continue to be regenerated from time to time.[37]

The gods of polytheistic religions are in all likelihood transformed versions of the gods and other supernatural beings found in shamanic and communal religions. But a major difference is that most gods in the latter religions take no real interest in human affairs. Polytheistic gods, by contrast, have intense interest in human affairs, and their worshipers try to appease them precisely because of this. These gods are greatly elevated in status compared to earlier gods or spirits, and their appeasement is undertaken by political rulers primarily to help them avoid harm and to achieve their most important goals, such as success in war. The priests of polytheistic religions either are closely allied with secular political rulers or *are* the political rulers themselves, which is why the polytheistic religions are often called *state religions*.

Again, it is important to keep in mind the distinction between official and popular religions discussed earlier.

And then why the transition to monotheism? What was happening around 600 BCE that would have changed or intensified people's religious needs? Space does not permit a detailed explication of my argument here,[38] but I emphasize the massive increase in the scale of war during the period of the Axial Age. The number of war deaths soared shortly after the beginning of the Axial Age, undergoing an 18-fold increase between the sixth and the fifth centuries BCE, and a dramatic 51-fold increase between the sixth and first centuries.[39] This dramatic increase in the scale of war created new needs for security and comfort. Many more people died, and many of those who lived were uprooted and displaced from their homes. One of the major themes of the emerging Axial Age religions was love and mercy: God's compassion.

Another major change that we see in the historical record in the time period after 600 BCE was a major increase in the level of urbanization. In the two centuries between 650 and 430 BCE, the number of cities of 30,000 or more inhabitants increased from 20 to more than 75.[40] The increase in urbanization created new religious needs in much the same way as the increase in warfare: rapid and large-scale urbanization was tremendously disruptive.[41] People's kin networks were disrupted and they were increasingly living in a world of strangers. During the period when Christianity arose, urban life was a source of chaos, misery, and crisis everywhere.[42] All of this led to higher levels of insecurity and anxiety, and an all-powerful, loving God was an excellent prescription for people's new sense of threat and danger.

SHAMANS, PRIESTS, AND PROPHETS

There have been essentially three major types of religious practitioners in world prehistory and history—shamans, priests, and prophets—and each is appropriate to a specific socioecological context. Shamans, as we have said, are the primordial type of practitioner. Priests are shamans transformed by the institutionalization of ecclesiastical religions. Although at first sight there would appear to be few similarities between priests and shamans, a closer look reveals some. Eliade calls shamans *psychopomps*, religious specialists who conduct souls to another world. But priests are psychopomps as well. Shamans do it through altered states of consciousness and ecstacy, whereas priests do it through urging individuals to accept and conform to elaborate doctrines. And there are other similarities. Shamans all over the world usually wear elaborate costumes, often adorned with feathers. This heightens their sense of importance, both to themselves and to their clients and audiences. Although most Christian denominations use distinctive ritual wear, Roman Catholic priests wear elaborate costumes, for example, the elegant robes, headgear, and other paraphernalia of the pope and cardinals. Once again the importance of the religious specialist is emphasized. In addition, the priests of the major world religions, like shamans everywhere, are concerned with suffering, misfortune, and tending to the sick. They are also concerned with restoring or saving souls.

Prophets tend to emerge under socioecological circumstances of massive disruption, suffering, and misery. They, like priests, are in essence shamans transformed by radically different socioecological circumstances, but in this case very different circumstances. The monotheistic religions were, by and large, brought into existence by the actions of prophets: Jesus in Christianity, the Buddha in Buddhism, Confucius in Confucianism, Mohammed in Islam, and so on. Of these and other prophets, perhaps the most stunning similarities between a prophet and a shaman were found in the case of Jesus Christ. Consider the following:

- Shamans often spend periods of time in seclusion undergoing intense ordeals, during which they hone their skills; Christ spent 40 days alone in the wilderness as part of his development.

- Shamans have special contact with the world of spirits; Christ was in direct contact with God the Father.

- Shamans above all heal and cure; Christ healed the sick and lame.

- Shamans enter the world of spirits and often ascend to the sky; Christ upon resurrection ascended to the sky.

- Potential shamans often undergo an initiatory ritual death from which they are resurrected; Christ, of course, is purported to have been resurrected.

- Shamans in some regions, such as Australia, undergo initiation in caves; Christ's body was put in a cave and he was resurrected in this cave.

- Shamans always have spirit helpers; Christ had "helpers" in the form of disciples, angels, etc.

- In their curing rituals shamans often look for the sick person's lost soul in order to restore it to the person; and, even though shamans attempt to achieve their effects in the here and now and Christ in the long hereafter, Christ saves your soul from eternal damnation.

Prophets are also found in so-called revitalization and millenarian movements, and these movements are most likely to occur during periods of major social disruption or stress. In the late nineteenth century in several islands in Melanesia, revitalization movements known as cargo cults appeared.[43] These movements prophesied that modern Western goods (cargo) were on their way to the indigenous societies for the benefit and enjoyment of their members. One cult was led by a prophet in Papua New Guinea named Evara, who claimed to have divine revelations. Similarly, on the island of Tanna in the New Hebrides a cargo cult formed around a prophet named John Frum. In the same century, well-known revitalization movements occurred among some North American Indian tribes.[44] The best known was the Ghost Dance, led by a prophet named Wodziwob, who prophesied a cataclysm in which the earth would open up and swallow the whites. Wodziwob's successor, Wovoka, prophesied that the whites would be blown away by high winds but that their possessions would remain for the benefit of the Indians. All of these movements occurred in situations in which European or Euro-American societies had set themselves up in a colonial or semicolonial situation in the lands of the indigenous peoples, and as a result severely disrupted their traditional ways of life and sense of security and well-being.

In addition to being transformed shamans, priests are also transformed prophets. New religions founded by prophets, if they do not die out, almost always become established and institutionalized. They experience what Max Weber[45] called the "routinization of charisma," and what Weber's student Ernst Troeltsch[46] identified as the transition from sect to church. Once this occurs, the new religion produces new priests, and they take over religious practices.

CONCLUSION: RELIGION'S TWIN EVOLUTIONARY FOUNDATIONS

Religion is an evolutionary phenomenon in a double sense, both biological and social. Winkelman and sociologist James McClenon contend that shamanism is neurophysiologically grounded, and McClenon has provided a plausible scenario for how shamanic rituals could have evolved by natural selection in the human ancestral environment, perhaps as early as 30,000 years ago. Along a different line, in recent years several scholars have noted a number of striking similarities between religious rituals and the emotional disorder known as Obsessive Compulsive Disorder (OCD).[47] There may be a "ritual module" in the brain that strongly predisposes humans to engage in collective religious rituals, and OCD may be a form of individual pathology that results when this module is somehow hyperactivated.

Discussion of the biological basis for various kinds of religious activity is grist for the mill of human ethology. However, even if religious impulses are grounded biologically, these impulses are greatly affected by the socioecological context in which people find themselves. And thus religion has evolved socially through a series of general stages, from the shamanic to the communal, the communal to the polytheistic, and the polytheistic to the monotheistic. Religious evolution did not end with the emergence of the monotheistic world salvation religions, for the monotheistic religions have themselves changed in various ways over time. Nevertheless, they have all remained monotheistic, and no new stage of religious evolution has been reached. It is therefore tempting to say that the transcendent monotheistic religions could represent the "final" stage of religious evolution. But then again, nothing lasts forever. The sociologist Daniel Bell declared in 1960 that we were seeing the "end of ideology,"[48] and more recently the political scientist Francis Fukuyama claimed that with modern liberal capitalism we had reached the "end of history."[49] The former has already been shown to be untrue, and the latter will certainly not prove to be true. There is no end of history, and thus there can be no end to the continued historical evolution of religion. It is difficult, of course, to predict what might lie ahead. After all, could ancient hunter-gatherers even remotely have imagined states and empires, let alone modern industrial capitalism and the world economy?

NOTES

1. Tylor, E. B. (1913). *Primitive culture: Researches into the development of mythology, philosophy, religion, language, art, and custom.* London: J. Murray.

2. Spencer, H. (1898). *The principles of sociology* (Vol. III). New York: D. Appleton & Co.

3. Bellah, R. N. (1964). Religious evolution. *American Sociological Review, 29*, 358–374.

4. Wallace, A. F. C. (1966). *Religion: An anthropological view*. New York: Random House.

5. Ibid., 75.

6. Murdock, G. P., & White, D. R. (1969). Standard Cross-Cultural Sample. *Ethnology, 8*, 329–369.

7. Eliade, M. (1964). *Shamanism: Archaic techniques of ecstasy*. Trans. W. R. Trask. Princeton, NJ: Princeton University Press; Walter, M. N., & Fridman, E. J. N. (2004). *Shamanism: An encyclopedia of world beliefs, practices, and cultures* (Vol. 1). Santa Barbara, CA: ABC-CLIO.

8. Wallace, *Religion: An anthropological view*.

9. O'Leary, T., & Levinson, D. (Eds.). (1990). *Encyclopedia of world cultures* (Vol. 4). Boston: G. K. Hall.

10. Winkelman, M. J. (1990). Shamans and other "magico-religious" healers: A cross-cultural study of their origins, nature, and social transformations. *Ethos, 18*, 308-352; Winkelman, M. J. (2000). *Shamanism: The neural ecology of consciousness and healing*. Westport, CT: Bergin & Garvey.

11. McClenon, J. (2002). *Wondrous healing: Shamanism, human evolution, and the origin of religion* (p. 134). DeKalb: Northern Illinois University Press.

12. Ibid.

13. Winkelman, *Shamanism*; Walter and Fridman, *Shamanism*.

14. Winkelman, *Shamanism*, 61.

15. Winkelman, *Shamanism*.

16. Wallace, *Religion: An anthropological view*.

17. O'Leary, T., & Levinson, D. (1990). *Encyclopedia of world cultures* (Vol. 9). Boston: G. K. Hall.

18. Armstrong, K. (2006). *The great transformation: The beginning of our religious traditions*. New York: Knopf.

19. Harris, M. (1977). *Cannibals and kings: The origins of cultures* (p. 119). New York: Random House.

20. Atran, S. (2002). *In gods we trust: The evolutionary landscape of religion*. New York: Oxford University Press.

21. Harris, *Cannibals and kings: The origins of cultures*.

22. Atran, *In gods we trust*.

23. D'Altroy, T. N. (2002). *The Incas*. Oxford: Blackwell.

24. Smart, N. (1976). *The religious experience of mankind* (2nd ed.). New York: Scribner's.

25. Zeitlin, I. (1984). *Ancient Judaism: Biblical criticism from Max Weber to the present*. Cambridge, U.K.: Polity Press.

26. Smart, *The religious experience of mankind*.

27. McNeill, W. H. (1963). *The decline of the West: A history of the human community*. Chicago: University of Chicago Press.

28. Smart, *The religious experience of mankind*.

29. Johnston, S. I. (2004). *Religions of the ancient world: A guide*. Cambridge, MA: Harvard University Press.

30. Ibid.

31. Woolley, C. L. (1965). *The Sumerians* (p. 129). Oxford: Oxford University Press.

32. Sharot, S. (2001). *A comparative sociology of world religions: Virtuosos, priests, and popular religion*. New York: New York University Press.

33. Weber, M. (1978 [1922]). *Economy and society* (Vol. 1). Trans. G. Roth and C. Wittich. Berkeley: University of California Press.

34. Thomas, K. (1971). *Religion and the decline of magic*. New York: Scribner's.

35. Sanderson, S. K., & Roberts, W. W. (2008, December). The evolutionary forms of the religious life: A cross-cultural, quantitative study. *American Anthropologist, 110*, 454–466.

36. Eliade, M. (1958). *Patterns in comparative religion* (p. 332). Trans. R. Sheed. New York: Sheed & Ward.

37. Ibid., 335.

38. But see Sanderson, S. K. (2008). Religious attachment theory and the biosocial evolution of the major world religions. In J. Bulbulia et al. (Eds.), *The evolution of religion: Studies, theories, and critiques* (pp. 67–72). Santa Margarita, CA: Collins Foundation Press.

39. Eckhardt, W. (1992). *Civilizations, empires, and wars: A quantitative history of war*. Jefferson, NC: McFarland.

40. Chandler, T. *Four thousand years of urban growth*. Lewiston, NY: St. David's University Press.

41. McNeill, *The decline of the West*.

42. Stark, R. (1996). *The rise of Christianity: A sociologist reconsiders history*. Princeton, NJ: Princeton University Press.

43. Worsley, P. (1968). *The trumpet shall sound: A study of "cargo cults" in Melanesia*. New York: Schocken.

44. Lanternari, V. (1963). *The religions of the oppressed*. New York: Knopf.

45. Weber, M. (1978 [1922]). *Economy and society* (Vol. 1). Trans. G. Roth and C. Wittich. Berkeley: University of California Press.

46. Troeltsch, E. (1931). *The social teaching of the Christian churches*. Trans. O. Wyon. London: Allen & Unwin.

47. Dulaney, S., & Fiske, A. P. (1994). Cultural rituals and obsessive-compulsive disorder: Is there a common psychological mechanism? *Ethos, 22*(3), 243–283; Fiske, A. P., & Haslam, N. (1997). Is obsessive-compulsive disorder a pathology of the human disposition to perform socially meaningful rituals? Evidence of similar content. *Journal of Nervous and Mental Disease,*

185, 211–222; Boyer, P. (2001). *Religion explained: The evolutionary origins of religious thought*. New York: Basic Books; Boyer, P., & Liénard, P. (2006). Why ritualized behavior? Precaution systems and action parsing in developmental, pathological, and cultural rituals. *Behavioral and Brain Sciences, 29*, 595–650; Liénard, P., & Boyer, P. 2006. Whence collective rituals? A cultural selection model of ritualized behavior. *American Anthropologist, 108*, 814–827.

48.   Bell, D. (1960). *The end of ideology: On the exhaustion of political ideas in the fifties*. Glencoe, IL: Free Press.

49.   Fukuyama, F. (1992). *The end of history and the last man*. New York: Free Press.

CHAPTER 2

Toward a Testable Definition of Religious Behavior

Lyle B. Steadman, Craig T. Palmer, and Ryan M. Ellsworth

The scientific study of religious behavior, like the scientific study of anything, requires rigorous objectivity, precise definitions of the concepts used, and a certain amount of healthy scientific skepticism. However, the scientific study of religious behavior is more complicated than the scientific study of many other human behaviors because it verges on paradox. The accuracy of religious statements is not empirically demonstrable (i.e., observable with the senses). Yet, in order to increase our knowledge of religion, it is essential that the accuracy of *our* propositions be demonstrable. The seeming paradox is that in the scientific study of religious behavior we are confronted with the problem of making statements that must be subjected to skepticism about statements whose acceptance depends on nonskepticism.

The anthropologist Edward Evans-Pritchard points out that one of the paramount questions that has historically guided the study of religion has been the following: "how does it come about that people capable of logical behavior so often act in a non-logical manner?" [1] We suggest, however, that this may not be the question that needs to be answered. The reason for this is because we do not assume that religious behavior is necessarily nonlogical. To understand the reason for this fundamental departure from earlier approaches, we must examine exactly what identifiable behavior the word "religious" refers to. In order to do this we must make explicit the reasons scholars of religion and their readers classify some behaviors, but not others, as religious. In short, we must *define* religious behavior.

By defining religious behavior, we refer to the act of specifying all of the elements needed to distinguish all behavior that is religious from all behavior that is nonreligious. This would specify not only what an explanation of religious behavior needs to account for, but what to test hypotheses against. A proposed definition of religious behavior must fit the literal, but not the metaphorical, uses of the term. For example, a definition of the word "religious" does not have to fit the metaphorical use of the word in the following statement: She goes to work religiously. However, a proposed definition of religious behavior that fits only some of the literal uses of the term is unacceptable. If the definition fits only some of the literal uses of the term, the definition would need to be expanded to become congruent to all observed cases of its literal use. On the other hand, if a proposed definition includes elements that are not always present when behavior is identified as "religious," the scope must be narrowed.

Other chapters in this book address the fact that religious behavior sometimes occurs with make-oneself-lower-or-smaller-or-more-vulnerable behaviors associated with the nonvocal aspect of petitioning prayer,[2] feasting and fasting,[3] various kinds of gaze behaviors,[4] and various in-group prosocial cooperative behaviors.[5] However, some of the occurrences of these behaviors written about in other chapters of this book are not considered religious in other contexts. In addition, many behaviors that are called religious do not include these behaviors. These other chapters cover important areas of research about specific behaviors; however, none of these areas address directly the questions of what *is* religious behavior, how is it recognized, and how can it be defined.

THE SUPERNATURAL

According to almost all scholars of religion, it is the supernatural—meaning literally "beyond nature" and hence beyond identification by the senses—that distinguishes that which is religion. For example, David Levinson defines religion as "the relationship between human beings and the supernatural world."[6] Evans-Pritchard, although specifically rejecting the term "supernatural," associates religion with "mystical" ideas that are not derived or logically inferred from observation.[7] He points out that "religion concerns beings which cannot be directly apprehended by the senses." [8] Sir Edward B. Tylor, who is often referred to as the "father" of cultural anthropology, based his definition of religion on "spiritual beings." [9] The French sociologist Lucien Levy-Bruhl equates religion with the "mystical" or "prelogical" (which, he argues, "wholly" characterizes primitive mentality).[10] He points out that such thought is not verifiable by the senses.[11] Robert Lowie, along with Robert Marett and Alexander Goldenweiser, specifies "supernaturalism" as "the differentia of religion." [12] Robin Horton defines religion by reference to entities "inaccessible to normal observation" and "unobservable beings";[13] Felicitas Goodman, on the basis of "alternative realities";[14] Jan van Baal, as the "non-verifiable world";[15] Milton Yinger, as the "superempirical";[16] William James, as "the belief that there is an unseen order";[17] and Melford Spiro, as "culturally patterned interaction with ...'superhuman beings.' " [18]

Recent evolutionarily informed approaches to religion also assume that religion is defined by reference to the supernatural. For example, Andrew Newberg and colleagues refer to "a realm of beings and forces beyond the material world." [19] Walter Burkert calls religion a "tradition of serious communication with powers that cannot be seen." [20] Robert Hinde defines religion as "systems of beliefs that have always been unverifiable." [21] Scott Atran refers to "supernatural agents" [22] and Pascal Boyer states that religion "is about the existence and causal powers of nonobservable entities and agencies" [23] or, in other words, "supernatural matters." [24] Finally, Richard Sosis and Candace Alcorta (a contributor to this book) refer to the "ineffable and unknowable aspects of religion that separate it from ordinary perceptual experience...." [25]

As can be seen from this literature review, even definitions of religion not explicitly based on something supernatural still imply the importance of something unidentifiable in distinguishing religion. For example, William Garrett noted that Peter Berger's definition of religion based on *transcendence* (God is separate from the observable world) refers to the "non-empirical." [26] Emile Durkheim's definition based on the "sacred," which he defines as something "set apart" or "forbidden" and that "inspires respect," also requires a supernatural aspect. To just be set apart, forbidden, and respected is not necessarily to be sacred (and hence, not necessarily religious).[27]

Reference to something supernatural is crucial to any *functional* definition of religious behavior. A functional definition of behavior is one that identifies the behavior on the result or outcome of the behavior. Some functional definitions in the literature have replaced the term "supernatural" with other words, such as "the transcendence of biology,"[28] "pervasive,"[29] and "ultimate."[30] Many of these terms used in various functional definitions having to do with religion have been repeatedly demonstrated to be overinclusive and to lack specificity.[31] However, the fundamental problem is that establishing the function of a behavior and then defining the behavior by this function still leaves the question of what the behavior is. This is why Spiro argues that unless religion is defined *substantively* (having a firm basis in material reality), it would be impossible to delineate its boundaries.[32]

Ake Hultkrantz, after pointing out the crucial role of unidentifiable things used in definitions, concludes that, "religion cannot be defined without reference to the concept of the 'supernatural.'"[33] W. R. Wells, after referring to the similar emphasis on the unidentifiable in the definitions of religion by Plato, Kant, and James, concludes that "regard for correct usage of the term requires that religion be defined in such a way as to include supernatural belief."[34] Thus, although there may be considerable disagreement among social scientists about what else religion involves, there is general agreement that it involves something "supernatural" (i.e., alleged elements, entities, or forces not identifiable by the senses).

Since the supernatural is "beyond nature" and hence beyond observation and identification by the senses, it itself cannot be used to identify or define religious behavior from a scientific perspective. The only thing that can be objectively observed and identified by an observer about supernaturals is what people *say* about them, the sound waves as well as the lip and tongue behaviors whose movements produce this vocalized speech. If no one said anything about supernatural things, they would have no discernible existence to an outside observer. To objectively identify religious behavior for an outside observer, therefore, it is neither necessary nor possible for the outside observer to identify supernatural phenomena. Only statements and claims about supernatural phenomena need be and can be observed and identified by the outside observer. Because supernaturals cannot be observed or identified, the accuracy of statements about supernaturals as well as correlations between supernaturals and anything else are unverifiable. This still leaves open the possibility that subjective feelings about the presence of the supernatural may be correlated with observable events by the religious practitioner. Indeed, it still leaves open the possibility that supernatural things exist. However, we again want to emphasize that both of these possibilities are beyond the reach of objective science. As stated in Chapter 9 by Lluis Oviedo, science has its limits in the study of religion.[35] We are trying to make clear in this chapter what some of these limits are.

During behavioral activities traditionally called religious, statements referring to supernaturals are regularly made.[36] While many other activities accompany these statements, they are not necessarily religious. For example, in the *milamala* ceremony of the Trobriand Islanders there is feasting, dancing, rejoicing, and gift giving. None of these behavioral activities are distinctive of religious behaviors. All occur in the Trobriands in other contexts that would not be considered by anyone as religious. Even the *ritual* performance of these activities (i.e., performances where the activities are performed in a stereotyped or repetitive manner) is not necessarily considered religious. In modern societies, the feasting, dancing, rejoicing, and gift giving occurring at parties, social dances, football games, birthdays, or parades all qualify as rituals, but they are not necessarily called religious. Many activities occur at a Christian church service. However, gathering together in a building, singing, speaking, reading, dressing up, and consuming bread and wine may also occur in contexts not considered religious. Yet going to a "House of God," singing hymns, listening to sermons, reading from the Bible, and taking communion are all commonly regarded as religious. It is not the eating or gathering together, even in a ritual way, that is religious, therefore, but rather the prayers—statements referring to supernaturals. The vocalized prayers and statements referring to supernaturals are what put these otherwise general-purpose behaviors into a religious realm.

The term "religious" is often extended in ordinary usage to include activities that tend to be associated with religious behavior, but that are not themselves distinctively religious. These activities may be explained or justified by the participants in terms of something supernatural, and it is this talk that is considered religious. Certain activities, like taking communion or spinning a prayer wheel, are almost always justified or explained by religious statements. A political candidate may claim that her activities are inspired by God, and while this statement itself is certainly religious in the strictest sense, there may be considerable disagreement over whether her political campaign is religious. Similarly, a "holy war" may involve many religious statements and be justified by the participants by invoking God; yet many aspects of the war—conduct of the battles, strategies, consequences for the victor—are more similar to nonreligious wars than they are to any distinctly religious behavior. Thus, while statements referring to supernaturals are regularly used to distinguish religion, activities merely associated with such statements are not necessarily religious.

BELIEF

Social scientists almost invariably equate supernatural statements with "belief in the supernaturals," which is also the most widely accepted general or short-version definition of religion. A recent article summarizing the latest evolutionary explanations of religion demonstrates the continued focus on religious belief.[37] The problem with this kind of definition is that unlike knowledge, which is identified in others by the correlation between identifiable phenomena and their behavior, *religious belief* cannot be identified by correlations with *supernatural* phenomena. Hence, such beliefs can only be *assumed* to exist in the minds of individuals, to motivate their behavior, and to be identifiable simply by observing the individual's *talk*. It is this assumption of belief, and only this assumption of belief, that has made the explanation of religion an attempt to explain "non-logical" behavior.

Untestable assumptions about beliefs have contributed to social science's quandary of trying to reconcile how people capable of logic can believe things that are seemingly counterintuitive and counterfactual, which are often-used characterizations of many religious beliefs. While it may be true that various religious rituals and statements are consequences of beliefs in supernaturals, the problem of how to observe and identify religious beliefs to study them is rarely addressed. An author's claims about the supernatural beliefs of the people he or she studies are often supported by no more than citing people's statements. What is wrong with this methodology?

First and most obvious, people can consciously and deliberately lie about what they say they believe. It may be difficult if not impossible to discover these lies. How is one to determine who is the "true believer" and who is not? This question is, of course, different from the question of whether the belief itself is true. The issue is how an outside observer knows if someone, who says that he/she believes something, truly holds that particular belief.

Many authors have pointed out problems with the "simplistic approach to religious belief" that assumes an equality between people's statements about what they believe and their actual beliefs.[38] Evans-Pritchard, who has studied native religions, warned that "statements about a people's religious beliefs must always be treated with the greatest caution, for we are then dealing with what neither European nor native can directly observe." [39] Authors making such criticism almost invariably assume that the problem of identifying beliefs can be solved "indirectly," merely by observing other behaviors. For example, some cognitive psychologists use a terminology that distinguishes between "explicit beliefs" (what people say they believe) and their actual or "implicit beliefs" (what they hold to be true). Thus, some cognitive psychologists assert that they can determine someone's implicit (i.e., actual) beliefs through observing their nonverbal behaviors.[40] The problems with this assertion are illustrated by Evans-Pritchard's claim that members of the Azande Tribe in north central Africa invariably consult the poison oracle (a prophet who divines the future) before making important decisions. Evans-Pritchard argues that their behavior is evidence that they "believe" in the efficacy of consulting the poison oracle.[41] However, that is obviously an unjustified inference since consulting a poison oracle could be done by someone who does not believe in the oracle's efficacy, but simply for the social consequences of such behavior.

As another example of this line of thinking, many anthropologists argue that a taboo requires people to state their belief about the taboo and then actually follow the taboo, rather than doing just one or the other.[42] However, a study of Maine lobster fishermen found that some fishermen actually observed taboos that they denied "believing in" and other fishermen failed to observe taboos in which they professed belief.[43]

The above examples illustrate the problem with trying to infer beliefs from either vocalized speech or nonverbal behavior. Just as humans can say things they do not believe, they can also behave as if they are someone they are not. Humans can be actors. When faced with contradictions between vocalized claims and accompanying behaviors, how can we choose with certainty whether it is the vocalized claim, the behavioral action, or neither that reflects the person's true belief? Any of these choices appear to be arbitrary—merely an untestable guess—and, hence, unacceptable in scientific analyses. As Alfred Radcliffe-Brown so aptly noted, "For as long as we admit guesswork of any kind social anthropology cannot be a science." [44] Even if brain imaging studies identify differences in the brain activity of people who communicate acceptance of a supernatural claim and people who do not communicate acceptance of that supernatural claim, this will not identify who is the true believer and who is not. Such studies will only identify correlations between different kinds of talk and different brain activities. Given the importance of influencing the behavior of others in specific ways through specific verbal communications, such correlations are to be expected.

There are many behavioral activities, which when observed, are inconsistent with vocalized statements made about religious beliefs by the participants. Adolphus Elkin reports that Australian Aboriginal peoples "believe" that a man can be killed through sorcery by pointing a sharpened stick or bone at him and singing a special chant.[45] Yet, when Aboriginal peoples decide that an overly active sorcerer should be stopped, they try to kill him with an actual spear. Why would they do this if they truly "believed" that sorcery is sufficient? We are not claiming that these behaviors prove the participants do not believe their supernatural claims. Rather, we are arguing that from their behavior we cannot tell with any degree of scientific certainty what supernatural beliefs they actually hold.

Individuals who study religious behavior scientifically, as opposed to theologically, do not use statements made about supernaturals as evidence that supernaturals exist. They do, however, often use statements about religious beliefs to conclude or at least presume that those religious beliefs exist. There is an inconsistency here. People *may* make statements about what is inside their heads. If a person says he or she believes in ghosts, he or she *may* believe in ghosts. There *may* even be ghosts. There is no evidence that can disprove a claim as to what the person says he or she believes. However, when religious beliefs are claimed by someone to be the cause of his or her behavior, the cause of the behavior then becomes unidentifiable, and the truth value of the claim unverifiable as well.

Several authors have come close to recognizing this problem of using beliefs in the scientific study of religious behavior but have failed to adequately address it. Roy Rappaport recognizes that what distinguishes religious ritual from nonreligious ritual is not beliefs but rather supernatural claims, or what he calls "unverifiable propositions."[46] For example, he states that, "a religious ritual always includes an additional term, such as a statement about or to spirits."[47] The realization that certain verbalized claims, rather than certain beliefs, are what identifies a ritual as religious leads Rappaport to then ask the question of whether or not participants in religious rituals actually believe the supernatural claims they make. Although he has just finished stressing the fact that humans can lie, he ignores this possibility and concludes: "It is thus plausible to assume a belief on the part of at least some of the participants in the existence of deceased ancestors; to assume otherwise would make nonsense of the proceedings." [48] In this statement Rappaport acknowledges that he cannot tell how many or which of the participants actually believe the supernatural claim, which would make the behavior of believers and nonbelievers indistinguishable. Thus, there is no logical basis for his conclusion that it is safe to assume that "some" must believe. Tradition itself can keep rituals alive.[49]

Probably the clearest example of the belief problem has been the statements made by Rodney Needham regarding the Penan tribe of interior Borneo. Needham reports that, although he had been accustomed to saying that "they believed in a supreme god," he suddenly realized that he had no evidence at all to this effect. Not only this, but:

> I realized that I could not confidently describe their attitude to God, whether this was belief or anything else. . . . In fact, as I had glumly to conclude, I just did not know what was their psychic attitude toward the personage in whom I had assumed they believed.[50]

Needham is also virtually alone in realizing the profound implications of this fact:

> The question then was whether the reports of other ethnographers were much better founded, and what evidence these really had that their subjects believed anything. Clearly, it was one thing to report the received ideas to which a people subscribed, but it was quite another matter to say what was their inner state (belief for instance) when they expressed or entertained such ideas. If, however, an ethnographer said that people believed something when he did not actually know what was going on inside them, then surely his account of them must, it occurred to me, be very defective in quite fundamental regards.[51]

Indeed, the uncertainty, controversy, and lack of progress characterizing most studies of religion ("stagnation" is the term used by Clifford Geertz[52]) may be at least in part a direct result of the use of claims about beliefs whose accuracy cannot be assessed. It needs to be stressed again that the issue we are addressing is only if the individual who claims to harbor a religious belief actually does so. This issue can digress into endless philosophical discussions beyond the scope of this chapter,[53] but the point remains that because counterclaims against what someone claims to believe cannot be logically resisted, such analyses often lead to either cult-like devotees to certain points of view, disagreement, or confusion. Thus, while beliefs are not empirically observable, behavior is. This includes the behaviors that produce the vocalized claims about communicated acceptance of supernatural claims. The study of the supernatural claims that people communicate acceptance of throughout the world can increase knowledge, but the study of beliefs may or may not.

IDENTIFYING AND DEFINING RELIGIOUS BEHAVIOR

We propose that the scientific study of religious behavior should be restricted to phenomena that are observable and identifiable by the senses. We also propose that testable hypotheses about religious behavior be limited to correlations between such phenomena. We can examine only those things that are examinable, look only at the things that can be looked at, and listen only to those things that can be heard.

We assume that behavior, as well as vocalized speech produced by behavior, can be identified by the senses of seeing and hearing. We also assume that English speakers mean something by the literal use of the terms "religion" and "religious." We therefore conclude that religious behavior (including the vocalized speech it produces) is observable and identifiable. Given that religious behavior is observable and identifiable, if it can be reliably and verifiably distinguished from other kinds of behavior, there should be no reason why a careful examination of religious behavior and its observable correlates should not be able to increase our scientific understanding of religion. Although religion *may* encompass more than that which can be identified by the senses of an observer, this does not threaten the assumption that our verifiable understanding of religious behavior can be increased significantly by focusing on what is observable and identifiable. Indeed, the scientific study of religion has made some real progress because of the detailed accounts of what has actually been observed.[54]

For those who wish to argue that statements not verifiable by our senses are nevertheless true, the burden is on them to propose a standard to evaluate the accuracy of such statements. Neither the internal consistency of an argument nor a popular vote is sufficient to establish its truth. Theological arguments can be both entirely consistent and said to be true by whole populations, and yet contradict one another.

How then can attempts to scientifically explain religion proceed once the need to exclude unidentifiable beliefs from those explanations is accepted? We suggest the answer is simply by restricting hypotheses to what can be identified as religious: certain *talk*, and the identifiable effects of that talk. In other words, religious behavior can be studied in the same way as any other form of communication.

But exactly what kind of talk distinguishes behavior as religious? Or more broadly, what is the definition of religion? While a claim of the existence of something unidentifiable by the senses appears necessary for behavior to be distinguished as religious, such a claim alone is not sufficient. A claim asserting the existence of something nonidentifiable may be considered evidence of the speaker being demented, perhaps even the basis for incarceration. An outright lie, a claim of seeing a unicorn, dragon, or flying saucer, the interpretation of a dream, a claim of being a teapot, a claim based on misperception, may all be "supernatural" assertions by definition, but are not normally considered religious.[55] Certainly none is distinctively or necessarily religious.

To make further progress toward a definition of religion that specifies its necessary and sufficient elements, one that can withstand skepticism based on our senses, let us focus on the first element in the definition of religion being "belief in the supernatural." According to the *Shorter Oxford Dictionary* cited by Hinde, "belief" means *"mental* assent to or acceptance of a proposition, statement, or fact, as true, on the ground of authority or evidence."[56] Religious beliefs, since they "are not subject to empirical verification,"[57] can be defined as *mental* assent to or acceptance of a *supernatural* proposition or statement on the grounds of authority. While it may be that such a statement was made by a supernatural itself, such a source cannot be verified. More importantly, while it is also possible that the person is experiencing *"mental* assent," the only thing that can be identified, by both social scientists and "believers," is the *explicitly communicated* assent or acceptance of another person's claim about something supernatural.

When a person makes a supernatural claim, we do not necessarily conclude he or she is religious. But when others regularly communicate their acceptance of that claim, it would be difficult to conclude that such behavior is not religious. For example, most current claims about the existence of *Sasquatch*, or "Bigfoot," are considered a joke or perhaps a sign of mental instability (see Chapter 11 by John Price[58]). However, in many Native American ethnographies such claims can be found in the description of peoples' *religion*. The only identifiable difference responsible for the classifications of "crazy" and "religious" is the absence of people communicating their acceptance of the claim in the former case and the presence of such behavior in the latter. Communicated acceptance of another person's supernatural claim communicates commitment. Does that imply belief? Of course not. Communicating acceptance of another person's supernatural claim can be seen as a promise to *behave* in a certain way in the future. Hence, the sincerity of the communication will be judged by the receiver, and others, in the same way we judge any sincerity—by subsequent *behavior*, not by identifying beliefs. What behavior? In this case, by behavior that shows continued acceptance of the speaker's influence.

CONCLUSION

Thus, we propose, as a testable hypothesis, that religious behavior is distinguished by, and hence can be defined as, the *communicated acceptance of a supernatural claim*. That is, *the communicated acceptance of another person's claim as true that cannot be shown to be true by the senses* constitutes the necessary and sufficient elements for identifying behavior as religious.

Here is the challenge to those who would remain skeptical: If it can be shown that something that reliably is called literally "religious" is not, nor has ever been, associated with the communicated acceptance of supernatural claims, the definition proposed above will have been falsified, and the scientific study of religion will have taken a progressive step forward.

NOTES

Parts of this chapter have been adapted with permission from L. B. Steadman & C. T. Palmer. (2008). *The supernatural and natural selection: The evolution of religion*. Paradigm Publishers: Boulder, CO. The right covers all editions, in all media, in all languages (world rights) and that permission is secured from all copyright holders.

1. Evans-Pritchard, E. E. (1965). *Theories of primitive religion* (p. 94). Oxford: The Clarendon Press.

2. Feierman, J. R., Chapter 5, this volume.

3. Goldberg, R., Chapter 12, this volume.

4. Ellis, T. B., Chapter 3, this volume.

5. Yamamoto, M. E., Leitão, M., Castelo-Branco, R., & Lopes, F., Chapter 14, this volume.

6. Levinson, D. (1996). *Religion: A cross-cultural dictionary* (p. vii). New York: Oxford University Press.

7. Evans-Pritchard, E. E. (1937). *Witchcraft, oracles, and magic among the Azande* (p. 12). Oxford: The Clarendon Press.

8. Evans-Pritchard, *Theories of primitive religion*, p. 108.

9. Tylor, E. B. (1958). *Religion in primitive culture* (p. 9). New York: Harper Torchbooks. (First published in 1871 as vol. II of *Primitive culture*.)

10. Levy-Bruhl, L. (1966). *Primitive mentality* (pp. 96, 447). Trans. L. Clare. Boston: Beacon Press. (First published 1922).

11. Ibid., p. 1.

12. Lowie, R. H. (1952). *Primitive religion* (p. xvi). New York: Crossett & Dunlap.

13. Horton, R. (1960). A definition of religion and its uses. *Journal of the Royal Anthropological Institute, 90*(2), 201–226.

14. Goodman, F. D. (1988). *Ecstasy, ritual and alternative reality: Religion in a pluralistic world.* Bloomington: Indiana University Press.

15. van Baal, J. (1981). *Man's quest for partnership.* Assen, The Netherlands: Van Gorcum.

16. Yinger, M. J. (1977). A comparative study of the substructures of religion. *Journal for the Scientific Study of Religion, 16*(1), 67–86.

17. James, W. (1902). *Varieties of religious experience* (p. 53). London: Fontana Press.

18. Spiro, M. E. (1966). Religion: Problems of definition and explanation. In M. Banton (Ed.), *Anthropological approaches to the study of religion* (p. 96). London: Tavistock Publications.

19. Newberg, A., D'Aquili, E., & Ruse, V. (2001). *Why God won't go away: Brain Science and the biology of belief* (p. 66). New York: Ballantine Books.

20. Burkert, W. (1996). *Creation of a sacred: Tracks of biology in early religions* (p. 177). Cambridge, MA: Harvard University Press.

21. Hinde, R. A. (1999). *Why gods persist: A scientific approach to religion* (p. 2). London and New York: Routledge.

22. Atran, S. (2002). *In gods we trust: The evolutionary landscape of religion* (p. 4). New York: Oxford University Press.

23. Boyer, P. (2001). *Religion explained: The evolutionary origins of religious thought* (p. 7). New York: Basic Books.

24. Boyer, *Religion explained: The evolutionary origins of religious thought,* p. 307.

25. Sosis, R., & Alcorta, C. (2003). Signaling, solidarity, and the sacred: The evolution of religious behavior. *Evolutionary Anthropology, 12*, 264–274 [265].

26. Garrett, W. R. (1974). Troublesome transcendence: The supernatural in the scientific study of religion. *Sociological Analysis, 35*(3), 167–180 [168]. See also Schneider, L. (1970). The sociology of religion: Some areas of theoretical potential. *Sociological Analysis, 31*(3), 131–145.

27. Durkheim, E. (1961). *The elementary forms of the religious life* (First published 1912). New York: Collier Books. See also Goody, J. (1961). Religion and ritual: The definitional problem. *British Journal of Sociology, 12*(2), 142–164; Swanson, G. (1964). *Birth of the gods.* Ann Arbor, MI: University of Michigan Press; Eliade, M. (1987). *The encyclopedia of religion.* New York: Macmillan.

28. Luckmann, T. (1967). *The invisible religion.* New York: MacMillan.

29. Geertz, C. (1966). Religion as a cultural system. In M. Banton (Ed.), *Anthropological approaches to the study of religion* (pp. 1–46). London: Tavistock Publications.

30. Bellah, R. N. (1964). Religious evolution. *American Sociological Review, 29*, 258–374. See also Yinger, M. J. (1970). *The scientific study of religion.* New York: Macmillan.

31. See Berger, P. L. (1974). Some second thoughts on substantive versus functional definitions of religion. *Journal for the Scientific Study of Religion, 13*(2), 125–134; Machalek, R. (1977). Definitional strategies in the study of religion. *Journal for the Scientific Study of Religion, 16*(4), 395–401; Weigert, A. J. (1974). Functional, substantive, or political? A comment on Berger's second thoughts on defining religion. *Journal for the Scientific Study of Religion, 13*(4), 483–486; Spiro, M. E. (1966). Religion: Problems of definition and explanation. In M. Banton, (Ed.), *Anthropological approaches to the study of religion* (pp. 85–126). London: Tavistock Publications.

32. Spiro, Religion: Problems of definition and explanation, p. 90 (emphasis in original).

33. Hultkrantz, A. (1983). The concept of the supernatural in primal religion. *History of Religions, 22*(3), 231–253 [231].

34. Wells, W. R. (1921). Is supernaturalistic belief essential in a definition of religion? *The Journal of Philosophy, 18*(10), 269–274 [275].

35. Oviedo, L., Chapter 9, this volume.

36. Boyer, *Religion explained: The evolutionary origins of religious thought,* pp. 1–2.

37. Boyer, P., & Bergstrom, B. (2008). Evolutionary perspectives on religion. *Annual Review of Anthropology, 37*, 111–130.

38. Hilty, D. M. (1988). Religious belief, participation and consequences: An exploratory and confirmatory analysis. *Journal for the Scientific Study of Religion, 27*(2), 243–259 [243]. See also Hahn, R. A. (1973). Understanding

beliefs: An essay on the methodology of the statement and analysis of belief systems. *Current Anthropology, 14*(3), 207–229; Saler, B. (1973). Comment. *Current Anthropology, 14*(3), 227.

39. Evans-Pritchard, *Theories of primitive religion*, p. 7.

40. Boyer, *Religion explained: The evolutionary origins of religious thought*, p. 305. See also Barrett, J. L. (2004). *Why would anyone believe in God?* Walnut Creek, CA: AltaMira Press. See Slone, J. (2004). *Theological incorrectness: Why religious people believe what they shouldn't.* New York: Oxford University Press.

41. Evans-Pritchard, E. E. (1937). *Witchcraft, Oracles, and Magic among the Azande* (p. 261). Oxford: The Clarendon Press.

42. Mullen, P. (1969). The function of magic folk beliefs among Texas coastal fishermen. *Journal of American Folklore, 82,* 214–225; Poggie, J. J., Jr., Pollnac, R., & Gersuny, C. (1976). Risk as a basis for taboos among fishermen in southern New England. *Journal for the Scientific Study of Religion, 15,* 257–262; Tunstall, J. (1962). *The fishermen.* London: Macgibbon and Kee; Poggie, J. J., Jr., & Pollnac, R. (1988). Danger and rituals of avoidance among New England fishermen. *Maritime Anthropological Studies, 1*(1), 66–78; van Ginkel, R. (1987). Pigs, priests and other puzzles: Fishermen's taboos in anthropological perspective. *Ethnologia Europea, 17,* 57–68; Zulaika, J. (1981). *Terranova: The ethos and luck of deep sea fishermen.* Philadelphia, PA: Institute for the Study of Human Issues.

43. Palmer, C. T. (1989). The ritual taboos of fishermen: An alternative explanation. *Maritime Anthropological Studies, 2*(1), 59–68.

44. Radcliffe-Brown, A. R. (1979). Taboo ("The Frazer lecture"). In W. A. Lessa & E. Z. Vogt (Eds.), *Reader in comparative religion: An anthropological approach* (4th ed.). New York: Harper Collins. (First published in 1939.)

45. Elkin, A. P. (1964). *The Australian Aborigines.* Garden City, NY: Doubleday & Co., Inc.

46. Rappaport, R. (1979). Ritual, sanctity, and cybernetics. In W. A. Lessa & E. Z. Vogt (Eds.), *Reader in comparative religion: An anthropological approach* (4th ed., p. 262). New York: Harper Collins. (First published in 1971.)

47. Ibid., p. 260 (emphasis in original).

48. Ibid., p. 262.

49. Palmer, C. T., Steadman, L. B., & Goldberg, R. (2008). Traditionalism and human evolutionary success: The example of Judaism. In R. Goldberg (Ed.), *Judaism in biological perspective* (pp. 139–164). Boulder, CO: Paradigm Publishers.

50. Needham, R. (1972). *Belief, Language, and Experience* (p. 1). Chicago: University of Chicago Press.

51. Ibid., pp. 1–2.

52. Geertz, Religion as a cultural system, p. 1.

53. Saler, B. (2001). On what we may believe about beliefs. In J. Andresen (Ed.), *Religion in mind: Cognitive perspectives on religious beliefs, ritual, and experience* (pp. 47–69). Cambridge: Cambridge University Press.

54. Murdock, G. (1971). Anthropology's mythology. *Journal of the Royal Anthropological Society*, 17–21.

55. Douglas, M. (1975). Heathen darkness. In M. Douglas (ed.), *Implicit meanings* (p. 75). London: Routledge and Keegan Paul.

56. Hinde, *Why gods persist: A scientific approach to religion*, p. 34.

57. Ibid.

58. Price, J., Chapter 11, this volume.

CHAPTER 3

Natural Gazes, Non-Natural Agents: The Biology of Religion's Ocular Behaviors

Thomas B. Ellis

What devotees do and do not do with their eyes has been a point of sustained interest in many religious traditions.[1] Similarly, whether or not an image of the deity is to be constructed is of equal import. Of the many ways to categorize the world's religious traditions, one strategy considers whether the tradition in question is generally *iconoclastic* (hostile to images) or generally *iconolatrous* (reverent of images). Iconoclasm and iconolatry reflect, respectively, prohibitions and sanctions concerning ocular behaviors, that is, movement of the eyes. A cursory glance at the Abrahamic traditions—Judaism, Christianity, and Islam—quickly reveals that these are generally iconoclastic.[2] Taught to label iconolatry idolatrous, Jews, Christians, and Muslims generally find anathema those traditions that not only allow but positively condone image worship. Complementing this iconoclastic prohibition regarding sight is the prescription of audition, that is, the injunction to listen attentively to the deity. Where Exodus 19:21 relates Yahweh's instructions to Moses to "warn the people not to break through to the Lord to look," Deuteronomy 6:4 and 9:1 commence with the injunction, "Hear, O Israel."[3] Most significant for the present discussion, the Abrahamic devotee routinely closes the eyes and often bows the head when engaging in petitioning prayer, behaviors clearly in the service of forestalling any direct eye contact with God.

Noticeably different from Abrahamic iconoclasm, South Asian iconolatry positively incorporates ocular engagement with the deity. As one scholar of Hinduism put it, "The central act of Hindu worship . . . [is] to see and be seen by the deity."[4] Such visual reciprocity constitutes the central Hindu practice of *darshan*. What for the Abrahamic practitioner is an abomination, for the Hindu practitioner is most desirable. Where the one suspects, the other celebrates the eyes. Wherein rests the difference?

Minimally defined, religion is social intercourse with *non-natural* agents. An *agent* is any object whose behavior is internally generated. Pesky philosophical problems pertaining to free will notwithstanding, humans act according to their desires and intentions.[5] Humans are agents, rocks are not.

Naturalism—a philosophical worldview enjoying a growing consensus amid the scientific and philosophical communities—methodologically dismisses the non-natural as such. Concerning agency, the naturalist maintains that intentions and desires are emergent properties of an exhaustively physical organ, the brain.[6] Non-natural agency violates this precondition. Though capable of embodiment, non-natural agents (e.g., deities) enjoy disembodied sentience. Non-natural agency presumes in this way what the philosophical community calls substance dualism, a position underwriting most beliefs in God as well as the putative distinction between the immaterial soul and the material body.[7] Religion presumably stands and falls with substance dualism.[8]

Biologically speaking, religious beliefs and behaviors betray a natural history and foundation. Natural agents are models for non-natural agents. Likewise, behaviors in the service of communicating with natural agents serve as models for religion's social intercourse with non-natural agents. Among the many behaviors employed in social intercourse, ocular behaviors are singularly significant in communicating social intention. Depending on the social other with whom one is interacting, certain ocular behaviors are more appropriate than others. I argue that religion's ocular behaviors indicate the natural agents upon which the non-natural agents or deities are modeled.

Several authors have addressed the natural models humans employ in their representation of deity. For instance, Sigmund Freud infamously favors the paternal model.[9] Ana-Maria Rizzuto favors the paternal and maternal.[10] Scott Atran favors the protector and the predator.[11] Lee A. Kirkpatrick favors the attachment figure.[12] Though finding something of significance in each author's contribution, I maintain that they collectively fail to articulate the *four* models of deity formation presented in this chapter. I propose that the three types of ocular behavior observed in religious practice (affiliative, affiliative-or-agonal, and agonal) reveal four types of others with whom one naturally interacts and upon which one naturally models deity:

- attachment figure
- intratribal rank-superior
- conspecific aggressor (an aggressor of the same species)
- extraspecific aggressor (an aggressor of a different species).[13]

The fifth type of social other—the *coalition partner*—seldom, if ever, serves as a model for deity.[14]

BIOLOGICAL BASES OF SOCIAL INTERCOURSE

Biologically speaking, there are two primary tasks humans must accomplish—survival and reproduction. Accomplishing the former facilitates the latter. Over evolutionary time, humans faced several obstacles standing in the way of these accomplishments. Behaviors most effective and efficient in negotiating these ancestral, environmental obstacles enjoyed greater reproductive success and thus adaptive fitness. Contemporary human behaviors reflect this natural history.

Of singular import to the reproductive success of humans is sociality. Because our ancestors were particularly bad at outrunning or overpowering extraspecific aggressors, banding together and using wits and tools (i.e., weapons) proved most effective. Only by acting in concert, using technology, and exchanging information could the human survive. In this way, we came to inhabit the "cognitive niche": "What humans especially need ... are ... *information* about the world around them; and ... *cooperation* with other members of the species."[15] While there were many types of information pertinent to survival in the ancestral past, social information was paramount.

Social intercourse falls into two general classes, *affiliative* (friendly) and *agonal* (nonfriendly and perhaps even fatal).[16] Agents seek either to establish or to maintain a social connection with another agent or, alternatively, forestall or discontinue such social contact. With the attachment figure, intratribal rank-superior, and coalition partner, we pursue affiliation; with conspecific and extraspecific aggressors, we pursue social avoidance. Such concerns and attendant behaviors are the principal domain of attachment theory.

Attachment theory examines the human's *proximity* (closeness)-seeking and exploratory behaviors.[17] Proximity to stronger and wiser others facilitates protection from conspecific and extraspecific aggressors. Originally addressing the relationship between primary caregivers and infants/young children, attachment theorists now apply the theory and the terminology to relationships beyond the nursery. For instance, and according to Kirkpatrick, the relationship between a religious devotee and the deity is not just like an attachment relationship; it is an attachment relationship.[18] This is only partially true.[19] As we will see below, not all deities are protective and nurturing.

While affording the infant protection in a hostile world, the caregiver also needed the protection of the social group, which continually increased in size throughout human evolution.[20] Such an increase led to more complicated social hierarchies. Social hierarchies determine not only the distribution of resources and reproductive opportunities (especially for males) but also who rightly commands and who rightly performs subordination.

Whereas social intercourse with the attachment figure is most often characterized by full affiliation, social intercourse with the intratribal rank-superior combines both affiliative and agonal qualities. The rank-superior enjoys the capacity to protect as well as harm his (almost always male) subordinates. Precisely for this reason, and from the subordinates' perspective, predicting the rank-superior's next move was (and continues to be) of great importance.

Agents are singularly unpredictable. Even with regard to the attachment figure, there is always the possibility that he or she will not be available when needed. Unpredictability is clearly the case with conspecific and extraspecific aggressors. To be sure, all five social and equally unpredictable others (attachment figure, intratribal rank-superior, conspecific aggressor, extraspecific aggressor, and coalition partner) were thus objects in the struggling-to-survive organism's horizon of immediate social concern: "The *recurring problem* that the organism would need to solve is predicting another organism's next move."[21]

Predicting another organism's next move was and remains most difficult. The other's intentions are not on display. What are on display, however, are the other's bodily movements, that is, behavior. Because behavior is—at least for an agent—an expression of intention, it behooved our ancestors to become fluent in "body language." And this they did. Some scientists suggest, in fact, that the ancestral human slowly developed cognitive means for discerning intention in the movements of the other's body. One behavior proved most effective in predicting the other's next move—ocular behavior. Ocular behaviors—the movement of the eyes—either intentionally advertise or unintentionally betray intention. Precisely for this reason, "any theory or account of social behavior that fails to mention gaze is ... completely inadequate." [22] Predicting intention through ocular behaviors requires sophisticated cognitive abilities.

COGNITIVE NEUROSCIENCE

According to some cognitive neuroscientists, the human *mind*—the cognitive or information-processing functions of the brain—comprises several different functionally defined *modules* dedicated to specific cognitive tasks. [23] One of these modules—the *theory of mind module*—is responsible for what is called the *intentional stance*. [24] The intentional stance identifies the capacity to attribute intentions and thus agency to another individual. Because I cannot directly observe your intentional states, I am left to infer from your contingent behavior that you are not externally compelled: you have a mind with its own hidden-to-the-outside-world agendas. Troubling for me, your agenda may not have my best interests in mind. Consequently, I need to know in advance what it is that you intend to do next so that I can plan and then act accordingly. Because other agents were so crucial to the survival or demise of the human animal, the cognitive science community suggests that it was and continues to be advantageous for humans to overattribute agency to various objects in the world. It is safer to assume something is an agent than not. [25] Our theory of mind module thus appears trip wired for detecting agents, including non-natural agents. Significantly for the present discussion, tracing the development of the theory of mind module takes us back to the emergence first of the eye direction detector and then the shared attention mechanism. [26]

Simon Baron-Cohen argues that prior to the emergence of theory of mind, humans and other species (nonhuman primate and otherwise) first evolved (yet-to-be-identified) brain structures cognitively dedicated to detecting eye direction. Concerning "the recurring problem," "the enduring property of the environment that natural selection is postulated to have exploited to solve this problem is that an animal's eye direction reliably correlates with its next move."[27] Understandably then, eye direction detecting first determines that a pair of eyes are in the environment and then determines whether or not those eyes are focused on you, at least when in close proximity.[28]

Although detecting eye direction was an advantageous cognitive function for many species seeking to avoid aggressors, it became of central significance for ancestral humans for whom the foremost aggressor was (and still is) the other hominid.[29] Flat faces and bipedal (two-legged) gait militated against using simple body orientation as an indication of future behavior. Eye direction thus became of paramount importance. Reflecting this importance, the human eye's naturally selected, disproportionally larger sclera (white of the eye) with respect to the size of the iris enables the ability to pay particular attention to the conspecific other's eye direction.[30]

If the cognitive function of detecting eye direction emerged at least partially—if not in full—as a means of discerning the extraspecific or conspecific aggressor's next move, then an important survival strategy would be to stay out of the other's sight. Indeed, detecting eye direction contributes directly to H. Clark Barrett's *predator-prey schema*.[31] From the perspective of a prey species or a defensive conspecific, once a pair of eyes is detected the next task is to avoid becoming the object of the aggressor's attention by either freezing or fleeing.[32]

Opposing the "desire" to stay out of the other's line of sight is the "desire" to be the object of the other's affiliative intentions. Unlike predator-prey interaction, infant and primary caregiver often engage in the intentional exchange of gazes.[33] Prolonged gaze reciprocity facilitates, in certain contexts to be sure, the affiliative bond. In this respect, yet-to-be-determined brain tissues whose functions are detecting eye direction become utilized in both the *predator-prey schema* and the *caregiver-careseeker schema*.

Elaborating upon the eye direction detector, hominids eventually developed the capacity for *shared attention*. Capitalizing upon the *dyadic* (two-individual) aspect of detecting eye direction, the capacity for shared attention pursues *triadic* representations (e.g., me, you, and the object of your or my attention). The capacity for shared attention allows one organism to take note of a third object depending on the other's gaze. For instance, if I see you looking at something intently, then I have detected your eyes, detected that you are not looking at me, and then detected that you are instead looking at some object that may be of interest to me as well. In a most sophisticated cognitive task, I can actually look at some random object with the intention of deceiving you by drawing your attention away from something in which I may be most interested. As we will see shortly, this becomes a central tactic in the battle against the evil eye, at times a deity-related phenomenon.

OCULAR BEHAVIORS, SOCIAL OTHERS, AND RELIGION

Nathan J. Emery discusses three particular functions of ocular behavior: "The eyes are often used as symbols of curse (*evil eye*) or as warning signals, but are also one of the first points of contact between infants and their mothers." [34] While there are two general types of social intercourse—affiliative and agonal—I suggest that a continuum exists along which we find pure and mixed types, types that employ particular ocular behaviors. On the extreme form of affiliation we find an open exchange of gazes. On the extreme form of agonism we find a desire not to engage in visual exchange for fear of harm or a "curse." The third type involves what Emery refers to as "warning signals." Emery disaggregates here what the preeminent human *ethologist* (behavioral biologist) Irenäus Eibl-Eibesfeldt calls the "threat stare." I associate the "curse/threat" stare with the extraspecific and conspecific aggressor. The "warning/threat" stare issues from the intratribal rank-superior. The "curse" promises attack, the warning potential attack. Should one challenge the rank-superior, he may and likely will respond first with a warning stare and then with agonistic behaviors should one not desist from the perceived provocation.

The three types of ocular behaviors (fully affiliative, affiliative-or-agonal, and fully agonal) accompanying social intercourse with four of the five general types of social others (the attachment figure, intratribal rank-superior, conspecific aggressor, and extraspecific aggressor) animate the various patterns of social intercourse with non-natural agents found amid the world's religions. Accordingly, and in much the same way that we use the ocular behaviors of others to predict their intentions, I suggest we use the religious practitioner's ocular behaviors to divine the type of non-natural agent with whom that practitioner is engaged.

In the Abrahamic traditions, icons of God[35] are generally frowned upon, if not, in fact, completely forbidden as is the case with Islam. I argue that prohibitions against iconolatry are in effect prohibitions against looking at God, alternative theological explanations notwith-standing. The Torah clearly states that the devotee is not to break through to the presence of the god to look, and this under penalty of capital punishment: "warn the people not to break through to the Lord to look; otherwise many of them will perish" (Exodus 19:21). The Torah similarly prohibits the creation of images: "You shall not make for yourself an idol" (Exodus 20:4). Clearly, and far more often than not, the Abrahamic god is understood to be a Lord, a king, that is, a male, intratribal rank-superior.[36] *Approaching* the rank-superior god—for instance, through petitioning prayer—one naturally averts one's gaze by closing the eyes and/or bowing the head.

Despite widespread admonitions against looking at God in both the Bible and the Qur'an,[37] we find some confounding passages. Psalm 25:15 declares, for instance, "My eyes are ever toward the Lord." Psalm 145:15 says, "The eyes of all look to you." Ethology (behavioral biology) and cognitive psychology offer an explanation for the discrep-ancy. According to ethology, once the subordinate displays submission by gaze aversion, the same subordinate will then ocularly attend to the rank-superior.[38] In a social group, dominance hierarchies are often indexed by which individual is the object of the most ocular attention, a phenomenon called "the social structure of attention." Subordinates ocularly attend to the rank-superior to monitor the superior's where-abouts as well as to monitor what captures the superior's attention. Of course, should the rank-superior turn toward the rank-inferior, the rank-inferior would duly avert his or her eyes.[39] The Book of Psalms presents in this regard "the social structure of *esoteric* attention."

The psalmist's social structure of esoteric attention betrays a certain "theological incorrectness."[40] Theological incorrectness reflects the cognitive limits of the human mind. Indeed, theology is notoriously, cognitively burdensome. In this particular context, theological incor-rectness issues from the thought that the god may have a particular object capturing his attention. In other words, that God's focus is not on the rank-inferior devotee confounds the theologically correct notion of an all-seeing deity, a quality equally represented in biblical passages: "For the eyes of the Lord range throughout the entire earth" (2 Chronicles 16:9) and "The eyes of the Lord are in every place" (Proverbs 15:3). Theology's official position on the all-seeing, omnipotent, omnipresent deity is cognitively difficult to maintain in unreflective moments. It takes cognitive muster to keep up with theol-ogy. Much to theology's consternation, humans often default to rather anthropomorphic characterizations when casually considering the deity.[41] For instance, humans often conceive of the god doing one thing first and then another second. I propose that the psalmist betrays unknowingly his cognitive infidelity to theology when he suggests that the eyes of all turn toward the god: the eyes of all turn toward the god when the god is looking elsewhere.

In petitioning prayer, the devotee's closed eyes betray the sense that he or she is now the focus of the non-natural agent's attention. When one prays to god, god attends the prayer. Moreover, if we take into consideration that prayers to the Abrahamic god are regularly petitions, then we would be well advised to take stock of Eibl-Eibesfeldt's comment: "a person talking to someone and uninterruptedly fixating on them will make the impression of being aggressive and dominating. In normal speech we note, therefore, that the speaker always interrupts visual contact while the listener may maintain contact uninterruptedly." [42] Surely, God need not blink.

We may similarly note that the very nature and existence of gods are by default strange.[43] Accordingly, and again from ethology, we know that children avert their gaze in the ocular company of strangers. As "children of God," we default to a certain fear stance when in proximity to the god, that is, we hide our eyes. I thus suggest that the Abrahamic god is not only ontologically strange—as all gods are—but more importantly often modeled upon the intratribal rank-superior and as such the religious practitioner's ocular behaviors reflect those of the intratribal rank-*inferior*.[44]

The most curious exception to Abrahamic iconoclasm is Mariolatry, that is, devotion to Mary, a saint. Opposing the closed eyes of the prayerful when approaching the god as rank-superior, Roman Catholics and Eastern Orthodox in particular—at least the ones I have repeatedly observed and interviewed—often petition images and statues of the Virgin Mary with eyes open (not unlike social intercourse with other non-natural saints). Here is precisely where we witness a shift in model for deity or deity-like other. Instead of social intercourse with the rank-superior, I suggest we witness here social intercourse with the attachment figure. Devotees of attachment figure gods approach the god with open eyes in just the same way that infants and young children approach with eyes open the loving mother or father as attachment figure.[45] This we find repeatedly not only amongst Roman Catholics and Eastern Orthodox in their ocular behaviors before specific icons but throughout the Hindu religious world as well.

At the heart of Hindu religious practice is *darshan*, that is, reciprocal gazing. In direct opposition to the Abrahamic traditions with their emphases on the rank-superior deity[46] who will not tolerate reciprocal gazes as displays of challenge, the Hindu deities are often sought out precisely for an exchange of gaze. In such situations, the devotee wishes to be the object of the other's ocular attention. Unlike the crucifix's inanimate representation, the Hindu image or *murti* is understood to be fully animate. If the dominant form of Abrahamic deity is based on the rank-superior, the dominant form of Indic deity is based on the attachment figure, exceptions certainly notwithstanding.

The third and final ocular phenomenon in religion has to do with that which is unswervingly agonal, an ocular behavior associated primarily with "the evil eye." The evil eye, I argue, is associated with deities modeled on either the conspecific or extraspecific aggressor, and quite possibly a combination of both. Indeed, many "devils" and "demons" appear to be part human and part beast. Moreover, these chimeric (combination) gods are often explicitly predator-like in their rapacious appetite. The medieval paintings of Hieronymus Bosch, for instance, often depict a chimeric devil *eating* his victims. Likewise in South Asia, the "hot deities" are often associated with the consumption of young children.[47] In fact, the predation anxiety attending social intercourse with such deities leads Hindus to tread circuitous paths through villages in order to avoid crossing in front of the "hot gazes" of the fierce gods' images.[48] Like a predator, the fierce god will not attack the individual if he or she does not see the individual.[49] Unlike the Abrahamic deity's all-seeing eye, the Hindu hot god's intentions and desires are seemingly limited to that god's eye direction.

The phenomenon of the evil eye obviously extends beyond the devotee's interactions with deity. Equally capable of deploying the evil eye is the coalition partner. In the South Asian world, for instance, mothers often refrain from doting on their infants.[50] Hindu mothers are particularly encouraged not to lavish ocular attention on their children because such investment may draw the evil eye. Classically associated with envy, the coalition partner's evil eye may cast a curse on the infant. In much the same way as other species will attempt to distract the predator from discovering the nest/home wherein rest the young, a Hindu mother will direct her attention away from the child in order to deceive any potential onlookers, natural and non-natural alike, a defensive strategy manipulating the shared attention mechanism and rooted in predator-prey dynamics.

According to some, jealousy is the emotional expression associated with cheater detecting.[51] Jealousy erupts when one believes the other has ill-gotten goods. In this regard, evil eye phenomena and suspicions are most often found in groups whose members (coalition partners) are of equal status.[52] Jealousy erupts when one coalition partner believes the other partner has cheated. The evil eye betrays in this regard coalitional strategies and concerns. Those who give the evil eye are "overreacting cheater-detectors." [53] This is the case because in an evolutionary past, group cohesion was essential to survival. Detrimental to group cohesion is the cheater. Deterrence of cheating was for these reasons paramount to the group's cohesion. The social punishment *par excellence* for cheaters was ostracism.[54] To be ostracized was to be most vulnerable to advancing predators.[55] In this way, to be found cheating, to be detected by the coalition partner's jealous ("evil") eye is indirectly related to being espied by a real predator's eye. The ostracizing eye of the jealous coalition partner becomes the devouring eye of the real predator.

CONCLUSION

There are three ocular behaviors (affiliative, affiliative-or-agonal, and agonal) associated with five general types of social other (attachment figure, intratribal rank-superior, coalition partner, and conspecific and extraspecific aggressor). These behaviors and social others (generally excluding the coalition partner) serve as natural models for how humans conceive of and relate to deities. With attachment figure deities and saints, such as Mary, devotees seek out visual reciprocity in much the same way that humans exchange gazes with attachment figures. With the intratribal rank-superior deities, such as the Abrahamic god, devotees avert their gaze in an act of respectful submission. Especially when petitioning through prayer the rank-superior, devotees avert their gaze so as not to appear demanding and thus challenging. With the conspecific and extraspecific aggressors, on the other hand, we wish to avoid ocular engagement. We do not want to be the object of the aggressive other's ocular attention for such attention facilitates attack. Similarly, we do not wish to direct the aggressor's attention to any objects we wish to keep safe from harm. Biologically speaking, specific combinations of the eye direction detector, the shared attention mechanism, and finally the theory of mind module enable all of these religiously deployed behaviors.

Our task as social beings is to be able to predict the other's next move. Ocular behaviors are a window onto the other's intentions. Because these are the natural, biological means by which we socially interact, I argue that they likewise animate religious performance, performances minimally involving social intercourse with non-natural agents. Religion's ocular behaviors are natural gazes redeployed in a non-natural idiom. Where authors in the past have identified either one or two naturally occurring others as models for deity representation, I argue that there are, in fact, four: attachment figure, intratribal rank-superior, conspecific aggressor, and extraspecific aggressor. The three ocular behaviors—affiliative, affiliative-or-agonal, and agonal—attending social intercourse with these others animate religion.[56] To look or not to look, to be seen or not to be seen, these are the biological questions underlying religion's ocular behaviors.

NOTES

1. Argyle, M., & Cook, M. (1976). *Gaze and mutual gaze*. London: Cambridge University Press.

2. A qualification is appropriate here. Amid the Christian community, iconoclasm has been at the heart of the Protestant traditions. However, and admittedly, icons find their place in Roman Catholicism and Eastern Orthodoxy. To cite the most significant instance, at the center of Roman Catholic and Eastern Orthodox sanctuaries is a crucifix, that is, an image of the crucified Christ on the cross. While one could perhaps suggest a certain iconolatry here, I believe we must recognize an irreducible quality of iconolatry—the icon is alive. The representation of an *inanimate* Christ forestalls the true iconolatry of and, for example, the Hindu traditions to be addressed below. The crucifix actually enables the *an*-iconolatry at the heart of Christian Eucharist. To be sure, the *living* Christ is either symbolically represented by or identified with the bread and wine, aniconic substances. The "dead icon" becomes the "living anicon." In this regard, and despite the plethora of images, the central Christian rite of Holy Communion is justifiably aniconic and by indirect extension iconoclastic.

3. In this chapter, all biblical citations are taken from the New Revised Standard Edition.

4. Eck, D. L. (1998). *Darsan: Seeing the divine image in India* (3rd ed., p. 3). New York: Columbia University Press.

5. On the problem of free will see Dennett, D. C. (2004). *Freedom evolves*. New York: Penguin; Flanagan, O. (2002). *The problem of the soul: Two visions of mind and how to reconcile them*. New York: Basic Books.

6. Searle, J. R. (2004). *Mind: A brief introduction*. Oxford: Oxford University Press.

7. Flanagan, *The problem of the soul*.

8. Guthrie, S. (1993). *Faces in the clouds: A new theory of religion*. New York: Oxford University Press; Boyer, P. (2001). *Religion explained: The evolutionary origins of religious thought*. New York: Basic Books; Atran, S. (2002). *In gods we trust: The evolutionary landscape of religion*. New York: Oxford University Press; Barrett, J. (2004). *Why would anyone believe in God?* Lanham: AltaMira Press.

9. Freud, S. (1961 [1927]). *The future of an illusion*. New York: W. W. Norton.

10. Rizzuto, A-M. (1979). *The birth of the living God*. Chicago: The University of Chicago Press.

11. Atran, *In gods we trust*.

12. Kirkpatrick, L. A. (2005). *Attachment, evolution, and the psychology of religion*. New York: The Guilford Press.

13. By "extraspecific aggressor," I mean those organisms not belonging to the species *homo* that threatened the survival of the human. While predators immediately come to mind, we must also countenance, for example, ungulates, reptiles, and insects.

14. A note concerning romantic partners as models for deity is appropriate here. Many mystical traditions view the relationship to the god as one of intense romantic involvement. Coalition partners may, of course, become romantic partners. The behavioral autonomy of romantic partnering is, however, rightfully questioned. Some authors persuasively argue that romantic love is an integration of three behavioral systems—attachment, caregiving, and sex. See Kirkpatrick, L. A., & Shaver, P. R. (1992). "An attachment theoretical approach to romantic love and religious belief." *Personality and Social Psychology Bulletin, 18*(3), 266–275. As for these systems informing ocular behaviors, I believe we can rule out the sex system. No doubt one flirts with eyes, but the sex system is in the business of sexual intercourse; it is blind to the eyes. Likewise, seldom, if ever, do religious traditions envision actual sex with the god; even in Hinduism, a tradition with a highly erotic component, the devotee understands a difference between *kama* and *prema*, that is, carnal love and sublimated love, the latter characterizing the relationship to the deity. As for the caregiving system, seldom do devotees actually take care of the god. While many traditions engage in the feeding and bathing of the deity, I argue that this is more an aspect of what I call "esoteric allogrooming" than it is actual caregiving. Certainly, deities do not really need our care. I propose in this regard that the attachment system serves as the dominant behavioral system amid the traditions of mystical love. The "love stare" is in effect a redeployed "attachment stare."

15. Boyer, *Religion explained*, p. 120.

16. Eibl-Eibesfeldt, I. (1989). *Human ethology: Foundations of human behavior*. New York: Aldine De Gruyter.

17. Bowlby, J. (1969). *Attachment*. New York: Basic Books.

18. Kirkpatrick, *Attachment, evolution, and the psychology of religion*.

19. Atran, *In gods we trust*, pp. 73–74.

20. King, B. 2007. *Evolving God*. New York: Doubleday.

21. Baron-Cohen, S. (1995a). The eye direction detector (EDD) and the shared attention mechanism (SAM): Two cases for evolutionary psychology. In C. Moore & P. J. Dunham (Eds.), *Joint attention: Its origins and role in development* (pp. 41–59, emphasis added). Hillsdale: Lawrence Erlbaum.

22. Argyle & Cook, *Gaze and mutual gaze*, p. 167.

23. Pinker, S. (1999). *How the mind works*. New York: W. W. Norton & Co. For a dissenting view, see Fodor, J. (2001). *The mind doesn't work that way*. Cambridge: The MIT Press. For a persuasive response to Fodor, see Pinker, S. (2005). So how *does* the mind work? *Mind and Language, 20* (1), 1–24.

24. Dennett, D. C. (1987). *The intentional stance*. Cambridge: The MIT Press.

25. Guthrie, *Faces in the clouds*.

26. Baron-Cohen, S. (1995b). *Mindblindness: An essay on autism and theory of mind*. Cambridge: The MIT Press; Emery, N. J. (2000). The eyes have it: The neuroethology, function and evolution of social gaze. *Neuroscience and Biobehavioral Reviews, 24*, 581–604.

27. Baron-Cohen, The eye direction detector (EDD) and the shared attention mechanism (SAM), pp. 46.

28. It is true that olfaction is and has always been a major factor in predator-prey relations, especially when the predator and prey are out of eye-gazing and eye-gaze-detecting distance. For the human animal, however, olfactory senses are particularly weak and thus the eyes played and play a much larger role in predator-prey relations relative to other species.

29. Atran, *In gods we trust*, p. 69.

30. Kobayashi, H., & Kohshima, S. (2001). Unique morphology of the human eye and its adaptive meaning: Comparative studies on external morphology of the primate eye. *Journal of Human Evolution, 40*(5), 419–435; Emery, The eyes have it, pp. 582–583.

31. Barrett, H. C. (1999). Human cognitive adaptations to predators and prey. Ph.D. dissertation, University of California, Santa Barbara; Barrett, H. C. (2005). Adaptations to predators and prey. In D. M. Buss (Ed.), *The handbook of evolutionary psychology*. Hoboken, NJ: John Wiley & Sons, Inc.

32. Barrett, Adaptations to predators and prey, p. 202.

33. Stern, D. (1985). *The interpersonal world of the infant: A view from psychoanalysis and developmental psychology*. New York: Basic Books.

34. Emery, The eyes have it, p. 584.

35. Despite the iconography of Jesus and various saints found in the Roman Catholic and especially Eastern Orthodox churches, iconic images of God are noticeably less frequent.

36. A point of clarification is due. While Christians certainly speak of God as "Father"—and also as "King" and "Lord"—this need not dissuade us from maintaining that the Abrahamic god still functions *primarily* as an intratribal rank-superior. Deity can, to be sure, take on alternative functions as the particular situation or context demands. I am not precluding, in this regard, the possibility that for Christians in particular God may on occasion function as an attachment figure (perhaps also as a conspecific aggressor as well!). My point here is simply that the Abrahamic god appears more often than not to be an intratribal rank-superior. Certainly, the ocular *behavior* attending those engaging in petitionary prayer is clearly associated with the intratribal rank-superior and not the attachment figure: our behaviors often belie our conscious intentions. Moreover and importantly, a parent need not be an attachment figure. Parents, of course, can be and often are attachment figures, but this is not a necessary qualification for parenthood. As Abelow notes in Chapter 6 (this volume), the father god can be quite punitive and this with or without being simultaneously an attachment figure. In fact, one could suggest that undeserved punishment issuing from a father could forestall the establishment of that father as a true attachment figure.

37. The Qur'an 5:91 states, "O ye who believe . . . idols . . . are but abominations."

38. Chance, M. R. A. (1976). Attention structure as the basis of primate rank orders. *Man*, 5(2), 503–518; Eibl-Eibesfeldt, *Human ethology*.

39. Eibl-Eibesfeldt, I. Personal communication.

40. Barrett, *Why would anyone believe in God?*; see also Slone, D. J. (2004). *Theological incorrectness: Why religious people believe what they shouldn't*. New York: Oxford University Press.

41. Guthrie, *Faces in the clouds*.

42. Eibl-Eibesfeldt, *Human ethology*, pp. 173.

43. Boyer, *Religion explained*.

44. This is not to deny the possibility that the Abrahamic god can on occasion function as an attachment god. As noted in note 2 above, sometimes the Christian mystic will relate to Jesus as a mystical lover. The "mystical stare" is the "attachment stare." Moreover, some authors actually argue that Jesus occasionally functions as a mother, a more direct instantiation of the attachment figure. See Bynum, C. W. (1982). *Jesus as mother: Studies in the spirituality of the High Middle Ages*. Berkeley: University of California Press.

45. Mary is not only an attachment figure; she is a maternal attachment figure. This may also affect eye behavior, especially of males. Social dominance hierarchies are generally sex-specific. As a result, a male would not feel the same degree of submission in approaching a high-ranking female compared to a high-ranking male. There would be less fear of punishment

associated with an intratribal female rank-superior than an intratribal male rank-superior. As a result, a male approaches an intratribal female rank-superior with deference more so than with submission.

46. Although some suggest that Jesus is more often a brother and a friend, I maintain that the ocular behaviors attending prayers to the Christ reflect behaviors more appropriate to the rank-superior than not.

47. White, D. G. (2006). *Kiss of the Yogini: "Tantric sex" in its South Asian contexts.* Chicago: The University of Chicago Press.

48. Mines, D. P. (2005). *Fierce gods: Inequality, ritual, and the politics of dignity in a South Indian village.* Bloomington: Indiana University Press.

49. It may be of interest to note here that the Qur'an contains the following sura (50:16): "Assuredly, We have created man and We know well what kind of doubt his mind throws up. We are closer to him than his jugular vein [*habl al-warid*]." Predators, of course, often went and go for the jugular.

50. Trawick, M. (1992). *Notes on love in a Tamil family.* Berkeley: University of California Press.

51. Boyer, *Religion explained*, p. 199.

52. Maloney, C., ed. (1976). *The evil eye.* New York: Columbia University Press.

53. Boyer, *Religion explained*, p. 200.

54. Baumeister, R. F., & Tice, D. M. (1990). Anxiety and social exclusion. *Journal of Social and Clinical Psychology, 9*(2), 165–195.

55. Wilson, D. S. (2002). *Darwin's Cathedral: Evolution, Religion, and the Nature of Society.* Chicago: The University of Chicago Press.

56. Again, and to be sure, I argue that the affiliative, gaze reciprocity often found between lovers is the behavior of the attachment system now confounded with caregiving and sexual behavior systems. In this regard, mystics may longingly gaze into the eyes of an icon, but this is not a gaze different in kind from that employed by the attachment system at large.

CHAPTER 4

Religion and Hidden Patterns in Behavior: Religion as a Biological Phenomenon

Magnus S. Magnusson

I work in a factory that produces graduates.
> —Said by a much loved teacher now long since gone,
> my father, to whose memory and passion for understanding
> this chapter is dedicated.

"Analogy as a source of knowledge" [1] means that something may be learned from similarities between otherwise very different phenomena or in the exact words of the Nobel Prize winning biologist and ethologist Konrad Lorenz:

> Whenever we find, in two forms of life that are unrelated to each other, a similarity of form or of behavior patterns which relates to more than a few minor details, we assume it to be caused by parallel adaptation to the same life-preserving function. [2]

With this in mind, the following chapter aims to describe some rather striking analogies across widely different levels of biological organization: biological cells and human cities. That such comparisons are not new or unique can be seen through Web sites dedicated to "Cell City." [3] But only the latest scientific and technical progress is finally allowing such work, as seen in the words of science writer and former editor for *Nature*, Philip Ball:

A modern view of biology is concerned with *organization* in time and space. How do the molecules of life arrange themselves amongst the cell's compartments, how are they shifted around, how do they communicate, so as to synchronize their action? We can ask these questions only because we can now inspect the working cell at the molecular level, taking measurements and snapshots of molecules going about their business. And so the cell becomes a community.[4]

The focus in this chapter is on long segmented patterned *strings* (ordered sequence of elements; a sentence is a string of letters and spaces) containing patterns of a particular type, called a t-pattern[5] (see definition below), which seem amazingly "universal"; that is, they appear in the string patterns of DNA, RNA, and proteins as well as in the temporal organization of at least a large proportion of the behavior of organisms from neurons to humans.[6] Special focus is also on an analogy between the functions of the cellular organelle called a *ribosome* (the site of protein synthesis) and human "schools," referring to any secular or religious institutions of education or training. The focus in this chapter thus differs, for example, from viewpoints based on the concept of a *meme* (a unit of cultural information),[7] which is, moreover, closely linked to the concept of imitation that is not implicated here.

Religious behavior is here understood as behavior implicating supernatural beings. The chapter focuses on religions based on standard texts such as the Holy Bible and the Koran, but should be relevant to (all?) other religions. Earlier versions existed of both these highly segmented texts, but a standard version of each was finally agreed upon,[8] thus minimizing conflicting influence on behavior within the corresponding communities, which now implicate nearly half of all humans.

This chapter aims to draw parallels to another, recently discovered type of long segmented pattern strings, DNA molecules, which are the fundamental biological means for the shaping and coordination of specialized behavioral potentials amongst the members of the very large protein populations of biological cells. It should be kept in mind that biological cells and their giant DNA information molecules had already existed for billions of years before the recent arrival of humans (themselves consisting of cells with DNA), who finally discovered DNA with its numerous patterns and special code only a few decades ago, a split second in both biological and cultural evolution. Surely, much remains to be learned from the astonishing discovery of a biologically fundamental molecule with information coded in a manner that seems to be in many ways a precursor to human language (with its repeated letters, words, and phrases) and to writing and text in that they exist as separate relatively durable entities. Recently, further analogies have been indicated between DNA structure and Chinese iconic writing.[9] DNA also appears as a precursor to the way the DNA-based humans store information in computers as bytes composed of eight bits (each 0 or 1) and complex information as combinations of bytes. Actually, DNA patterning was discovered about a decade after the creation of the first electronic computer.[10]

BEHAVIOR

Thoughts, feelings, physiological mechanisms, and other internal processes are not amongst the issues of this chapter. Nor is this chapter about beliefs or what individuals say they will or would do. Far from denying the importance of such issues, it is simply assumed that inner workings can or even should sometimes be ignored to gain clarity as, for example, when studying train schedules, consideration of clutches, engines, or conductors is usually less than useful.

In his book *Principles*, the great economist Alfred Marshall (1842–1924) asks: "whether there need be large numbers of people doomed from their birth to hard work in order to provide for others the requisites of a refined and cultured life, while they themselves are prevented by their poverty and toil from having any share or part in that life." [11] This truly disturbing situation suggests the presence of massive interindividual behavior control mechanisms sometimes known to have religious components. But delving into the physiological processes of each of those involved may be frustrating. Covert (internal) phenomena can neither oppress nor kill others, while overt behavior often does. Here a kind of "bird's eye" view of some aspects of overt behavior and its products is instead attempted with special attention to religious behavior with its characteristic repeated standard patterns such as rituals, ceremonies, and standard buildings, as well as the copying, teaching, and distribution of (vocal and written) religious verbal strings.

Should verbal behavior be considered as essentially different from nonverbal behavior? This question is important here and the position adopted is best indicated through the words of a leading twentieth-century linguist, Kenneth L. Pike: "The activity of man constitutes a structural whole, in such a way that it cannot be subdivided into neat 'parts' or 'levels' or 'compartments' insulated in character, content, and organization from other behavior. *Verbal and nonverbal activity is a unified whole*, and theory and methodology should be organized or created to treat it as such." [12] (Emphasis added.)

New conditions constantly arise in complex dynamical systems such as cities with thousands or even millions of interacting individuals, so any approach must consider the creative aspect of such behavior as has, for example, been underlined by Noam Chomsky regarding verbal behavior. [13] That is, even if their fundamental form is the same, new verbal patterns are constantly being produced along with older ones. However, all seem to involve the same general form (pattern type; see below) as other human behavior and interactions. But perpetual creativity also means perpetual uniqueness as is expressed in unison by two pioneers of human interaction research, Adam Kendon and Michael Argyle: "a conversation, . . . a complex system of relationships which nonetheless may be understood in terms of general principles which are discoverable and generally applicable, even though the course of any specific encounter is unique." [14]

Thus, looking at behavior as the repetition of patterns of a general structural type does not deny that their content and meaning (function) may be endlessly innovative and subject to selection whether through slow DNA evolution or the much faster cultural evolution. Either way, the long segmented strings of human wisdom have deep roots as reflected in this passage from Samuel Noah Kramer:

> If you ever begin to doubt the brotherhood of man and the common humanity of all people and races, turn to their sayings and maxims, their precepts and adages . . . The Sumerian proverbs were compiled and written down more than thirty-five hundred years ago, and many had undoubtedly been repeated by word of mouth for centuries before they were put in written form . . . We have little difficulty in recognizing in them reflections of our own drives and attitudes, foibles and weaknesses, confusions and dilemmas. [15]

RELIGIOUS BEHAVIOR

In numerous human cities, omnipresent religious rituals such as the massively repeated prayers, baptisms, and masses of Christian societies are usually expected to influence individual behavior in somewhat predictable and constructive ways. Performed by numerous citizens at particular times and even at fixed locations in standard structures (for example, churches, mosques, chapels, and monasteries) this per se must have a strong synchronizing and organizing effect.

However, the presently dominant world religions can hardly be imagined without their very long and standardized verbal strings. The Holy Bible and the Koran are amongst the best-known and influential examples of such giant verbal strings that, moreover, are often also considered the foundations of law, culture, and politics in their respective communities. Other such examples are the extensive religious poems of ancient Greece and India implicating numerous supernatural beings. Control or influence thus extends naturally from a long, old, and stable verbal string usually through compatibility of any new (and often derived) texts. Laws will not contradict the constitution, which generally will not contradict the holy text (except, for example, some outdated parts).

Holy texts, however, are mostly composed of everyday words, and their sentences look the same as secular ones. They also frequently concern worldly matters such as rules of social conduct amongst mortal humans. As essential aspects of human and even primate interaction have probably remained similar for a very long time,[16] this may partly explain the "eternal value" of some parts of holy scriptures initially oriented toward highly diverse and mostly illiterate, superstitious, and, by modern standards, uneducated populations. While secular texts also contain guidelines for worldly social conduct, one defining aspect of religious speech and text is to also provide guidelines for conduct vis-à-vis supernatural beings.

REPEATED PATTERNS AND BIOLOGICAL PHENOMENA

Repeated patterns appear to be of essential importance in all things biological. In the words of one of the discoverers of the structure of DNA,[17] the Nobel Prize winning biologist Francis Crick: *"Another key feature of biology is the existence of many identical examples of complex structures."* [18] (Emphasis added.) The central place of *patterns* in the biology of *behavior*, as well as their often "hidden" character, is also clearly expressed by the opening words of Irenäus Eibl-Eibesfeldt's[19] book *Ethology: The Biology of Behavior:*[20] *"Behavior consists of patterns in time.* Investigations of behavior deal with sequences that, in contrast to bodily characteristics, are *not always visible."* (Emphasis added.)

However, the concept of "pattern" is broad to say the least, since most mathematicians view mathematics as the science of patterns as witnessed, for example, by Keith Devlin's recent history of mathematics entitled *Mathematics, the Science of Patterns: The Search for Order in Life, Mind and the Universe*.[21] The pattern type of special interest here, t-patterns, will be defined below in a relatively nontechnical way, as an intuitive understanding of their essential characteristics is sufficient for the purpose of this chapter.

Because behavior patterns are "not always visible," long-standing attempts to deal with the definition and detection of hidden behavioral patterns in general have contributed much to the proposed biological view of religious behavior in particular based on the concept of repeated patterns.[22] Human behavior and interactions involve a complex stream of events in time and space. While repeated patterning is often sensed by participants as onlookers, pinpointing exactly what *kind* of patterns is involved and detecting them has proven difficult. However, t-pattern detection using the specially developed detection software THEME[23] has been successfully applied to the behavior and interactions of very different "organisms": neurons,[24] *Drosophila* (fruit flies),[25] and humans, as witnessed by the recently published work of nearly 40 scientists.[26] Its use for the detection of t-patterns in DNA and proteins has also begun.[27]

THE T-PATTERN

The ideas and motivations behind the development of the t-pattern type come from a number of sources such as ethology (the biology of behavior), linguistics, Skinnerian behaviorism, artificial intelligence, statistics, and computer science. As the essential defining aspect, a t-pattern happens when various types of elements on a single dimension (such as time) occur together more often than expected by chance[28] in the same order and with similar distances (intervals, windows) between them each time. For a more formal part of the definition, see the Appendix.

The following is an example of a pattern where the critical intervals have been determined:

I.   A [3, 7] B [20, 30] C [4, 6] D

In this case, when A occurs, B will occur 3 to 7 units later and then C will occur, 20 to 30 units later followed by D, 4 to 6 units later. If such a pattern occurs more often than expected by chance within some interval (period) on a single dimension, then it is a t-pattern.

Moreover, a t-pattern is generally hierarchical and *recursive* (objects are defined in terms of other objects of the same type)[29] as well as *self-similar* (looks "roughly" the same on any scale)[30] structures, in the sense that a t-pattern is composed of t-patterns of t-patterns, etc., always of the same kind down to their simplest elements. For example, pattern I could be considered and detected as the following:

$$\text{II.} \quad ((\,A\,[\,3,7\,]\,B\,)\,[\,20,30\,]\,(\,C\,[\,4,6\,]\,D\,))$$

where the simpler t-patterns (A [3, 7] B) and (C [4, 6] D) may each occur more frequently than the more complex pattern II, which will involve only those occurrences of the simpler patterns that are related by the critical interval [20, 30]. Note especially that each time a t-pattern occurs any number of other elements may occur between those of the pattern, which often has made both direct and computational detection difficult or impossible.

T-patterns, such as phrases and melodies (t-patterns of notes), can be produced at different speeds and with other temporal modifications; that is, they have limited elasticity as indicated by their critical intervals, as can be seen above and in the Appendix. A melody if played sufficiently fast will simply become an accord and if played sufficiently slowly just a series of unrelated notes.

Any standard sentence (such as "How are you today?" or "You shall not murder") is an example of a t-pattern as each time it occurs it is composed of the same words in the same order. Each time there are highly predictable time distances between its words (elements), and its words (elements) can be similarly described in terms of simpler elements: phonemes (or in text, letters).

Everyday secular routines or rituals such as a dinner, a lunch, a coffee break, or a car wash are t-pattern examples, as are a multitude of religious rituals such as baptism and marriage ceremonies, which are all characterized by particular behavioral elements occurring sequentially and with somewhat flexible but limited distances between them. Moreover, and essentially, considering the frequency and distribution of each of the elements per se, they would not be expected just by chance to occur together so often in this order and with such similarity in relative timing.

Figure 4.1 illustrates one occurrence of a t-pattern with six subpatterns (AB and CD are called subpatterns of pattern II above), which

Figure 4.1. This figure illustrates an instance of a t-pattern composed of other t-patterns (its subpatterns, which may again have subpatterns, etc.) here marked as black segments, while the white intervals between them are either insignificant or empty, but may also contain various other elements, which sometimes influence the effect or meaning of the pattern. The t-pattern is elastic and can be thought of as a rubber band where any part can be stretched to some extent. This structure can, for example, be interpreted either as a behavioral routine with six parts (subpatterns) such as a dinner or a religious ritual or as a gene, in which case the dark segments represent exons (the active part of a gene used to make a protein).

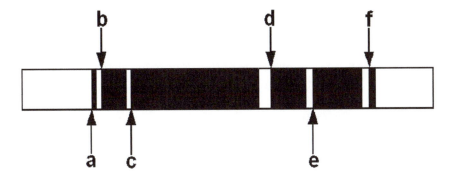

could, for example, be seen as a representation of a dinner: (a) sits down at table, (b) takes an appetizer, (c) takes a main course, (d) takes a dessert, (e) takes coffee, and (f) stands up from table. Here the letters a, b, c, d, e, and f stand for the beginning of each of those subpatterns. Using more letters the endings could also be explicitly included in the pattern. Any religious ritual (here with six steps) would correspond to the t-pattern structure and look similar even if the exact timing were different.

Instead of time, measured in some discrete unit, written verbal strings (text) can be measured in letters. In this case, examples of verbal t-patterns are repeated phrases, paragraphs, sections, and texts, etc., within all (secular or holy) books and libraries, and even within the totality of text of a whole community, here called its *textome*.

PATTERNS AND INDIVIDUALS IN CELL CITY

A biological cell contains a DNA molecule that is called its *genome* and is divided into "chapters" called *chromosomes*. DNA is a long string of four different molecules,[31] called *bases* and noted A, C, G, and T. Thus GTGCTTGAGTTACTCCCCCTATTATTTGGAT... is a tiny DNA segment. Many DNA segments, called *genes*, are essential to the existence of the cell. Much (most) of the genome has no genes and is often referred to as "*junk* DNA" (as opposite to *coding* DNA).

Each gene[32] is a template for the creation of a particular *protein*[33] type, the specialized individuals (workers) of Cell City. Proteins are strings of a few hundred to a few thousand (amino acid) molecules of 20 different kinds (and thus conveniently represented using the alphabet). For example, MKGEPKTYSMSDLSYYGEKAQQQNEKQQ KQY... is a part of a protein sequence. The population of all proteins in a cell at each moment is called its *proteome*.[34] The series of bases in the gene is interpreted or read three at a time, that is, as a series of triplets of bases called *codons*[35] (for example, "GTG" or "AGT") with each combination specifying one of the 20 possible elements along the sequence of the protein. The genes are first transcribed (in adapted relative rates) into *relatively short-lived* molecules called *RNA*, which in the *ribosome* structures serve as templates for the creation of proteins with a corresponding sequence that determines its behavioral potential (relative to the various tasks).

Proteins may be "building materials" but also "specialized workers" (here *work proteins*), which like many living creatures have special parts for interactions (communication modules) and show strong selectiveness regarding their protein "interlocutors," which results in fairly well defined social networks.[36]

The genes of humans and numerous other species are made of two types of segments called *exons* and *introns*[37] (see Figure 4.1). During the translation into a protein only the exons are used while the introns are ignored[38] as basically meaningless separators, a kind of "junk" DNA, much as those segments separating the genes on the DNA molecule. Such separator segments, however, sometimes contain important information on how to read the significant parts. Thus, for example, just as some types of poetry may be read meaningfully in different ways (for example, forward and backward), the same DNA (gene) segment can be read in various ways, resulting in different proteins.

Between the complexity levels of codons and genes, a relatively small number of basic components exist: "Genes, we know, are long stretches of DNA code. Each is build up of smaller modules, like a mosaic. We don't know exactly how many such modules there are, but it looks as though there may be *as few as a thousand or two*. So these modules must be shared by a large number of genes." [39] (Emphasis added.) This number of modules is apparently close to the number of signs needed for essential communication in Chinese iconic writing, which may look more complex than it is: "All the 30–40,000 known characters are formed from combinations of these basic elements. There are only 200–300 of them; most are characters with specific meanings in their own right." [40]

Thus, relatively few special modules occur repeatedly within multibillion units (bases) long DNA strings, which also contain a large proportion of junk. However, various subsets of these modules (just as, for example, subsets of words in language) intermittently occur together in a particular order and with relatively strict limits on the number of units (bases) between them (see t-pattern definition above and Figure 4.1). Under such distributional circumstances, the patterning of the DNA molecule, its crucial segments called genes, and consequently their RNA transcripts and their resulting protein sequences correspond to the t-pattern model.

Thus, in Cell City, there is a highly patterned information molecule (DNA) with numerous crucial segments (genes) and numerous short-lived (RNA) transcripts of these that shape and coordinate the behavioral potentials of the citizens, but, interestingly, this ultimately leads to the same type of patterns in time, that is, for example, temporal t-patterns in neuronal interactions and ultimately in the behavior and interactions of their hosts, for example, humans.

THE RIBOSOME: FACTORY AND SCHOOL

Speech is momentary and dependent on the speaker. The invention of writing made it more like DNA as speech was represented by durable objects, written verbal strings or text that could be distributed independently of the speaker/writer. The consequences have since been incalculable for human life and apparently right from the start. In the words of Kramer: "The Sumerian school was a direct outgrowth of the invention and development of the cuneiform system of writing, Sumer's most significant contribution to civilization." [41]

When focusing on the ribosome's production of proteins that serve, for example, as building materials in the cell, the natural human analogy is the factory. [42] But when considering specialized work proteins in the ribosome shaping other types of specialized work proteins, the analogy turns toward human institutions of education and training and their specialized workers (teachers, preachers, etc.) who create specific behavioral potentials in individuals preparing them for a particular city's tasks.

In humans this means that special combinations of relatively short-lived verbal strings (such as, for example, teaching materials) derived (by writers with analogous DNA to RNA translation workers in cells) from a selection of segments of relatively long and long-lasting strings (such as, for example, religious scriptures, classical literature, legal texts, and knowledge and know-how literature) are copied into human brains by specialized individuals such as teachers or preachers. Each combination often has a name such as engineer, lawyer, pilot, geologist, captain, chemist, behavioral scientist, physicist, medical doctor, theologian, economist, astronaut, teacher, and priest.

In the cell, specialized proteins in the ribosome take care of translating relatively short-lived transcripts of the various segments of its giant DNA string into the corresponding molecular strings, the proteins, whose behavioral potential is determined by their particular molecular sequence. But in the human case behavioral potentials are rather installed in the existing human individual relying on a multitude of internal mechanisms (molecular, physiological, etc.), some little known. However, the net effect can still be seen as equivalent since the specialized proteins and humans are enabled to perform the tasks of their respective cities (see Figure 4.2). And they are "produced" in numbers approximately adequate for the needs of the city. As a matter of fact, the ribosome may thus still be likened to a factory, if an educational institution is seen as a "factory that produces graduates (specialists)."

SOCIAL INSECT CITIES VERSUS THOSE OF HUMANS AND PROTEINS

The hives of social insects such as ants and termites (which like humans are also composed of cells) could seem better models of human cities than are the cities of proteins if only for the more similar size and complexity of the inhabitants. But no simple relation seems to exist between body size, brain size, or general intelligence of citizens and the complexity of their social organization. Even amongst humans, there exist both tiny villages and giant cities. The Great Apes thus have far bigger bodies and brains than social insects whose societies have far larger populations (up to tens of millions) and are more

Figure 4.2.   This sketch outlines a mechanism that seems to be common to both Cell City and the human city: Long and long-lived string patterns (DNA or fundamental texts; for example, religious or legal) provide templates for shorter and shorter-lived strings (RNA or "teaching materials"), which provide the templates used in the "shaper" (ribosome or "school"; i.e., educational institution, religious or secular) to form specialized citizens. See text.

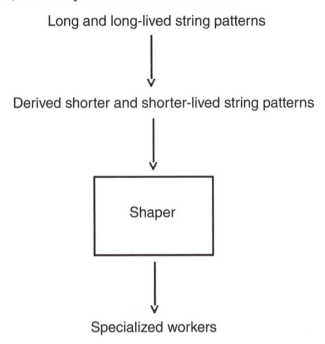

Long and long-lived string patterns

Derived shorter and shorter-lived string patterns

Shaper

Specialized workers

complex. Actually, there are no nonhuman primate hives or cities at all. But the great cities of humans and those of the microscopic brainless proteins are far more complex and populous than those of any insects that notably lack the others' means of shaping and coordinating the behavioral potentials of the citizens: the giant long-lasting highly segmented information strings and the regulated copying of their segments into durable strings, which exist outside the individuals (citizens) and serve as templates for the shaping of such potentials.

Cell City thus becomes a more tempting model of human cities and not the least with regard to religious behavior, which frequently relies on some of the oldest, longest, and most stable segmented information (control) strings in each city.

TALKING MOLECULES REFLECT THEIR OWN IMAGES AND DISCOVER THEMSELVES

Cultural transmission is about transmitting behavior between individuals and generations through non-DNA means such as verbal behavior. Humans thus started copying verbal control strings fairly exactly, first by vocal means and then through *writing*, a fundamental invention as the written verbal control strings become highly durable independent objects that can be stored, accumulated, and elaborated, thereby constituting an endlessly extendable external memory. Giant strings have thus emerged containing numerous segments, each with fairly predictable effects on the behavioral potential of the specially prepared (literate) receivers of ever-larger communities. Besides the standardized religious texts with all their derived speech and texts, this also includes the extremely voluminous and complex legal, scientific, and technological texts that today fill the huge structures called libraries.

Thus ever-more complex superorganisms continue to evolve together with their giant control strings as the evolution of DNA molecules has finally led to the elements needed for the discovery and understanding of the DNA molecule itself and possibly also of the role and place of supernatural beings in human life.

Watching a military parade with thousands of human individuals moving identically and in perfect rhythm, one wonders what controls this behavior: the individuals' brains or the "superorganism" (city, community, state, or society). Actually, in this situation the brain simply appears to be the body part *used* by the superorganism as a kind of handle to control the behavior of each individual, and frequently this is achieved through the use of verbal string patterns.

CONCLUSION

The visual verbal string in this chapter has been about mechanisms involved in the organization of (social) systems of interacting entities or individuals with varying behavioral potentials. Some of the oldest, longest, most pervasive, and influential verbal control strings are here called religious due to their implication of supernatural beings. The behavior and interactions of nearly half of humanity is influenced by only two such strings, both from the same geographical region and related to the same supernatural being: the Koran and the Holy Bible. Interestingly, however, long verbal strings have played somewhat similar roles in very large communities, such as those associated with the names of known mortals, for example, Confucius, Buddha, and Marx.

So, DNA molecules, in their own image and through their increasingly well-prepared (literate) human hosts, spin ever-more complex and voluminous external control strings, which gradually take control and mediate interindividual and intergenerational transfer of ever-more complex behaviors, within communities of increasing sizes, without any need for changes in their own molecular (DNA) patterns.

Verbal and molecular strings thus serve as a database of collective social intelligence. While they operate on different time scales, their segments guide behavior in somewhat predictable ways. Unlike Cell City, both types of strings act on the individuals of a human city: molecular from within and verbal from outside. The total set of inside and outside control strings in a human city, that is, the genomes of all its individuals plus its textome, could be called its *stringome*. Considering either the stringome or the textome alone, humans could thus be seen not only as "naked apes" [43] but also as *string-controlled apes* or just "string-apes," being both puppets and weavers of evolving control strings.

Religious behavior depending on relatively old, long, and stable verbal strings containing numerous crucial segments with the frequency of use of each depending on community needs, as well as large unused parts, could thus apparently be viewed not only as natural, but rather as a prototypical biological phenomenon.

APPENDIX

Thus, for a particular observation period and with X_i as the ith element within the pattern of m elements, the following represents a t-pattern:

$$X_1 \, [d_{11}, d_{12}] \, X_2 \, .. \, X_i \, [d_{i1}, d_{i2}] \, X_{i+1} \, .. \, X_{m-1} \, [d_{(m-1)1}, d_{(m-1)2}] \, X_m$$

The general term $X_i[d_{i1}, d_{i2}]X_{i+1}$ means that when X_i occurs at t as a part of the pattern, then within the interval $[t + d_{i1}, t + d_{i2}]$ it is followed by X_{i+1}; $[t + d_{i1}, t + d_{i2}]$ is called a critical interval and $0 \leq d_{i1} \leq d_{i2}$. (For concurrent elements within a t-pattern $0 = d_{i1} = d_{i2}$.) A pattern of length m thus has $m - 1$ different critical intervals.

NOTES

1. The title of Konrad Lorenz's Nobel lecture in 1973.

2. Lorenz, K. (1992 [1973]). Analogy as a source of knowledge. In J. Lindsten (Ed.), *Nobel lectures, physiology or medicine 1971–1980.* Singapore: World Scientific Publishing Co.

3. See notably the BBCi and Open University site: http://www.open2.net/science/cellcity/.

4. Ball, P. (2001). *Stories of the invisible: A guided tour of molecules* (p. 44). New York: Oxford University Press.

5. Magnusson, M. S. 2000. Discovering hidden time patterns in behavior: T-patterns and their detection. *Behavior Research Methods, Instruments and Computers, 32*(1), 93–110. Regarding the close relationship between linguistic analysis of verbal strings and modern DNA analysis, see, for example, Sankoff, D., & Kruskal, J. (Eds.). (1999). *Time wraps, string edits, and macromolecules. The David Hume series: Philosophy and cognitive science reissues.* Stanford, CA: Center for the Study of Language and Information.

6. Anolli, L., Duncan, S., Magnusson, M.S., & Riva, G. (Eds.). (2005). *The hidden structure of interaction: From neurons to culture patterns.* Amsterdam: IOS Press.

7. Dawkins, R. (1976). *The selfish gene.* New York: Oxford University Press; Blackmore, S. (1999). *The meme machine.* New York: Oxford University Press.

8. Onfray, M. (2008). *Atheist manifesto: The case against Christianity, Judaism, and Islam.* New York: Arcade Publishing.

9. Noble, D. (2006). *The music of life: Biology beyond the genome* (pp. 101–103). Oxford: Oxford University Press.

10. "The first electronic computers date to the mid-20th century (1940–1945)." See, for example, Burks, A. R., & Burks, A. W. (1989). *The first electronic computer: The Atanasoff story.* Ann Arbor, MI: University of Michigan Press.

11. Marshall, A. (1930; first published 1890). *Principles of economics* (8th ed.; pp. 3–4). London: MacMillan. Here cited from Bowels, S. (2004). *Microeconomics: Behavior, institutions, and evolution* (p. 7). Princeton, NJ: Princeton University Press.

12. Pike, K. L. (1960). *Language: In relation to a unified theory of the structure of human behavior* (p. 138). Glendale, CA: Summer Institute of Linguistics.

13. Chomsky, N. (1965). *Aspects of the theory of syntax.* Cambridge, MA: MIT Press.

14. Kendon, A. (1990). *Conducting interaction: Patterns of behavior in focused encounters* (p. 4). Cambridge and New York: Cambridge University Press. See also Argyle, M., & Kendon, A. (1967). The experimental analysis

of the social performance. In L. Berkowitz (Ed.), *Advances in Experimental Social Psychology* (Vol. III, pp. 55–98). New York: Academic Press.

15. Kramer, S. N. (1956). *History begins at Sumer* (p. 117). Philadelphia, PA: University of Pennsylvania Press.

16. See, for example, a special issue of *Science*, November 7, 2008, regarding the genetics of behavior including human social behavior.

17. J. D. Watson and F. Crick discovered the double helix structure of the DNA molecule in 1953 for which they later shared the Nobel Prize.

18. Crick, F. H. C. (1988). *What mad pursuit: A personal view of scientific discovery* (p. 138). New York: Basic Books.

19. Irenäus Eibl-Eibesfeldt, a long time collaborator of Konrad Lorenz, is often referred to as the father of human ethology, the biology of human behavior.

20. Eibl-Eibesfeldt, I. (1970). *Ethology: The biology of behavior* (p. 1). New York: Holt, Rinehart and Winston.

21. Devlin, K. J. (1997). *Mathematics, the science of patterns: The search for order in life, mind and the universe*. New York: Scientific American Library.

22. Magnusson, M. S. (2003). Analyzing complex real-time streams of behavior: Repeated patterns in behavior and DNA. In C. Baudoin (Ed.), *L'éthologie appliquée aujourd'hui* (Volume 3—Ethologie humaine). Levallois-Perret, France: Editions ED. ISBN 2-7237-0025-9; Magnusson, M. S. (2004). Repeated patterns in behavior and other biological phenomena. In D. K. Oller & U. Griebel (Eds.), *Evolution of communication systems: A comparative approach* (Vienna Series in Theoretical Biology). London: The MIT Press; Magnusson, M. S. (2005). Understanding social interaction: Discovering hidden structure with model and algorithms. In L. Anolli, S. Duncan, M. S. Magnusson, & G. Riva (Eds.), *The hidden structure of interaction: From neurons to culture patterns*. Amsterdam: IOS Press.

23. See www.hbl.hi.is, www.patternvision.com, and www.noldus.com.

24. Nicol, A. U., Kendrick, K. M., & Magnusson, M. S. (2005). Communication within a neural network. In L. Anolli, S. Duncan, M. S. Magnusson, & G. Riva (Eds.), *The hidden structure of interaction: From neurons to culture patterns*. Amsterdam: IOS Press.

25. Arthur, B. I., & Magnusson, M. S. (2005). Microanalysis of *Drosophila* courtship behaviour. In L. Anolli, S. Duncan, M. S. Magnusson, & G. Riva (Eds.), *The hidden structure of interaction: From neurons to culture patterns*. Amsterdam: IOS Press.

26. Anolli, L., Duncan, S., Magnussson, M. S., & Giuseppe, R. (Eds.). (2005). *The Hidden structure of interaction: From neurons to culture patterns*. Amsterdam: IOS Press.

27. Magnusson, M. S. (2005). Understanding social interaction: Discovering hidden structure with model and algorithms. In L. Anolli, S. Duncan, M. S. Magnusson, & G. Riva (Eds.), *The hidden structure of interaction: From neurons to culture patterns*. Amsterdam: IOS Press.

28. Assuming a zero hypothesis, there is independent random uniform distribution for each element type.

29. The definition of "recursive" is taken from http://mathworld .wolfram.com/Recursion.html.

30. This definition of "self-similarity" is taken from http://mathworld .wolfram.com/Self-Similarity.html.

31. In human DNA there are 3 billion bases.

32. The DNA segment of a gene generally has associated with it some elements (notably, so-called promoters and repressors) that help determine when and in what quantities it is translated into proteins.

33. Petsko, G. A., & Ringe, D. (2004). *Protein structure and function*. London: New Science Press.

34. A fast-growing research area, *proteomics*, is now dedicated to the structure, functions, interactions, and organization of proteins within cells. See, for example, Campbell, A. M., & Heyert, L. J. (2007). *Discovering genomics, proteomics, and bioinformatics*. New York: CSHL Press, Pearson Benjamin Cummings.

35. The codon is similar to a byte, but with three positions and four possible values (A, C, G, and T) instead of eight positions with two (0 or 1) possible values.

36. Giot, L., et al. (2003, December 5). A protein interaction map of *Drosophila* melanogaster. *Science, 302*(5651), 1727–1736.

37. In some species there are no introns.

38. In this connection, it is interesting to note that when speech is transcribed, hesitation or pauses are generally not reflected (are cut out) in the resulting text.

39. Noble, D. (2006). *The music of life: Biology beyond the genome* (p. 103). Oxford: Oxford University Press.

40. Ibid., p. 103.

41. Kramer, *History begins at Sumer*, p. 3.

42. For example, on the Open University Cell City Web site, http:// www.open2.net/science/cellcity/, the ribosome in Cell City is likened to a factory in the human city.

43. Morris, D. (1967). *The naked ape: A zoologist's study of the human animal*. New York: McGraw-Hill.

PART TWO

The Evolutionary History of Religious Behavior

Some but not all human behaviors have evolved in ways that allow one to look for the same behaviors (called *homologous behaviors*) in lower organisms. To do this, one has to look for behavior that has the same form, rather than the same function. This is similar to looking for the same anatomical forms, such as the bones of the human arm and hand, in lower organisms. Finding homologous forms in ancestors allows one to establish the relationship between two species as well as trace the evolutionary history of the form. In biology *phylogeny* is the term for tracing the evolutionary history of a form. The single chapter (Chapter 5) in Part Two traces the evolutionary history of religious behavior that can be defined by its form. It also explores the other religious behaviors whose forms are variable and therefore can be defined only by their functions.

CHAPTER 5

The Evolutionary History of Religious Behavior

Jay R. Feierman

Human evolutionary history involves tracing human features back over time. When the features are passed across generations by DNA, this is called biological evolution and the tracing process is called *phylogeny*. Darwinian natural selection is the most common form of biological evolution.[1] When the features are passed across generations by social learning, this is called "cultural evolution." The two are interrelated.[2] All of the features of any organism can be divided into forms (also called "structures") and functions. Only forms, which have structural or architectural mass, can be directly traced back through evolutionary time either biologically or culturally. Functions cannot.[3] Throughout this chapter the terms "form" and "structure" are used interchangeably. As an example, a leg has form or structure but walking is a function. This relationship between form and function will be important to keep in mind in trying to understand the evolutionary history of religious behavior.[4]

Nobel Laureate ethologist (behavioral biologist) Niko Tinbergen said that to fully understand any behavior one has to understand four things about the behavior, which are often called the four questions of Tinbergen:[5] (1) What is the behavior's evolutionary history? (2) What is the behavior's developmental history over the life span of the individual? (3) What are the behavior's causes within the life span of the individual? (4) Does the behavior have survival value or adaptiveness? These four questions also form the part headings of this book. This chapter will be concerned with the first question of Tinbergen. However, before that is undertaken, more needs to be said about religion and behavior in general.

RELIGION

Religion is so broad a concept that most definitions fail, as there are always exceptions. However, religion can be described. Ethologist Robert A. Hinde describes most religions as containing at least some of the following elements: structural beliefs, narratives, and rituals; prayer, sacrifice, and other aspects of religious practice; a code of personal and group conduct; religious experience; and social aspects.[6] For simplicity in this chapter these elements will be reduced to religious behavior, beliefs, values, moods, and feelings. When one does this, religious beliefs, values, moods, and feelings become contributing causes of religious behavior.[7]

BEHAVIOR

There are many ways that behavior (the movement of an individual) can be divided into categories. Each way may be useful for a different purpose. For the purpose of understanding human religious behavior from a behavioral biology perspective, the following classification, which is derived from previous work of the author,[8] is useful.

Type I Behavior: Definable by form and function in a natural environment and species-universal in form.

Type II Behavior: Describable by form and *definable* by function in a natural environment and not species-universal in form.

Because the terms *describable* and *definable* are used above as one of the ways to differentiate between Type I and Type II Behaviors, it may help to clarify the differences between them and then show how this applies to behavior. When something is *defined,* it is first put into a recognizable general category; then one says how it is different from the other items in the same general category. A good definition allows one to identify or recognize something without missing it or without confusing it with something else that is similar. In addition, a definition tells what something is by equating the definition with its referent by using the verb "to be."

In contrast, a *description* is a transformation of some of the perceivable features of what is being described using a different format. For example, what is seen visually gets transformed into a verbal representation of some of the visual features. The more words that are used to describe something, the more likely it is that one will be able to recognize what is being described and not confuse it with something that is similar. Definitions are what create categories with sharp boundaries in science.

To *define* behavior by its form, one states "the change of positions of parts of the body relative to other parts and to environmental coordinates."[9] Then one states how this movement is different from other movements that are a similar change of position in reference to the same reference points. When behavior shows lots of variation in form when repeated by the same or different individuals, it can only be defined by its function, although its form can still be described. For example, imagine a child is "playing," which is a functional characterization of the child's behavior. One cannot *define* "playing" by its form because there are too many behaviors that can be used when a child is playing. Yet, for any specific example of a particular child playing, one can easily *describe* the child's behavior.

The other concept used to understand behavior is *function*. Both Type I and Type II Behaviors can be defined by their function. A function can be thought of as the nonstructural result or outcome of one form (or structure) interacting with another form (or structure) in space and over time where at least one of the two forms (structures) is a part of the behaving individual. For example, "clapping," which is a function, is the result or outcome of the palm of one hand briskly contacting the palm of the other hand in a rhythmic manner. The type of function referred to above has been called the nonhistorical, causal role (CR) type of function. Another synonym is *proximate* (meaning near) use function.[10] This CR concept of function is in contrast to what is called the selected effect (SE) type of function in which the function of a trait, often called the trait's adaptive function or ultimate function, is considered the same as its evolutionary purpose or the reason why the trait evolved by natural selection. In this chapter when the term "function" is used, it only refers to CR or proximate function, which is its meaning when used by comparative anatomists and physiologists when they study the forms and functions, respectively, of the various structural organs of the body. The form and function of behavior (movement) can be studied biologically in ways similar to how the form and function of structural organs of the body are studied.[11] This similarity is what allows us to study religious behavior from a biological perspective.

It may be useful to say more about Type I and Type II Behaviors that will help when these terms are applied to religious behavior. First, the instructions for executing Type I Behavior biologically evolve and are passed across generations by DNA. In contrast, most of the instructions for executing Type II Behavior culturally evolve and are passed across (and within) generations by social learning. There are actually two types of Type I Behaviors: reflexes and coordinated motor patterns. A coordinated motor pattern is in-between a reflex and the more flexible types of behaviors seen in humans. Reflexes tend to be independent of mood, whereas coordinated motor patterns are mood dependent. Reflexes also tend to be all or none and only exhibit variation in intensity with muscle fatigue or in neurological disorders. In contrast, coordinated motor patterns have more variation in intensity from the subtle smile to the ear-to-ear grin. Specific stimuli in the environment can "release" specific Type I Behaviors whether they are reflexes or coordinated motor patterns.[12] These principles will be applied to Type I religious behavior in the next section of this chapter.

Type I Behaviors are seen in all vertebrates (animals with backbones) from bony fish to humans. All of the instincts of animals are executed by Type I Behaviors.[13] Common examples of Type I Behaviors (coordinated motor patterns) can easily be seen in one's family dog: wagging the tail, fetching something that is thrown, burying a bone or food, baring the canine teeth when aggressive, lying on the back when submissive, etc. In humans common examples of Type I Behaviors are the various facial affects (happy, sad, anger, surprise, disgust, fear, and neutral)[14] as well as much of our courtship,[15] mating, maternal-infant care, and dominance and submissive behaviors.[16] As one moves up the evolutionary tree of life from bony fish to humans, the individual has more volitional control over the execution of Type I Behavior.

All societies have what are called "display rules,"[17] which regulate the context and intensity for Type I Behaviors, such as where and how displays of anger can be shown. Different societies also have display rules for which of several variations on a common theme of a Type I Behavior are shown. For example, bond-establishing and maintaining rites (greeting and departing ceremonies) have many local variations on a common theme.[18] The common theme is some type of reciprocated mirrored behavior in close proximity that is a part of our universal human "social grammar." [19] However, the variations on the common theme can be different across societies as in the American handshake, the European kiss on both cheeks, the Japanese bow, the Inuit *kunik*, and the Maori *hongi*. This concept of intersocietal variation on a common theme will be important in terms of understanding the local variations in Type I Behavior across different religions.

Type II Behaviors are not seen in all vertebrates. They have been described, although not by the name "Type II Behaviors," in some primates, sea mammals, and birds. Type II Behaviors are all behaviors (movements) that are not Type I Behaviors. When a species that is only capable of executing Type I Behavior learns, only the timing, orientation, intensity, and function of the coordinated motor pattern gets modified. The behavior's form remains the same. In contrast, the actual form of Type II Behaviors can be modified through learning. In humans postinfancy maternal caring behavior (a functional characterization of behavior) is an example of Type II Behavior. Think of all of the forms of behavior that a human mother uses to care for her toddler, preteen, and teenage child. Many of these behaviors are "flexible" in their execution and only have one thing in common—the function of postinfancy maternal caring. All of the behaviors that are used in vocally articulating as well as in writing human symbolic languages are Type II Behaviors.

It helps to realize that so-called present participle verbs that end in "ing" are functions. Examples include such things as playing, throwing, dancing, hiding, cooking, baptizing, and praying. Functions are ephemeral (temporary) states rather than more permanent, structural traits. Features or characteristics that can only be defined by their function do not have mass. One cannot hold them in one's hand. Because only forms (structures) can be traced back in biological evolution, one cannot trace the biological evolutionary history of functions per se. There is a reason for this. The information that is passed across generations through genes (DNA) is structural information. Most active genes code for the instructions to make structural proteins, which are enzymes that control specific biochemical reactions. It is an old principle in biology that genes code for structures and then the structures have functions. The functions of the structures that genes code for can change through the developmental lifetime of a single individual as well as over the evolutionary history of the species. Therefore, Type II Behavior (the movement of individuals) that can only be defined by its function cannot have the same type of biological evolutionary history as the Type I Behavior that can be defined by its form and structure. As will be seen, most religious behaviors are Type II Behaviors.

Having given some general background about behavior and how to categorize and conceptualize it in terms of form and function, the next step is to apply this understanding to religious behavior. The next two sections will address Type I and Type II religious behaviors.

TYPE I RELIGIOUS BEHAVIOR

Many Type I Behaviors used in religion, such as smile and walk, are not specific to religion. However, there is a Type I religious behavior that appears to be present in all the major religions of the world and at least some tribal religions. It is seen in the nonvocal aspect of petitioning prayer. What can be seen is a local variation of make-oneself-lower-*or*-smaller-*or*-more-vulnerable behavior (*LSV behavior*).[20] Stated slightly differently, LSV behavior is the general theme upon which there is local variation. LSV behavior is an ancient, coordinated motor pattern whose various forms can be traced back through the earliest vertebrates. LSV behavior has had many functions over its long evolutionary history. Its likely first function was submission, which is an automatic response when two individuals of the same species have an aggressive interaction, one member is overwhelmingly more powerful, and escape or simple freezing (becoming motionless) is not possible. Submissive behavior acts as a "releasing stimulus" or "social releaser" to the aggressor and decreases the aggressor's aggressiveness.[21]

Submissive behavior in humans has many variations in form of the general LSV theme. For example, one of the first signs of submission is the volume of the voice gets reduced and the pitch gets higher. Then, questions are answered but not initiated, and the topic of conversation is not changed. There is less eye contact. The head often tilts and then the shoulders get squeezed inward. Signs of fear in the facial affect may appear. Empty, weaponless hands are brought together in front of the body and eventually above the head. If the threat is very serious, the submissive individual may drop to the knees. Thus, there are a number of different behaviors that are all variations on the LSV theme.

Another area where one can see LSV behavior is in the nonverbal aspect of human female courtship. In this context the function of the behavior has changed from submission to solicitation. The behavior is done in conjunction with simultaneously occurring or rapidly alternating approach-avoidance behaviors, producing the classic picture of coyness or teasing.[22] Also, in courtship there can be a variety of facial affects seen, but one facial affect is avoided—fear. Fear is the facial affect that accompanies the LSV behavior when it is used in true submission. Therefore the absence of a fearful affect makes it clear that the LSV behavior is being used as courtship solicitation and not submission. In contrast, in some of the earliest premammalian ancestors of humans the female courtship solicitation behaviors are indistinguishable from the behaviors whose function is submission.[23]

Lastly, one also sees variations of the LSV behavior associated with the nonvocal aspect of petitioning prayer in all major and at least some tribal religions of the world. Christians, Hindus, Buddhists, Muslims, and Jews all use different variations of the LSV theme. As discussed in Chapter 3, the eyes are often closed during prayer, making the praying individual even more vulnerable. Christians bow their heads and put their hands together in front of their chests in the nonvocal aspect of petitioning prayer. Most Christians pray with their hands in front pressed together pointing upward. However, members of the Church of Jesus Christ of Latter-day Saints (Mormon) faith often pray by folding both arms across their chest. Some Christian denominations also kneel at times. Sometimes Pentecostal Christians pray by putting their empty (weaponless) hands over their heads similar to signs of surrender.[24] Hindus can sit with their hands up. Buddhists exhibit various LSV behaviors when petitioning in front of statues of the Buddha for enlightenment. Muslims pray on their knees (smaller) and get even smaller, lower, and more vulnerable by putting their forehead on the ground with their eyes downward. Orthodox Jews as well as Muslims bow back and forth, which lowers them when they read sacred texts in prayer.

It is possible to ask the question, "Why do people engage in the nonvocal LSV behaviors associated with petitioning prayer?"[25] We know that as part of the socialization process, children interact with other children and adults in a variety of interactions, some of which are potentially or actually hostile or aggressive. In such an interaction when a child is confronted with an overwhelmingly more powerful adversary, often a punishing parent, and when this individual is corporally threatening or actually punishing or hurting the child, the child becomes fearful. The child's automatic response is to assume LSV behavior. In this context the function of the LSV behavior is submission. The submissive LSV behavior is an intraspecies signal. When seen by an aggressive adversary, it tends to decrease aggression. Submission signals to the overwhelmingly more powerful adversary that the submissively displaying individual has essentially given up. If decreased aggression occurs in the adversary, a decrease in fear by the individual who displayed the LSV behavior follows. It is not known for certain if simply engaging in LSV behavior reduces fear or if one learns through association in childhood that LSV behavior reduces fear. Under natural conditions fear reduction would almost always follow the execution of LSV behavior when it is used in the context of submission.

From the perspective of ethology (behavioral biology), LSV behavior, as a Type I coordinated motor pattern, can also be considered a "consummatory end act." The term "consummatory" derives from the Latin *summa*, which means a total or sum. Nothing literally (such as food) has to be consumed by the organism as a whole. The term is used to signify that an appetitive (derives from an appetite) search has just been ended.[26] There are other familiar examples of consummatory end acts that when executed raise the thresholds for their continued execution and make them less likely to occur through a change in mood. These acts (behaviors) have to do with food (eating), water (drinking), and sex (copulation). In reference to LSV behavior, if fear were motivating escape from an adversary but where escape was not possible, then executing the LSV behavior can be considered the consummatory end act that under natural conditions would almost always reduce fear. By whatever mechanism—innate, acquired, or both—the child comes to associate the execution of LSV behavior with fear reduction. The significance of this should be obvious, as LSV behavior is also used in the nonvocal aspect of petitioning prayer. When one eats, drinks, copulates, or makes a petitioning prayer, there is a clear endpoint when one feels satisfied after the consummatory end act.

As a result, whenever a child or an adult who has had such a fear-dissipation-through-submission type of upbringing was in a fearful mood and felt fearful, if he or she assumed the LSV behavior, even when not in a hostile interaction with another individual, the experience could be calming and fear reducing. Appreciate that in the nonvocal aspects of petitioning prayer, the function of the LSV behavior is prayerful petition rather than stopping punishment from an overwhelmingly more powerful adversary. Fear, which is associated with true submission, is seldom if ever seen on the face of someone praying. Petitioning prayer can ask for favors from a loving God as well as ask for mercy from what is believed to be a punishing God. In support of the above the historical relationship between childhood abuse and abandonment (which were rampant during the time the Judeo-Christian scriptures and other sacred narratives were being written[27]) and the thematic content of various sacred narratives will be presented in Chapter 6.

TYPE II RELIGIOUS BEHAVIOR

As previously developed in Chapter 1, most religious behaviors are Type II Behaviors that evolve culturally and are passed across generations by social learning. From the perspective of ethology (behavioral biology), Type II religious behaviors are "appetitive" proximity-seeking behaviors. As explained, the term "appetitive" derives from appetite. These behaviors seek proximity (nearness) by trying to get the attention of or call to God through religious rituals and ceremonies, including marriage, baptism, circumcision, funerals, rain dances, and healing ceremonies. They also include all of the behaviors that are used in the vocal aspect of petitioning prayer and in reciting and reading sacred narratives in local languages. And, they include all of the behaviors that have been used to write various sacred narratives such as the Holy Bible and Qur'an.

In addition to what has been said about Type II religious behavior's cultural evolution, can the same question be asked of Type II religious behavior that was asked of Type I religious behavior? Namely, do Type II religious behaviors have a biological, evolutionary history that can be traced back to our prehuman ancestors? There is evidence that some aspects of human morality, which is a component of religion often executed through Type II religious behaviors and which is based in part on values, can be traced back through our social vertebrate ancestors, especially the higher primates.[28] However, behaving morally often uses different forms of behavior in different species. Many of the Type II Behaviors used in human religious rituals, such as baptism, are just not seen in any nonhuman animal, including primates. These are human-specific, *functionally* defined behaviors. And, to review, all Type II Behaviors are only definable by their function.

What then would be the result or outcome of someone engaging in Type II religious behavior, such as reading sacred narratives, if in doing so it promotes survival in a particular society? Will the particular Type II religious behavior increase in frequency in the society (a population) over succeeding generations similar to how a Type I Behavior could? The answer is "Yes, through cultural selection," but only in the particular society in which such behavior currently is occurring. The specific Type II Behavior would not appear in succeeding generations if the person were adopted at birth into a different society that had a different religion.[29] This is not just a theoretical or hypothetical question. There is evidence that in modern pluralistic societies those individuals who are religious have better survival in their particular society.[30] Here is the important question. What changes (from a biological evolutionary perspective) when such individuals—who are engaging in Type II religious behaviors and where engaging in Type II behaviors leads to increased survival—increase in the population in a particular society over succeeding generations?

To understand what changes, one has to appreciate that the contributing causes of behavior can be divided into those causes that are intraindividual and those causes that are extraindividual. Of the intraindividual causes of behavior, there are those that actually are associated with movement, such as muscles in the arm contracting. There are also the nonmovement contributing causes of behavior that are associated with its motivation. As explained in the beginning of the chapter, religious beliefs, values, moods, and feelings can be considered intraindividual, contributing causes of religious behavior. Beliefs and values are "structural" meaning that the information (that which is necessary to make decisions) of which they are composed is a structure rather than a function. Information itself is thermodynamic/structural.[31] Living matter changes when it acquires information, such as a belief. What changes is structural. How can this knowledge be used to understand how religious beliefs and values, which are contributing causes of Type II religious behaviors, can be affected by natural selection?

In addition to being conceptualized as that which is held to be true, a belief can also be conceptualized as a unit of information that biases behavior (movement) in a predictable way. A value is then the rank order given to a belief and the entire rank-order hierarchy of beliefs is called a value system. The content of beliefs can be acquired through one's ancestors via DNA (e.g., heights are dangerous) or by social learning (e.g., Jesus is the Son of God).

If having the capacity to hold symbolically coded beliefs that were acquired through social learning led to an increase in survival, then the effectiveness, efficiency, and even the size of the structures in the brain that acquire and hold symbolically coded beliefs in general would have increased in subsequent generations.[32] In this respect, religious beliefs and the values that derive from their hierarchical organization would also have contributed to the capacity for humans to hold symbolically coded beliefs and values in general.

In contrast to the above, moods and feelings, which also are contributing causes of religious behavior, are functions rather than structures. As functions they do not have form. One cannot hold a mood or a feeling in one's hand. Nevertheless, the brain tissues whose functions are (or which produce) moods and feelings are structures that do have form and can evolve biologically by natural selection. As a result, if having certain religious moods and feelings led to an increase in survival, the brain tissues that generate moods and feelings in general and religious-related moods and feelings in particular would have increased in effectiveness, efficiency, and size in subsequent generations.

For example, there are a number of moods and feelings associated with spirituality that include such things as an increased capacity for commitment[33] as well as feelings of awe, love (attachment), trust (faith), compassion, gratitude, forgiveness, joy, and hope.[34] Most religions have such a spiritual component. Therefore, when individuals experienced these moods and feelings and as a result engaged in Type II Behaviors that increased their survival or the survival of their kin and co-ethnics (in tribal societies), the brain tissues that generated these moods and feelings would have increased in effectiveness, efficiency, and size in subsequent generations. The implication of this process is that, contrary to the more intuitive (and more secular) proposition that religious psychology evolved as a by-product of the mind,[35] believing in God may have been what contributed to the creation of many parts of the human mind. Some would call that a "gift." This perspective is in contrast to other perspectives that may have prematurely dismissed religion's value.[36]

CONCLUSION

This chapter began by giving a brief overview of religion as well as some ways to understand and classify behavior. The main question was whether religious behavior has a traceable, biological evolutionary history. It was shown that the Type I religious behavior that is seen in the nonvocal aspect of petitioning prayer does. Type II religious behaviors were also addressed, especially since they make up the majority of religious behaviors. When these Type II religious behaviors are executed, if by executing them there was an increased survival of individuals or the individuals' families or co-ethnics (in tribal societies), it was shown how this could have led to the increase in the effectiveness, efficiency, and even size of the brain structures responsible for the motivations of these behaviors in succeeding generations. Some of these brain structures would have been involved in the moods and feelings that underlie much of what is known as religious spirituality. Other brain structures that would have been selected if Type II religious behaviors conferred increased survival would have been those that were involved with some of the higher cognitive capacities of humans such as those that are responsible for symbolically coded beliefs and values.

In addition, much Type II religious behavior itself is symbolic as are many of the items that accompany the behavior. The meanings attributed to these symbols often divide the material world into the sacred, which has religious significance, and the profane.[37] Appreciate that the symbolically coded language with which sacred narratives were first spoken and eventually written were executed through Type II behavior. As a result, when the earliest humans engaged in Type II religious behavior, including speaking, writing, and transcribing sacred narratives, this could have had important consequences for human evolution if engaging in such behaviors led to an increase in survival. One such consequence could have been the emergence[38] of or improvement in human higher cognitive and intellectual capacities.

To date there have been two major biobehavioral scientific theories of how human higher cognitive and intellectual capacities could have emerged. The first theory was zoologist Richard Alexander's theory of social competition.[39] The second was evolutionary psychologist Geoffrey Miller's theory of sexual selection.[40] To these two theories one can now add a third. It can be called religious. This religious theory proposes that at least some human higher cognitive and intellectual capacities could have emerged and improved as humans began not only to pray but to search for some type of meaning in their lives.[41] These three theories on how human higher cognitive and intellectual capacities could have emerged and improved are not mutually exclusive. It would also be very difficult but perhaps not impossible to design a modern experiment that could choose among them. Note also that "religious" in this context does not mean intelligent design, as the proposed mechanism is Darwinian natural selection.

All of the above, some of which is admittedly speculative, begs the more provocative question of why people believe in God. To many true believers the answer is self-evident. To others it is yet to be discovered. Nevertheless, the evolutionary history of religious behavior probably began with the Type I make-oneself-lower-or-smaller-or-more-vulnerable behavior associated with the nonvocal aspect of petitioning prayer. It can therefore be predicted that with few exceptions, when individuals relate *directly* to a higher power, deity, or God, such behavior will still be executed. In fact, if one ever observes this type of behavior being exhibited anywhere in the world and it is not directed to someone else in close proximity, and if fear is absent on the face, one can be almost certain that one is witnessing the nonvocal aspect of petitioning prayer. It is in this simple behavior where religion—with all its current splendor, glory, and complexity—most likely had its humble evolutionary origin.

NOTES

1. Darwin, C. (1859). *On the origin of species by means of natural selection.* London: John Murray.

2. Boyd, R., & Richerson, P. J. (1985). *Culture and the evolutionary process.* Chicago: The University of Chicago Press.

3. Lorenz, K. (1981). *The foundations of ethology.* New York: Springer-Verlag.

4. Feierman, J. (2009). How some major components of religion *could* have evolved by natural selection. In E. Voland & W. Schiefenhövel (Eds.), *The biological evolution of religious mind and behavior.* New York: Springer-Verlag.

5. Tinbergen, N. (1963). *Zeitschrift für Tierpsychologie, 20,* 410–433. (Reprinted 2005 in *Animal Biology, 55,* 297–321.)

6. Hinde, R. (1999). *Why gods persist: A scientific approach to religion.* London: Routledge.

7. Technically, moods and feelings are functions. They do not have mass and cannot cause behavior (the movement of individuals) unless one believes in nonmaterial causation. The brain tissues whose functions are moods and feelings would be the actual contributing cause of the behavior. See Feierman, How some major components of religion *could* have evolved by natural selection. This issue also is addressed later in the chapter in reference to religious behavior.

8. Feierman, J. (2006). The ethology of psychiatric populations II: Darwinian neuropsychiatry. *Clinical Neuropsychiatry, 3*(2), 87–109.

9. Immelmann, K., & Beer, C. (1989). *A dictionary of ethology* (p. 27). Cambridge, MA: Harvard University Press.

10. Amundson, R., & Lauder, G. V. (1994). Function without purpose: The uses of causal role function in evolutionary biology. *Biology and Philosophy, 9*, 443–469. For a discussion of use function, see Love, A. C. (2007). Functional homology and homology of function: Biological concepts and philosophical consequences. *Biology and Philosophy 22*(5), 691–708. A selected effect function would be a *distal* (ultimate) use function.

11. Lorenz, *The foundations of ethology.*

12. Ibid.

13. Tinbergen, N. (1951). *The study of instinct.* New York: Oxford University Press.

14. Ekman, P., & Friesen, W. V. (1975). *Unmasking the face: A guide to recognizing emotions from facial clues.* Englewood Cliffs, NJ: Prentice-Hall, Inc.

15. Moore, M. M. (1985). Nonverbal courtship patterns in women: Contexts and consequences. *Ethology and Sociobiology, 6*, 237–248.

16. Eibl-Eibesfeldt, I. (1989). *Human ethology.* New York: Aldine de Gruyter. See also Morris, D. (1977). *Manwatching: A field guide to human behavior.* New York: Harry N. Abrams, Inc., Publishers.

17. Eibl-Eibesfeldt, *Human ethology.*

18. Eibl-Eibesfeldt, I. (1971). *Love and hate: The natural history of behavior patterns.* New York: Holt, Rinehart and Winston, Inc.

19. Eibl-Eibesfeldt, *Human ethology.*

20. First, note the conjunction is *or* rather than *and*, which means that someone can exhibit LSV behavior by being either lower *or* smaller *or* more vulnerable. Also, LSV behavior is reportedly absent in the behaviors of shamans in the Enga people of New Guinea, as per Polly Wiessner, personal communication, 2008. However, see a discussion of this in Chapter 15 in terms of LSV behavior in the recipients of the services of a Malaysian shaman.

21. Immelmann & Beer, *A dictionary of ethology.*

22. Feierman, J. R. (1994). Ethology and sexology. In V. L. Bullough & B. Bullough (Eds.), *Human sexuality: An encyclopedia* (pp. 190–193). New York: Garland Publishing, Inc. Also, Feierman, J. R. (2000). Gender ethology: Feminine mannerism as signals of sexual reciprocity. The Second International Behavioral Development Symposium. University of North Dakota, Minot.

23. Eibl-Eibesfeldt, I. (1990). Dominance, submission, and love: Sexual pathologies from the perspective of ethology. In J. R. Feierman (Ed.), *Pedophilia: Biosocial dimensions* (pp. 150–175). New York: Springer-Verlag. See also Medicus, G., & Hopf, S. (1990). The phylogeny of male/female differences in sexual behavior. In Feierman (Ed.), *Pedophilia: Biosocial dimensions* (pp. 122–149).

24. This behavior is in contrast to the victory leap in which one puts both hands above the head and jumps high, making oneself taller. This is seen in winning sports teams.

25. It has been shown that people invoke vertical perceptions (i.e., "Glory to God in the highest") when God-related cognitions are accessed. They also encode God-related concepts faster if presented in a vertical high position. They rate strangers whose pictures are presented in a high versus low position as more likely to believe in God. See Beier, B. P., Hauser, D. J., Robinson, M. D., Friesen, C. K., & Schjeldahl, K. (2007). What's "up" with God: Vertical space as a representation of the divine. *Journal of Personality and Social Psychology, 93*(5), 699–710. These findings may contribute to our understanding why people engage in the "lower" aspect of LSV behavior when they pray, as lower makes one more congruent with God being higher. Of course, being lower is also being more submissive to whomever or whatever is more dominant.

26. See Immelmann & Beer, *A dictionary of ethology*. According to classical ethological theory formulated more than half a century ago, the consummatory end act "consumes" the "energy" propelling the appetitive acts. This is a theoretical formulation that now has only historical interest. See Lorenz, *The foundations of ethology*.

27. Abelow, B. (2007). What a history of childhood reveals about New Testament origins and the psychology of Christian belief. *The Quarterly Review of the Committee for the Scientific Examination of Religion, 2*(1), 1–6.

28. de Waal, F. (1996). *Good natured: The origins of right and wrong in humans and other animals*. Cambridge, MA: Harvard University Press.

29. The issue is actually more complex, as components of religion may be subject to natural selection at the group level as well as at the individual level. See Wilson, D. S. (2002). *Darwin's cathedral: Evolution, religion, and the nature of society*. Chicago: The University of Chicago Press.

30. Reynolds, V., & Tanner, R. (1983). *The biology of religion*. London: Longman. See also Koenig, H. G., McCullough, M. E., & Larson, D. B. (2001). *Handbook of religion and health*. New York: Oxford University Press.

31. Lowenstein, W. R. (1988). *The touchstone of life: Molecular information, cell communication, and the foundations of life*. New York: Oxford University Press.

32. Brown, W. M. (2001). Natural selection of mammalian brain components. *Trends in Ecology and Evolution, 16*(9), 471–473.

33. Nesse, R. M. (Ed.). (2001). *Evolution and the capacity for commitment*. New York: Russell Sage Foundation.

34. Vaillant, G. (2008). *Spiritual evolution: A scientific defense of faith*. New York: Broadway Books.

35. Pinker, S. (2006). The evolutionary psychology of religion. In P. McNamara (Ed.), *Where God and science meet: How brain and evolutionary*

studies alter our understanding of religion. Volume I: Evolution, genes and the religious brain (pp. 1–9). Westport, CT: Praeger.

36. Dawkins, R. (2006). *The god delusion*. New York: Houghton Mifflin Company.

37. Eliade, M. (1958). *Patterns in comparative religion*. New York: Meridian, New American Library.

38. The term "emergence" is used rather than "evolved" because higher cognitive and intellectual capacities are functions rather than structures. The functions emerge as a by-product of the evolution of the structures whose functions they are.

39. Alexander, R. (1979). *Darwinism and human affairs*. Seattle: University of Washington Press.

40. Miller, G. F. (2000). *The mating mind: How sexual choice shaped the evolution of human nature*. New York: Doubleday.

41. Frankl, V. E. (1963 [1946]). *Ein Psycholog erlebt Konzentrationslager* [*Man's Search for Meaning*]. New York: Washington Square Press, Simon and Schuster.

PART THREE

The Development of Religious Behavior in the Individual

The development of behavior refers to three maturational stages in the life history of the individual: when the behavior first appears, when and for how long the behavior continues, and when it (sometimes) disappears. Of interest is whether the behavior changes in form or function during an individual's life history. If so, are the changes due to biological maturation or to learning processes? There is also the question of critical (sensitive) period learning, a term that refers to the fact that things learned at certain developmental periods in the life history of an individual often have different impacts than if the learning occurred at another period. The developmentally sensitive mechanisms that are *proximate* or near causes of behavior are also considered. The proximate causes are the mechanisms that operate within the life span of the individual. In biology, *ontogeny* is the term for biobehavioral development within the life span of an individual. The two chapters in Part Three address the effects of childhood and adolescence on the development of religious behavior.

CHAPTER 6

Religious Behavior as a Reflection of Childhood Corporal Punishment

Benjamin J. Abelow

Various scholars have discussed the possible influence of childhood on religion. Some of these scholars have argued that aspects of religion and religious life have been shaped by cultural norms of childhood punishment and submission, especially as occurring within the framework of patriarchal society.[1] In my own work, I have argued that New Testament narrative and salvation teachings were shaped by historically widespread patterns of childhood punishment and abandonment.[2]

In this chapter, I extend my analysis of Christianity to include behavior. Specifically, I examine the foundational rituals (or sacraments) of baptism and Eucharist; the well-known teaching, ascribed to Jesus, to "turn the other cheek"; and the broad religious-ethical prescription to imitate Christ. I argue that these behaviors are intimately tied to New Testament themes which themselves were shaped by childhood. I also consider the possibility that a biologically rooted mechanism of psychological trauma might influence religious behavior. To provide a foundation, I begin by recapitulating some of my work on links between childhood punishment and New Testament themes.[3] It should be understood that, in this chapter, my explanation of New Testament passages will at times diverge from those of traditional Christian interpreters.

NEW TESTAMENT THEMES REFLECT PATTERNS OF CHILDHOOD PUNISHMENT

Throughout history, children have been corporally punished to inculcate obedience. Such punishment has been both widespread and socially prescribed. Evidence on this point is substantial from ancient times to the modern period, though full documentary details are beyond the scope of this chapter. In general, the father has been the ultimate source of disciplinary authority and has often been the primary "hands on" disciplinarian.

In fact, physical discipline has historically been so central to the father's role that one finds reference to the idea that a child, especially a son, who is *not* punished by the father might be presumed illegitimate. This idea is expressed in the New Testament itself. The book of Hebrews, usually dated to around 65 CE, asserts that *all* sons are punished, and then asks, "what son is he whom the father does not chastise?"—and answers, "if you are without chastisement . . . then are you bastards and not sons" (Hebrews 12:5–8).[4] As recently as the nineteenth century, the Englishman John Epps (1806–1869) wrote of his childhood, "my father felt obliged to testify to the fact of my being his child, by correction." [5]

Holding in mind these endemic patterns of childhood punishment, it is instructive to consider New Testament narrative and salvation teachings. Doing so, one finds strong thematic parallels with the experiences of ordinary children.

To begin, observe that the Son, Jesus, suffers corporally according to the will of his heavenly Father. This teaching is emphasized throughout the New Testament. According to Paul, the Father "did not spare his own Son, but gave him up for us all" (Romans 8:32). In the Gospel of John, when Peter tries to prevent Jesus' capture, Jesus rebukes him, saying, "the cup which my Father has given me, shall I not drink it?" (18:11). The "cup" refers to the fate that Jesus knows awaits him. John's Gospel goes so far as having the Father himself, speaking in "a voice from heaven," indicate that He is responsible for the crucifixion (12:27–28). The Acts of the Apostles states that Jesus was "delivered up according to the definite plan and foreknowledge of God" (Acts 2:23). Acts even gives the impression that the Father, like a divine playwright, scripted the actions of everyone involved in the crucifixion: Herod, Pontius Pilate, Gentiles, and Jews all "were gathered together . . . to do whatever Thy hand and Thy plan predestined to take place" (Acts 4:27–28). In observing the central role of the Father in his Son's suffering, we find close thematic parallels with the historical situation of ordinary children.

As Jesus contemplates his fate, his sadness and fear is palpable. In the Gospels of Matthew (26:38) and Mark (14:34), Jesus is "very sorrowful, even to [the point of] death." In Luke's Gospel (22:44) we read of Jesus' emotional "agony." The book of Hebrews (5:7) describes Jesus' "loud cries and tears" and his intense "fear." [6] Filled with sorrow and fear, Jesus implores his heavenly Father to remove the "cup" of punishment, or pain, from before him: "Father, all things are possible for you; remove this cup from before me" (Mark 14:35–36 and parallels). In all this, Jesus' responses closely parallel the sadness, terror, and desperate pleading of ordinary children faced with impending punishment. Ultimately, Jesus resigns himself to his fate, saying, "Father...not what I will, but what you will" (Mark 14:36 and parallels). In so speaking, Jesus expresses a posture of filial submission that has, time immemorial, been forced upon ordinary children. And when Hebrews (5:8) says of Jesus, "he learned obedience by the things which he suffered," the parallels with ordinary childhood discipline are unmistakable.

Parallels with childhood are evident, also, within Christian salvation teachings. In childhood, historically and often still, disobedience leads to punishment by the father, whereas obedience leads to benign treatment. Starting with Paul's New Testament letters, we find the same pattern within Christianity. Disobedience—Adam's sin in the Biblical garden—leads to punishment for humans, whereas obedience to the Father—the action of Jesus—leads to salvation. Here are the seminal lines from Paul, which became foundational for later Christianity:

Then as one man's [Adam's] trespass led to condemnation for all men, so one man's [Jesus'] act of righteousness leads to acquittal and life for all men. For as by one man's disobedience many were made sinners, so by one man's obedience many will be made righteous. (Romans 5:18–19)

The strength of this salvational parallel with ordinary childhood becomes clear if we allow ourselves to apply the term "salvation" to childhood. Then we can say that for both the child within the family and the believer within the cosmos, salvation from punishment is attained through filial obedience. This parallel is rendered even more precise by two facts. First, human beings are themselves considered children of the heavenly Father. Thus, both in ordinary childhood and in Christian teachings about damnation, it is *children* who are subject to punishment by the father/Father. Second, Adam himself is sometimes described as a child—Luke's Gospel (3:38) calls him "the Son of God"—and his sin has a child-like quality to it;[7] thus, there is a sense in which Adam's sin is not simply disobedience, per se, but *filial* disobedience.

Finally, observe the central place of *fear* in the believer's relationship with the heavenly Father. Luke's and Matthew's Gospels have Jesus intone: "I will warn you whom to fear: fear him who, after he has killed, has power to cast into hell; yes, I tell you, fear him!" In the opening lines of the earliest surviving Christian text (ca. 50 CE), Paul recounts the conversion of the Thessalonians to Christianity: they turned from idols to God and waited for "Jesus who delivers us from the wrath to come" (1 Thessalonians 1:9–10). In the letter to the Ephesians (2:2–3), we read that the Father's wrath is provoked, specifically, by the disobedience of his human children.[8] Again, the parallels with ordinary childhood are unmistakable. Just as the righteous anger of human fathers has, throughout history, filled children with fear, so the heavenly Father's righteous anger is a source of terror for His human "children." Likewise, paternal wrath, both on earth and in heaven, is provoked by disobedience.

Thus, in New Testament narrative, salvation theology, and emotional experience we find striking parallels with patterns of ordinary childhood punishment. These parallels, I think most readers will agree, are too extensive and precise to plausibly be explained by chance. A likely explanation is that foundational New Testament traditions were shaped in response to the situation of children in the highly patriarchal formative matrix of early Christianity. Furthermore, punishment, especially by fathers, remained the cultural norm throughout the medieval and much of the modern periods; often, it remains the norm still. This fact raises the distinct possibility that New Testament traditions have been found meaningful and emotionally resonant, for most of the Christian era, at least partly because they portray the painful realities of human childhood. For those countless believers who, as children, suffered physical punishment by their fathers, New Testament teachings simply "made sense."

RELIGIOUS BEHAVIOR IN ITS THEOLOGICAL AND CHILDHOOD CONTEXTS

So far, I have focused on the *external* circumstances of children—that is, what is done *to* the child. But when children are compelled to obey, they also undergo a specific *internal* process. Because it is, ultimately, the child's will and "willfulness" that lead to disobedience and hence punishment, children reared with corporal discipline learn that, to avoid punishment, they must suppress the will and psychologically disengage from aspects of their inner selves that are associated with willfulness. Put differently, to avoid disobedient actions, and hence punishment, children learn to "nip the problem in the bud" by suppressing their own motivational tendency toward willfulness.

Remarkably, foundational Christian teachings reflect this inner psychological process. The internal childhood requirement to suppress, repudiate, and negate willful aspects of the self is expressed in the powerful language of religious metaphor: to avoid eternal punishment, the believer must "die to the self" and be reborn "in Christ." Here it is essential to recognize that the "self" which must die is the *disobedient* self, specifically, the self that is tainted with Adam's primal act of willful disobedience. Likewise, the Christ in whom the Christian is said to be reborn is the Son who, in his relationship with his heavenly Father, is the obedient child *par excellence:* the Son, obedient even "unto death," who says, "Father . . . not what I will, but what you will."

Once it is recognized that Adam and Jesus mythically exemplify and personify, respectively, disobedience and filial obedience, a key psychological element of the believer's engagement with the Adam-Jesus story becomes transparent. In pursuing the Christian path, believers attempt to metaphysically realign themselves from Adam to Jesus, that is, from disobedience to obedience, thereby avoiding punishment by the Father. In attempting this realignment, believers metaphorically but precisely *reenact* the childhood experience of subjugating the will—"dying to the [willful] self"—to avoid paternal punishment. Put differently, in undertaking the quintessentially Christian act of accepting and identifying with Jesus, believers voluntarily repeat, on the level of religious symbolism, an internal process that was *forced* upon them as children.

At this point we can begin speaking of behavior, specifically, baptism and Eucharist. For these two quintessential Christian rituals (and sacraments) are overt behavioral expressions of the believers' attempt to shift their affiliation from Adam to Jesus.

Baptism is the religious rite associated with becoming a Christian. It involves a ritual cleansing with water, often viewed as a washing away of sin. Some Christians understand baptism as the actual means by which believers enter into the mystical body of the Church, effecting the spiritual merger with Jesus Christ. These Christians take Paul literally when he says, "For by one Spirit we were all baptized into one body" (1 Corinthians 12:12–13). Other Christians, who accept Paul's words somewhat less literally, understand baptism as imparting a ritual or community seal on a process of inner conversion to Christ. Notice that, however understood, baptism is by no means an isolated "behavior" that can be understood outside its context of theological meaning. Rather, baptism is a behavioral *dimension* of a fully integrated symbolic system comprising cognition, affect, and behavior.

To better understand how closely behavioral and nonbehavioral elements are integrated within Christian ritual, consider some of the links, evident in baptism, among belief, behavior, and narrative. In becoming a Christian, one is said to become a new person. The old, willfully disobedient self, who is identified with Adam, is said to be metaphysically transformed into, or replaced by, a new, innocent, obedient self, who is identified with the Christ-Child, the preternaturally obedient Son. This transformation is often described as a death and rebirth: the believer dies to the old self and is reborn in Christ. This is one reason why, traditionally, many baptismal fonts have been constructed at ground level. During the immersion in water, the individual passes below ground level, as if entering a grave, signifying the death of the old self; and when the individual rises from this "grave," he or she is understood to be resurrected new, obedient, and Christ-like.

In fact, this sequence of ritually constructed death (of the willful self) and birth (of the obedient, Christ-willed self) is often understood as being mystically tied directly to the crucifixion and resurrection of Jesus: the disobedient self is said to be crucified with or through Jesus, just as the new self is resurrected with or through Him. Paul describes the process this way:

> When we were baptized into union with Christ Jesus we were baptized into his death. By baptism we were buried with him, and lay dead, in order that, as Christ was raised from the dead

in the splendor of the Father, so also we might set our feet upon the new path of life. (Romans 6:3–4)

Thus, the ritual, or sacrament, of baptism is inseparable from narrative and salvational themes involving Adam and Jesus, disobedience and obedience, punishment and salvation, and the Son's relationship to the Father. As I discussed, these themes closely parallel, and appear to have been shaped in response to, endemic patterns of childhood punishment and inculcated obedience. As much as the narrative and salvational themes themselves, I suggest, the rite of baptism appears to reflect the painful realities of childhood.

Let me emphasize this last point in a particular way. For the child, the regime of physical discipline produces a profound inner "conversion"—a changing of the mind—from disobedience to obedience, from willfulness to filial submission. Notice that the Christian convert is understood to experience an almost identical change of mind: from willfulness (Adam) to filial obedience (Christ). In both cases, the change is driven by fear of punishment and the desire for parental love—that is, a desire for "salvation." Thus, the adult's (voluntary, religious) conversion forms a striking parallel with the child's (compulsory, psychological) "conversion." The strength of this parallel, which itself is closely aligned with other parallels we have observed, leads me to suggest that the Christian conversion experience may have its ultimate psychological roots in the inculcation of childhood obedience. As I wrote a few paragraphs earlier: "[I]n undertaking the quintessentially Christian act of accepting and identifying with Jesus, the believers voluntarily repeat, on the level of religious symbolism, an internal process that was *forced* upon him as a child." Baptism provides the primary behavioral expression of this childhood repetition.

Consider now the Eucharist (aka communion, Holy Communion, the Lord's Supper). In the ritual, or sacrament, of Eucharist, the believer consumes consecrated bread, wine, or both, which are often conceived of as being the body and blood of Jesus Christ in either a physical or a spiritual sense. This sacrament is rooted in Jesus' words to his disciples: "Jesus took bread, and blessed it, and broke it, and gave it to them, and said, 'Take, eat: this is my body'" (Mark 14:22). According to the Gospel of John, Jesus stated that eating the Eucharist is necessary for salvation: "Unless you eat the flesh of the Son of man, and drink his blood, you have no life in you . . . [but] he who eats my flesh, and drinks my blood, has eternal life" (John 6:53–54). When the believer performs the Eucharist, he sees himself as ingesting Jesus' body and blood—literally, spiritually, or symbolically—and is nourished by them. The Eucharist thus enacts, on the level of physical substance, the notion that Christ is in the believer. One might even say the Eucharist *puts* Christ into the believer, making him more Christlike. As Jesus is quoted, "He that eats my flesh, and drinks my blood, dwells in me, and I in him" (John 6:56).

Like baptism, the Eucharist should be understood as a behavioral expression of an integrated process by which believers attempt to realign themselves metaphysically from disobedient Adam to the obedient Son, Jesus. As discussed, this realignment, and thus the Eucharist itself, forms precise thematic parallels with the child's compulsory "realignment" (or "conversion") to obedience. The Eucharist, like baptism, thus appears to provide a symbolic, culturally sanctioned behavioral reenactment of an internal process that has, throughout history, been forced upon children.

PSYCHOLOGICAL TRAUMA AS A POSSIBLE MECHANISM IN RELIGIOUS BEHAVIOR

In my initial discussion of New Testament themes, I referred to the prominent place of fear. Here it is useful to elaborate. In the New Testament context, fear arises primarily because the heavenly Father wields the threat of hell, which has often been understood as punishment of infinite intensity and duration. If one takes seriously this threat, then it is no exaggeration to say that one is contemplating a situation of ultimate trauma, a situation that, once entered into, is inescapable and unendurable. It is a perfect, eternal torture, a situation almost beyond the capacity of the mind to contemplate, much less to endure in reality.

If it is true, as I have suggested, that this theologically imagined punitive structure parallels, and was shaped in response to, the suffering of ordinary childhood, then it is natural to ponder more deeply about the nature and consequences of childhood punishments—to ponder, even, whether the long history of childhood punishment might actually be a history of socially sanctioned childhood trauma. Without attempting to answer this question in a specific way—for it is full of complexities and uncertainties[9]—it is noteworthy that reports spanning at least 2,000 years have described states of intense fear and terror arising from routine childhood punishments. A few examples follow. During the first century CE, in his *Institutio Oratoria* (1.3.16),

Quintilian hints that Roman children commonly became so terrified during beatings that they lost bowel or bladder control: "when children are beaten, the pain and fear often have results which it is not pleasant to speak of and which will later be a source of embarrassment." St. Augustine, reared in fourth-century Roman North Africa, described the unbearable terror he and his classmates experienced during school beatings; writing as an adult, Augustine compared these beatings to actual torture.[10] Closer to our own time, Winston Churchill described how merely witnessing a beating can terrify and produce involuntary physiological reactions. He tells how boys at his prep school, forced to watch beatings of wayward classmates, "sat quaking."[11] The twentieth-century evangelist Aimee Semple McPherson describes how beatings at home led her to a state of disorganized panic: "I stood looking wildly about for a way out of the dilemma. No earthly recourse was nigh.... Dropping to my knees on the side of my bed, I began to pray, loudly, earnestly."[12] In some cases, unexceptional experiences of punishment appear to have produced psychological dissociation and amnesia, responses often considered to be indicative of psychological trauma.[13]

Whether and to what extent corporal punishments are strictly traumatic, we are certainly dealing with a phenomenon that exists, at the very least, at the *margins* of trauma. For this reason, it is appropriate to discuss childhood punishments with reference to situations that are typically understood as traumatic, to see how childhood punishments are similar to and different from these other situations.

A variety of extraordinary events—including violent attack, physical torture, military battle, and natural disaster—can produce psychological harm. The events most likely to be harmful are those involving an inescapable threat of death, severe injury, or intense pain. Such unavoidable threats tend to produce an experience of overwhelming fear, horror, and helplessness. The terms "trauma" and "traumatic" have been used to describe these damaging events. Although no single definition for trauma has gained universal acceptance, a useful working definition is the following: a stressful event that is both inescapable and of a magnitude that tends to overwhelm the individual's normal coping mechanisms.

Following a psychologically traumatic event, some victims experience visual flashbacks, in which—with varying degrees of clarity—they see the event happening again. Trauma victims may also have repetitive nightmares, which portray the event with some combination of literal and figurative imagery. It has also been observed that some trauma victims repeat or reenact aspects of the trauma in their waking *behaviors*. Bessel A. van der Kolk, M.D., a professor and trauma expert at the Boston University Medical School, writes:

> Many traumatized people expose themselves, seemingly compulsively, to situations reminiscent of the original trauma. These behavioral reenactments are rarely consciously understood to be related to earlier life experiences.[14]

It has been suggested that behavioral repetitions of this sort are especially common among persons who enter into a state of psychological dissociation during the traumatic event. Thus, the Harvard psychiatrist and neurologist James Chu refers to post-traumatic reenactments as the "reliving of dissociated trauma."[15] There are documented reports of post-traumatic behavioral repetitions involving babies and children (including those with no conscious recollection of their traumas), adolescents, and adults.[16] As fantastic as it may seem, one medical study even raises the possibility that experiences at *birth* may be reenacted later in life.[17]

Although the underlying mechanisms responsible for post-traumatic repetition are poorly understood, studies in the biology of trauma may point to an explanation. Bruce Perry, M.D., Ph.D., a researcher in this area, writes:

> The prime "directive" of the human brain is to promote survival. ... Therefore, the brain is "over-determined" to sense, process, store, perceive and mobilize in response to threatening information. ... All areas of the brain and body are recruited and orchestrated for optimal survival tasks during the threat. This total neurobiological participation in the threat response is important in understanding how a traumatic experience can impact and alter functioning in such a pervasive fashion. Cognitive, emotional, social, behavioral and physiological residue of a trauma may impact an individual for years—even a lifetime.[18]

Essential to Perry's point is that, in situations of threat and extreme physiological arousal, the body processes information in extraordinary and redundant ways, via multiple pathways, leaving memory traces in numerous brain areas, some of which are not accessible to conscious awareness yet may still influence behavior and other functions. Recently, a neural network model has been proposed that attempts to explain trauma-related repetitions as pattern completions in hippo-campal and thalamocortical pathways.[19]

As noted, the inability to escape from a threatening situation—in other words, the experience of helplessness—is central to the phe-nomenon of trauma. Although helplessness plays a crucial role in vir-tually all traumas, the experience of helplessness is not the same in all types of trauma. During a natural disaster, say a flood or earth-quake, persons are sometimes able to improve their chances of survival through active and rational struggle. With even brief advance warn-ing, they can attempt to prepare for the event or to flee. They may be able to hide under tables or in doorways, climb out of rubble or onto rooftops, or attach themselves to flotsam. They can even curse the blind forces that confront them, if they wish. Even when events develop too quickly or massively for protective action to provide any benefit, it is relevant that there is nothing in principle that prevents victims from *attempting* to take action to save themselves—and, in fact, it is generally wise for them to make this attempt, even if the effort ultimately proves futile.

For the corporally punished child, the situation is rather different. This child is not merely overwhelmed physically by the superior power of the parent but is *forbidden* to take protective action of any sort. Consider a child who tries to protect himself during punishment by fleeing or by repositioning his body to shield the area being tar-geted for blows. Unlike the earthquake victim, such a child will not help his situation: he may well bring about a renewal, prolongation, or intensification of punishment. If the child adopts a more active strategy, for instance, trying to deflect or ward off blows with hands or feet, punishment may be additionally intensified. If the child goes further still and attempts to strike back, either in retaliation or in hopes of deterring continued punishment, he will be punished even more severely. The child quickly learns that to respond defensively, to resist in any way, is worse than futile; it is dangerous. As historian Philip Greven has written, "Children who resist are often hurt the most, since adults who intend to inflict corporal punishments usually do not allow children to retaliate or to resist."[20] In fact, both in modern writings on childhood discipline and in the historical litera-ture, parents are admonished to intensify punishment in response to a child's resistance. The terse recommendation of Italian Renaissance writer Giovanni Dominici—"Double the punishment if they deny or excuse their fault or if they do not submit to punishment"[21]—is just one of many comparable formulations.

More than this, children have long been compelled to actively *participate* in the very assault that is waged against them—for instance, to voluntarily strip and assume the position in which they will be beaten; or to go into the woods and pick the birch saplings with which they will be whipped; or to thank their parents for beating them; or even to kiss the rod with which they were just chastised. Children who refused to participate in these ways were considered to be acting willfully, and their punishments were intensified accordingly. Thus, if children are to be active at all during punishment, if they are to take concrete steps to ameliorate the punishment or diminish its extent, their activity must be of a paradoxical sort: they must *facilitate* the assault.

Keeping in mind this enforced pattern of paradoxical childhood behavior, consider the Christian ethical emphasis on acceptance of unearned suffering. According to Matthew's and Luke's Gospels, Jesus teaches that when one is struck on the cheek one should not strike back or even shield oneself. Instead, one should present the other cheek so it might be struck as well. Thus Matthew states, "Do not resist one who is evil. But if any one strikes you on the right cheek, turn to him the other also" (5:39). Notice that this ethical prescription almost perfectly depicts *the actual situation* of children during punishment: a child who must acquiesce in and facilitate his or her own punishment is, in essence, being made to turn the other cheek.

The ethical prescription to "turn the cheek" may, at first glance, seem idiosyncratic and unrelated to other Christian teachings. If this were so, then discussing the prescription would seem arbitrary and of little general importance. However, this singular teaching, in fact, epitomizes a central thrust of Christian ethics. To begin with, notice that the prescription to "turn the cheek" is entirely consistent with the underlying theological theme of the Gospel story. Jesus, who is innocent, is crucified for a sin he did not commit, and his voluntary acceptance of this suffering is seen as proper. Likewise, a person who is struck on the cheek without provocation is also, so to speak, being punished for a sin he did not commit. To expose one's other cheek to the same attack is to see the unearned suffering as proper and to extend its scope. To turn the cheek is to be voluntarily crucified, writ small; to be voluntarily crucified is to turn the cheek, writ large. The singular ethical prescription and the theologically central Passion narrative are cut from the same cloth.

Once one recognizes the fundamental thematic link between Jesus' admonition to turn the cheek and Jesus' own acceptance of unearned suffering, it becomes clear that the prescription to turn the cheek is an admonition to imitate Christ or, put differently, to follow in his footsteps. In fact, a core ethical injunction within Christianity has been to live in "imitation of Christ"—that is, to deliberately endure and even seek actual suffering in the manner of Christ: to live not only *in* Christ, through spiritual identification or mystical union, but to live *like* him as a deliberate lifestyle—i.e., behavioral—choice. This imitative injunction, which is often understood to be the foundation of the entire structure of Christian ethics, has its Biblical basis in lines such as these:

> Deny yourself, take up your cross, and follow me. (Luke 17:10)
>
> Are you able to drink of the cup that I shall drink of, and to be baptized with the baptism that I am baptized with? (Matthew 20:22)
>
> I appeal to you therefore, brothers, to present your bodies as a living sacrifice, holy and acceptable to God. (Romans 12:1)

When one considers these ethical teachings with an eye toward the experiences of ordinary children, one arrives at a remarkable conclusion: the very same modes of behavior that were *imposed* on children by overwhelming force, against their will, are now advocated *as models of adult virtue*. This conclusion is practically a tautology, since Jesus, the behavioral model, is, almost by definition, an innocent Child who suffered obediently according to the will of the Father. When the believer follows in Christ's footsteps, he or she, in essence, steps into shoes that corporally punished children throughout history have already worn—for these children, reared under patriarchy, have suffered corporally according to the will of the (earthly) father. For those countless believers, past and present, who have experienced traditional modes of childhood discipline, imitating the suffering of Christ has offered, and continues to offer, a ready-made path for the behavioral repetition of childhood.

CONCLUSION

In the quintessential sacramental rituals of Christianity (baptism and Eucharist), and in what is arguably Christianity's broadest and most foundational ethical injunction (imitation of Christ), one finds striking thematic parallels with the painful realities of childhood. In the performance of these rituals and this injunction, one seems to

encounter culturally sanctioned behavioral repetitions from childhood. These parallels and repetitions mesh seamlessly with key narrative and salvational elements of the New Testament, which themselves
appear to have been shaped by childhood.

As part of my presentation, I suggested that psychological trauma
may play a role in determining religious behavior. However, this is
just a possibility, for not enough is currently known about either
trauma or childhood punishment to reach firm conclusions. Therefore, I present this aspect of my argument as food for thought. However, even if one assumes that trauma-related mechanisms are
irrelevant, one still confronts a remarkable observed reality: precise
parallels between childhood punishment and Christian religious experience, including its behavioral dimension. Whatever the mechanism,
whether related to trauma or not, we must take these parallels seriously as an essential feature of religious experience and, accordingly,
seek to understand them.

Much of this chapter has focused, explicitly or implicitly, on the historical development of religious teachings and injunctions. Absent
plausible alternative explanations for the childhood-religion parallels
we have observed, it seems likely that historical patterns of childhood
corporal punishment helped shape religious narratives, salvation
teachings, and behaviors during the formative period of Christianity.
Perhaps a converse influence is now at work. Secularization is currently sweeping across Europe at the same time that corporal punishment is being legally banned in many European countries. It is
striking that Sweden, known for its low rates of church attendance
and sometimes considered the most secular of nations, was the first
country (1979) to outlaw all forms of childhood corporal punishment.
It is possible that a decrease in corporal punishment is leading to a
lessening of interest in traditional Christianity. To help clarify the
nature of these European relationships, a study could be done corre-
lating rates of corporal punishment by country with rates of church attendance. One would predict a positive relationship.[22] It is hoped that
some readers will take up the challenge of testing this prediction and
of constructing other hypotheses relevant to the concepts presented
in this chapter.

I have here focused exclusively on Christianity. I focused on one
religion because of space limitations, as well as for conceptual simplicity; I chose Christianity because its parallels with childhood are especially transparent. This transparency arises naturally from the central
place of the Father-Son relationship within Christian teaching.

However, other religions also contain parallels with childhood,[23] which are often more subtle than those found in Christianity. In my ongoing work, I am exploring childhood parallels in Judaism, Islam, and the religions arising from Indian culture. Thus, I end by suggesting that Christianity may provide not an isolated instance of childhood parallels, but an unusually clear example of what actually may be a widespread pattern in religious thought and practice.

NOTES

1. See, e.g., Greven, P. (1977). *The Protestant temperament*. Chicago: University of Chicago Press; Greven, P. (1992). *Spare the child: The religious roots of punishment and the psychological impact of child abuse*. New York: Vintage Books; Brock, R. N. (1989). And a little child will lead us: Christology and child abuse. In J. C. Brown & C. R. Bohn (Eds.), *Christianity, patriarchy, and abuse* (pp. 42–61). Cleveland: The Pilgrim Press; Brock, R. N. (1991). *Journeys by Heart: A Christology of erotic power* (esp. pp. 50–56). New York: Crossroad; DeMause, L. (2002). *The emotional life of nations* (Chapter 9). New York: Other Press Books; Levenson, J. D. (1993). *The death and resurrection of the beloved Son: The transformation of child sacrifice in Judaism and Christianity*. New Haven, CT: Yale University Press; Schatzman, M. (1973). *Soul murder: Persecution in the family*. New York: Random House; Feierman, J. R. (2009). How religion *could* have evolved by natural selection. In V. Eckart & W. Schiefenöhvel (Eds.), *The biological evolution of religious mind and behavior*. Berlin: Springer-Verlag (also see Chapter 5, this volume); Persinger, M. A. (1987). *Neuropsychological bases of God beliefs* (e.g., pp. 67–69, 113–122). New York: Praeger. Freud, of course, also suggested links between childhood and religion, though much of his work is rooted in a vision of prehistorical childhood that is itself highly mythical; see Freud, S. (1962). *Totem and taboo*. New York: Norton.

2. For example, Abelow, B. (2007). What the history of childhood reveals about New Testament origins and the psychology of Christian belief. *The Review of the Committee for the Scientific Examination of Religion, 2*, 11–16.

3. Ibid. Though a discussion of childhood abandonment could readily be built into my argument in this chapter, I will, because of space limitations, focus exclusively on childhood punishment.

4. In this chapter, I rely on the *Revised Standard Version* and a number of other Bible translations. In a few places I replace archaic words with modern equivalents or make minor changes in sentence structure to facilitate flow.

5. Pollack, L. (1983). *Forgotten children: Parent-child relations from 1500 to 1900* (p. 183). Cambridge: Cambridge University Press.

6. These New Testament images of suffering were, centuries later, reflected in formal church doctrine, which declared that Jesus is fully human

(and divine), capable of suffering the same physical and emotional pain as other humans.

7. As one important modern Biblical commentary notes, "When Adam has been caught in his transparent attempt at evasion [in the Garden], Yahweh speaks to him as a father would to his child: 'Where are you?' In this context, it is the same thing as, 'And what have you been up to just now?' This simple phrase—a single word in the [Hebrew] original—does the work of volumes. For what . . . [is] evoked is the childhood of mankind itself." [Speiser, E. A. (1964). *The Anchor Bible Genesis: Introduction, translation, and notes* (p. 25). Garden City: Doubleday. (General Editors of the Anchor Series: W. F. Allbright & D. N. Freedman.)]

8. Referring to the "sons of disobedience": "Among these we all once lived in the passions of our flesh, following the desires of body and mind, and so we were by nature children of wrath."

9. For example, childhood punishments have existed across a range of contexts and intensities and, therefore, the phenomenon in question is not homogeneous. Furthermore, basic questions about trauma (e.g., what, exactly, trauma is biologically and psychologically; the nature and consistency of its links with dissociation and repetitive phenomena; and how trauma should most appropriately be defined or diagnosed) are areas of ongoing investigation and theorizing.

10. Augustine, *Confessions*, 1.9.15.

11. Rose, L. (1991). *The erosion of childhood: Child oppression in Britain 1860–1918* (pp. 186–187). London: Routledge.

12. Quoted in Greven, *Spare the child*, p. 24.

13. See ibid., ix–x, for a personal example by a respected historian.

14. Van der Kolk, B. (1989). The compulsion to repeat the trauma. *Psychiatric Clinics of North America, 12,* 389–411.

15. Chu, J. A. (1991). The repetition compulsion revisited: Reliving dissociated trauma. *Psychotherapy: Theory, Research, Practice, Training, 28,* 327.

16. Terr, L. (1991). Childhood traumas: An outline and overview. *American Journal of Psychiatry, 148,* 12–13; Terr, L. (1988). What happens to early memories of trauma? A study of twenty children under age five at the time of documented traumatic events. *Journal of the American Academy of Child and Adolescent Psychiatry, 27,* 98–99; Terr, L. (1990). *Too scared to cry: Psychic trauma in childhood* (pp. 233–280). New York: Harper & Row. Herman, J. L. (1992). *Trauma and recovery: The aftermath of violence—from domestic abuse to political terror* (pp. 39–42). New York: Basic Books; Greven, *Spare the child,* pp. 178–186.

17. Jacobson, B., Eklund, G., Hamberger, L., et al. (1987). Perinatal origin of adult self-destructive behavior. *Acta Psychiatrica Scandinavica, 76,* 364–371.

18. Perry, B. D. (1999). Memories of fear. How the brain stores and retrieves physiologic states, feelings, behaviors and thoughts from traumatic events. Available at http://www.childtrauma.org/ctamaterials/memories.asp.

19. Javanbakht, A., & Ragan, C. L. (2008). A neural network model for transference and repetition compulsion based on pattern completion. *The Journal of the American Academy of Psychoanalysis and Dynamic Psychiatry, 36,* 255–278.

20. Greven, *Spare the child*, p. 123.

21. Quoted in Ross, J. B. (1974). The middle-class child in urban Italy, fourteenth to early sixteenth century. In L. DeMause (Ed.), *The history of childhood: The untold story of child abuse* (p. 214). New York: Psychohistory Press.

22. Current measures of corporal punishment might not accurately indicate rates during the preceding generation or two, which would likely be the period of interest. This and other complications and potential confounders would need to be addressed in the experimental design and/or interpretation of the study. A positive correlation in this study would not, of course, in itself prove causality or the direction of influence.

23. Scholars who have explored childhood links in non-Christian religion include Levenson, *The death and resurrection of the beloved Son;* DeMause, *The emotional life of nations;* and Freud.

CHAPTER 7

Religious Behavior and the Adolescent Brain

Candace S. Alcorta

None of us are born with religion. There are no inherently animist, Muslim, Buddhist, or Christian infants. Although religion is a universal feature of all known human cultures, like language, it must be learned, and the forms it takes are as varied as the languages we speak. Had King Frederick II of Hohenstaufen attempted to identify the original human religion rather than the original human language, it is likely that the experiment he conducted would have yielded the same negative results. The king found that infants reared without the benefit of human speech and interaction failed to acquire any language at all. Indeed, these babies not only failed to learn a language; they died.[1]

During the twentieth century Communist nations throughout the world embarked on an experiment similar to King Frederick's with regard to religion. These totalitarian atheist states attempted to eliminate all religious practice and belief. Today suicide rates in these countries, and in atheist nations in general, are among the highest in the world. In contrast, the lowest male suicide rates throughout the world are found in highly religious nations, even though many of these states exhibit severely depressed economic and social conditions. Sociologist Phil Zuckerman notes that suicide rates are "the one indicator of societal health in which religious nations fare much better than secular nations."[2]

We intuitively recognize that language is fundamental to our humanity. It is the means by which we consciously transcend the insularity of our individual experiences and forge a common culture. Yet, none of us are born with language. We all enter the world with an inherent capacity to learn language,[3] but the development of this capacity depends on both the culture we are born into and our unique individual socialization experiences during critical developmental periods.

This also appears to be true of religion. Like language, religion allows us to transcend our individual existence through submersion in a larger social body. In contrast to the conscious, cognitive mechanisms of language, however, the faith-based transcendence of religion operates predominantly on a subconscious, emotional level. At the heart of this transcendence is the music-based communal ritual that behaviorally defines religion across all human cultures.[4] The formality, sequence, repetition, and pattern of religious ritual, like the ritualized displays of our nonhuman relatives, focus our attention, enhance our memory, alter our neuroendocrine function, and engage our motivational systems.[5] Religion has the capacity to evoke our emotions, elicit empathy, and instill trust among adherents. This renders it a powerful mechanism for prescribing and proscribing individual behavior, and an effective tool for creating culturally defined, cooperative groups.

Just as we are born with an innate predisposition to learn language, we also appear to possess an innate capacity to "learn" religion.[6] We know that early childhood is the optimal time of life to learn language. It is during this developmental period that those areas of the brain responsible for language production and processing are undergoing their greatest growth and development. Anthropological and brain research suggests that humans may also have an optimal developmental period for "learning" religion; that period is likely to be adolescence.

ADOLESCENT RITES OF PASSAGE

Throughout the world adolescence is considered the "right" time for individuals to learn the sacred beliefs and behaviors of their culture. In nearly three-quarters of the societies studied by anthropologists, the transmission of these beliefs and behaviors is achieved through adolescent rites of passage.[7] These rites recur across hunter-gatherer, pastoral, agricultural, and industrial societies and are important components of animist, Buddhist, Muslim, Judeo-Christian, and other widely divergent religions. Although these rites differ dramatically from culture to culture in their intensity, duration, and beliefs, they all share a common purpose and structure. They have the explicit function of transforming children into adults, and do so by ritually initiating the adolescent into the group's sacred knowledge. This involves teaching initiates the cognitive schema of their respective religions—i.e., the symbols, counterintuitive narratives, and supernatural beliefs—but it also involves investing these schema with emotional and social meaning. Initiates "learn" their religion on a cognitive level, but by living it they also "learn" it on social and emotional levels. Ordinary narratives are thereby transformed into extraordinary, sacred symbols and beliefs with motivational significance.

In many societies initiates undergo prolonged and painful psychological and physical ordeals. Among the hunter-gatherer Walmadjeri of Australia initiates are subjected to sleep deprivation, scarification, and genital mutilation.[8] The agricultural Ndembu of Zambia kidnap, seclude, and ceremonially circumcise their adolescent girls and boys.[9] In contrast, the traditional rites of the Patagonian Ona, like the contemporary bat/bar mitzvahs of Judaism and the confirmation rites of modern Christianity, are relatively painless, involving little more than the oral transmission of sacred knowledge. Yet, no matter how widely these rites differ from culture to culture, they all have three elements in common: (1) all require that initiates participate in music-based communal ritual; (2) all evoke emotions; and (3) all seek to associate those emotions with sacred symbols and beliefs that prescribe and proscribe social behaviors.[10]

Adolescence is certainly not the only time of life that religious learning occurs (see Chapters 6 and 11). Children everywhere hear the narratives and witness the rituals of their culture's sacred beliefs, and adults convert to new faiths. Yet, in nearly all cultures including our own, adolescence is deemed to be the appropriate time of life for initiation into "the sacred." This close relationship between adolescence and religious initiation is something that "comes naturally" and is seldom questioned. But *why* is this so? What is it about adolescence that makes it the "right time" for transmitting sacred knowledge in cultures as different as those of Australian hunter-gatherers, African agriculturalists, and American industrialists? The answer to this question is likely to be found in the developmental patterns of our brains.

THE HUMAN BRAIN

The human brain is unique in several important ways. It is proportionally larger in comparison to body size than that of all other primates and it is also the least developed at birth. While chimpanzees are born with brains approximately 40 percent of their final size at maturation, humans develop between 75 and 80 percent of their total brain volume after birth. This development takes much longer in humans than it does in chimpanzees. By the second year of life, only about 50 percent of human brain development is complete. The human brain does not reach its maximum size until late adolescence. Thereafter our brains are actually reduced slightly in size through the elimination of synapses, or "pruning." [11]

The average human brain is made up of approximately 100 billion neurons. Each of these neurons receives electrochemical impulses from other neurons through specialized projections called dendrites that extend from the neuronal cell body. Environmental stimuli, both internal and external to the organism, generate these impulses. When electrochemical impulses are transmitted through the dendrites, they initiate an action potential in the neuron's cell body, which travels down the axon. A small gap, the synapse, separates the axon of each neuron from the dendrites of neighboring neurons. When impulses traveling down the axon reach the synapse, they cause it to "fire," thereby activating neighboring dendrites. This synaptic firing creates neuronal networks of information flow across adjacent neurons. The more frequently synapses fire, the stronger these associational networks become. Synapses that fire infrequently or not at all are "pruned" away as the brain reallocates its resources to more active neuronal networks.[12] Neuroscientist Timothy Murphy notes "the rules for synaptic strengthening work in a developmental and context-specific manner to ensure that neuronal networks both reward active connections (Hebbian) and ensure that networks contain a requisite amount of basal activity (homeostatic)."[13]

The sights, sounds, and people around us provide much of the stimuli responsible for the synaptic firing in our brains, but our own thoughts and emotions initiate firing as well. Since "neurons that fire together wire together," over time, the repeated firing of synapses shape and strengthen associational networks in our brains. These networks are then streamlined through pruning and the formation of myelin sheaths around the axons of existing networks, which speeds up impulse transmission and creates the "white matter" of the brain.

We are born with the neuronal scaffolding for all of the abilities basic to our survival and reproduction, such as sight, walking, and speech. The successful development of these abilities, however, requires environmental inputs during critical windows of brain maturation. Inputs experienced when neurons are undergoing maturation and pruning have the greatest impact on the development and sculpting of associational networks. Since the maturation rates of various brain structures differ, the optimal developmental periods for shaping and strengthening neural interconnections through experientially based "firing" of synapses differ as well. As a result, environmental stimuli are processed differently and have different impacts on the brain at various stages of development.[14]

If stimuli are absent and synapses fail to fire, the dormant synapses are pruned away and innate capacities remain undeveloped. Laboratory experiments show that covering the eyes of newborn kittens in the first few weeks of life functionally blinds them. Without the visual stimuli needed to initiate synaptic firing, the excitatory neuronal pathways originally allocated to vision are reshaped through pruning to fulfill other sensory functions.[15]

Our sensory and motor capacities emerge early in life as the areas of the brain responsible for these functions develop and mature. These neural circuits provide a foundation for the subsequent building of more complex associational networks that allow us to do such things as play baseball, master a language, or compose a symphony. Impulse inhibition, social judgment, and abstract reasoning are among the most complex human functions requiring the integration of many associational networks. As a result, brain regions responsible for these functions are among the last neural structures to mature.

The prefrontal and temporal cortices of the brain are particularly important in relation to social and "executive" brain functions. Language, music, facial recognition, and the processing of nonverbal cues are all social capacities processed predominantly in the temporal cortex. The prefrontal cortex is responsible for various "executive" functions, including emotion regulation, social judgment, and abstract, symbolic thought. The prefrontal cortex has direct interconnections with both the temporal cortex and the amygdala, a limbic structure that functions in the processing and evaluation of emotion. The prefrontal cortex also directly interconnects with the nucleus accumbens, the "pleasure center" of the brain, and the hippocampus, the brain's memory processing center. These interconnections across executive, social, emotional, and reward processing regions of the brain constitute the neural framework for our social and moral capacities, as well as for our concept of self.[16]

ADOLESCENT BRAIN CHANGES

During adolescence significant changes occur in all of the brain structures involved in our social and moral behaviors.[17] In early and mid-adolescence the temporal and prefrontal cortices attain their greatest volume through processes of dendrite growth and synapse proliferation. The amygdala, the emotional processing center of the brain, also increases in volume. In late adolescence and early adulthood these volumes are reduced through pruning and remaining associational pathways are streamlined through myelination. This results in faster and more efficient information flow across associational networks throughout the brain.

Neurotransmitters, the brain's chemical messengers, undergo significant changes during adolescence as well. The neurotransmitter dopamine is central to both our motor functions and the reward systems of the brain.[18] When dopamine is released in the nucleus accumbens, the "pleasure center" of the brain, it makes us feel good; it also initiates approach behaviors. The nucleus accumbens assigns incentive value to stimuli. Some things, such as food, sex, music, and psychoactive drugs, have intrinsic reward value and naturally stimulate the production of dopamine in our brain's reward circuitry. Neutral stimuli that do not have inherent reward value for us can acquire such value through a process of reinforcement learning. Brain imaging studies of cocaine addicts show that, over time, previously neutral stimuli, such as places and paraphernalia associated with cocaine use, are themselves capable of stimulating dopamine production in the nucleus accumbens even in the absence of cocaine.[19]

The nucleus accumbens is linked to the amygdala and the hippocampus via the dopaminergic reward system. This emotional/motivational system influences our behavior. Although it was once believed that our social judgments and behavioral choices derive from conscious, "rational" decision-making processes, clinical studies, laboratory experiments, and brain imaging data have since clearly demonstrated that our subconscious emotions play a critical role in all our behavioral choices. While behavioral judgments and decisions do engage "rational" prefrontal cognition, they also require the emotional valuation of choices provided by the amygdala. When the amygdala is damaged, or when a disconnect occurs between this limbic structure and the prefrontal cortex, individuals able to solve abstract social and moral problems fail to apply these solutions to their own choices and behaviors.[20]

According to neuroscientists Alison Wismer Fries and Seth Pollack, the "connection between the nucleus accumbens and hippocampal-amygdalar complex creates a neural network whereby associations and memories activated by attended emotion cues are able to directly influence the enactment of a motor response ... [Additionally,] the DA [dopaminergic] system appears to be critical for linking the PFC [prefrontal cortex] to other networks tied to emotional behavior regulation." [21]

During adolescence the associational networks linking the nucleus accumbens, the amygdala, and the prefrontal cortex undergo synapse formation and pruning. In early and mid-adolescence the emotion and reward processing centers of our brains dominate dopamine activation. By late adolescence/early adulthood, however, ongoing maturation of the prefrontal cortex results in a "shift" in dopamine activation with increasing predominance of the prefrontal cortex over the dopaminergic system.[22] This shift increases prefrontal control over both emotion regulation and impulse control. Since the prefrontal cortex is also responsible for symbolic and abstract thought, the ongoing maturation of the prefrontal cortex during adolescence and early adulthood creates a unique developmental window for investing abstract cognitive schema, such as symbols, relationships, and beliefs, with both reward value and emotional/motivational meaning.

ADOLESCENT BEHAVIOR

The neural and hormonal changes that occur during the teen years have important effects on adolescent behavior. Pediatric psychiatrist Ronald Dahl has described adolescence as a period "prone to erratic ... and emotionally influenced behavior." [23] Adolescents react more quickly and with greater intensity to environmental stimuli than do either children or adults, and they perceive events as relatively more stressful than individuals at other life stages. Basal levels of circulating stress hormones such as cortisol are highest during adolescence; physiological responses to stressors such as blood pressure and cardiac output increase, and amygdalar activation, particularly in response to social stimuli, peaks.[24] Simultaneously, sex steroid hormones undergo a dramatic rise with the onset of puberty.

Risk taking and novelty seeking also increase during the teen years, particularly in males. Human sensation seeking scores peak in late adolescence. Simultaneously, mental processing speeds increase, the ability to focus on task-relevant information improves, and abstract, symbolic reasoning develops. Social behaviors shift focus from predominantly kin to non-kin interactions as peer relationships, romantic interests, and sexual motivations become increasingly important. The interindividual play behaviors of childhood decline and participation in coordinated group activities, such as sports, dance, and work, increases.

This shift from kin to non-kin interactions requires the mastering of new social roles and behaviors. According to psychologist Laurence Steinberg, "adolescent thinking in the real world is a function of social and emotional, as well as cognitive processes . . . just as cognition has an important impact on emotion, emotion has an important impact on basic cognitive processes, including decision-making and behavioral choice." [25] Learning how to control our impulses and emotions, what risks are worth taking and when to take them, whom we can trust, and when to subordinate our immediate self-interest to the long-term interests of the group entails the integration of emotional inputs, reward valuations, social assessments, and abstract cognition. Much of this learning can only be achieved through experience.

Neuroscientist William Greenough has coined the term "experience expectant" to describe developmental periods during which the experiences of the individual are particularly important in shaping brain structures undergoing maturation.[26] Early childhood is such a period for learning language. Our growing knowledge of the adolescent brain suggests that this is also an "experience expectant" period for the experiential sculpting of our social[27] and moral[28] "brains."

RELIGION, EMOTION, AND BELIEF

Both our genes and our life experiences impact our social and moral development. Early relationships with primary caregivers lay the foundation for subsequent social interactions that influence and shape our social judgments and behaviors. While our initial social experiences most frequently occur within the context of kin, as we move through the life course social interactions with non-kin assume increasing importance. This shift from kin to non-kin relationships introduces potential genetic conflicts of interest, since there is no inclusive fitness benefit for subordinating individual self-interest to the interests of unrelated others. This problem is intensified as group size increases and genetic relatedness decreases. Yet, since larger groups have an advantage in warfare, economies of scale, and technological innovation, societies able to successfully solve this problem can out-compete smaller groups.

Religion, in general, and adolescent rites of passage, in particular, offer a solution to this problem. Religion's ability to elicit empathy and instill motivational "rules" for social behavior that subordinate individual interests to those of the group constitutes a successful mechanism for fostering cooperation (see Chapters 13 and 14). This appears to be particularly effective during adolescence. The music-based communal ritual, emotionally evocative experiences, and abstract symbols and beliefs of religion activate precisely those brain regions undergoing the greatest changes during adolescence. Music, an intrinsically enjoyable experience, engages the dopaminergic reward system, particularly when coupled with ritualistic movement. The a cappella chants of fundamentalist Islam, the hymns of American Protestants and Latin Pentecostalists, and the ecstatic song and dance of Sufi mysticism all stimulate the production of "feel good" neurochemicals such as dopamine, serotonin, oxytocin, and endorphins in our brains.[29] The same changes occurring in the brain's dopaminergic reward system that render adolescents more vulnerable to alcohol and drug addiction also increase their emotional and reward responses to music and movement. In modern secular cultures the popularity of iPods and dance concerts, or "raves," among adolescents suggest this increased reward value of music and dance. Throughout the vast majority of our evolution as a species, however, music and dance were not secular experiences but were, instead, intimately intertwined with religious ritual.[30]

Of course, religious ritual may also evoke powerful negative emotions. Dark, candlelit cathedrals, the specter of vengeful ancestral ghosts, the slaughtering of sacrificial animals, and the terrifying masks of gods and demons all activate our brain's alert systems, eliciting feelings of uncertainty, fear, and awe. Pain, an extremely effective mechanism for evoking emotional response, is also a ubiquitous element of religious ritual. Asceticism, self-flagellation, and circumcision are not confined to strange cults and sects, but are prominent in modern world religions as well. Fear-inducing and painful experiences are particularly prominent in adolescent rites of passage. Kidnapping, seclusion, food and sleep deprivation, scarification, tooth excision, genital mutilation, and other psychological and physical ordeals have been and continue to be prominent elements of such rites in many cultures throughout the world.[31] Even the relatively benign rites of modern Judeo-Christian traditions require initiates to engage in fear-evoking public performances. Such experiences activate the amygdala, etching indelible memories on both conscious and unconscious levels.[32]

The ability of ritual to evoke both positive and negative affect is, of course, not specific to religion. Secular dances, concerts, and sporting events also induce feelings of happiness and joy, and military boot camp can certainly elicit awe, fear, and pain. What is specific to religion, however, is the association of these evoked emotions with socially meaningful and unfalsifiable abstractions that prescribe and proscribe individual behaviors. The counterintuitive beliefs of religious systems are both metaphorical and memorable; they activate cognitive schema on a conscious level, but they also activate myriad unconscious social and emotional associations. And, because they are counterintuitive, they are readily remembered and difficult to "fake." Since they are unfalsifiable, they more readily endure. Unlike the superiority of Communism as an economic system, or the assertion that enemy combatants are "sub-human," it is impossible to empirically prove or disprove the existence of forest spirits, vengeful ghosts, or omniscient gods.[33] Belief in such abstractions is faith-based, and faith is seldom instilled through rational discourse; it is, instead, more commonly "found" through active participation in emotionally evocative ritual.

Survey results from 310 American college students suggest the importance of ritual participation to religious faith.[34] Nearly three-quarters of the students surveyed reported high levels of previous religious training, but at the time of the study only one-third of these students were actively involved in religious activities. Statistical analysis showed that those who were currently religiously involved differed significantly from those who were not in the religious activities they had previously experienced. Students who had previously attended communal religious services were twice as likely as others in the sample to be currently involved in religious activities. If those services had also involved music, the students were three times more likely to currently participate in religious activities, and if their previous religious experiences included prayer, they were four times more likely than other students in the sample to be currently involved in religion. Interviews conducted with middle and high school students further supported this correlation of ritual participation and religiosity. Students who only attended classroom religious training classes expressed consistently higher levels of skepticism regarding religious beliefs than students who also regularly attended ritually rich worship services.

The brain changes occurring during adolescence are precisely those relating to emotional, social, and symbolic functions. Religions throughout the world provide emotionally evocative experiences for adolescents that initiate neuronal firing in brain regions undergoing maturational processes, including the brain's reward circuitry, limbic nuclei, and temporal and prefrontal cortices. Both incentive learning and conditioned associations result, investing social and moral abstractions with emotional significance and motivational force. Participation in religious ritual engages the neural pathways that link our reward and emotional valuation systems with social and cognitive abstractions. This provides a mechanism for inculcating culturally derived social algorithms that influence individual judgments, decisions, and behaviors.

ADOLESCENTS, RELIGION, AND PROSOCIAL BEHAVIORS

In traditional societies adolescent rites of passage explicitly shape adult social values, expectations, and behaviors. In modern nation-states adolescent religious participation is also positively correlated with prosocial behaviors. A longitudinal study of Thai adolescents participating in Roman Catholic and Buddhist ordination programs demonstrated long-term changes in both psychological parameters and social behaviors of these groups.[35] Sociological studies conducted in the United States have repeatedly found a significant positive relationship between adolescent religious involvement and dominant social values[36] (see also Chapter 13). Adolescents who regularly attend religious services are significantly less likely to engage in delinquent behaviors, and less likely to use tobacco, alcohol, or drugs. They are also less likely to engage in premarital sex and risky sexual behaviors.[37]

In research conducted with American middle and high school students,[38] those who regularly participated in such religious activities as weekly worship services, youth retreats, and church-based community service projects were more likely than others in the sample to participate in nonchurch community service and less likely to ignore problems. Those who neither believed nor participated in religion reported nearly four times more difficulty concentrating than other teens in the sample, and teens who reported little or no participation in religious activities, regardless of their beliefs, had higher odds of getting angry quickly than other study participants. They were also four times more likely to have experienced school problems within the past year. These findings support previous research indicating beneficial psychological and social effects of religious participation.

CONCLUSION

Over the past four decades ongoing industrialization, urbanization, and secularization throughout the world have been accompanied by escalating rates of adolescent suicide and depression.[39] During this same period neuroscientists have imaged and explored the adolescent brain. Their research has shown adolescence to be a particularly critical developmental period for the development of reward valuation systems, emotional processing, social judgment, and abstract/symbolic thinking. During the teenage years the brain regions responsible for these functions are maturing through dendrite growth, synapse formation, pruning, and myelination. Associational neural circuits are strengthened and shaped as experiential inputs initiate synaptic firing.

We have long known that adolescence is marked by increased sociality, heightened sexual awareness, and greater novelty seeking/ risk taking behaviors. These changes all contribute to the transition from child to adult as teens venture away from their kin group to encounter unrelated mates, competitors, and collaborators. We also know that emotional responses are heightened during the teen years. Vulnerability to alcohol, drug, and nicotine addiction is increased due to changes occurring in the reward circuitry of the adolescent brain. Abstract and symbolic reasoning capacities develop as the prefrontal cortex matures. These simultaneous brain changes during adolescence provide a unique window of opportunity for assigning reward value to social and symbolic abstractions and for investing these abstractions with emotional and motivational meaning.

The widespread recurrence of adolescent rites of passage in highly diverse cultures throughout the world suggests that religion may constitute a particularly effective mechanism for doing just that. The central role of music in religious ritual across all cultures has innate reward value for humans. Both music and the emotionally evocative elements that typify adolescent rites of passage across widely diverse cultures are likely to prime the adolescent brain for incentive and associative learning. The metaphorical narratives and counterintuitive beliefs of religion comprise highly memorable abstract cognitive schema for creating such associations and subsequently accessing the largely subconscious, emotionally valenced social algorithms they represent.

Do adolescents "need" religion? One-quarter of societies throughout the world do not conduct adolescent rites of passage, and millions of adolescents in modern secular nations mature into well-adjusted and productive adults without ever having participated in any religious ritual. This suggests that religion is not necessary for normal adolescent social development. Indeed, if religion is an adaptation for achieving cooperation in non-kin groups, then we should not find expenditures of time and energy on religion in general, and adolescent rites of passage in particular, in those societies where this need does not exist. This includes small-scale kin-based societies, such as the Ache of South America, as well as modern large-scale nation-states that achieve cooperation through both economic and military means. Conversely, we would expect to see the greatest expenditures of time and energy on religion and adolescent rites of passage in large, non-state-level societies that depend on cooperation for their continued existence. Research by anthropologist Richard Sosis and his colleagues supports this hypothesis.[40] When there is no need for non-kin cooperation, or when other institutions more efficiently or effectively meet that need, then religion and adolescent rites of passage should be absent or greatly attenuated because the time and energy costs these entail are not offset by the benefits religion confers. Recent declines in religious participation in modern European nation-states suggest such a trend. In contrast, the high mobility, economic inequality, and cultural diversity of the contemporary United States should promote religious participation, particularly among disenfranchised groups.

Medical and sociological studies of contemporary American adolescents indicate that those who do participate in religion experience less cognitive dissonance, lower psychological distress, and less depression than their nonreligious peers.[41] Research further indicates that religiosity in teens is "inversely related to depression and suicide ideation"[42] and suicide rates are significantly lower for American youth who regularly attend worship services than for those who do not.

Although adolescents may not "need" religion, in economically and culturally diverse societies they may benefit from it. The social algorithms inculcated through participation in religious ritual and encapsulated in the metaphorical narratives and memorable counterintuitive beliefs of religious systems provide frameworks for social interactions that reduce indecision and anxiety and promote in-group cooperation. Changes occurring in emotional, social, and cognitive neural pathways during adolescence are likely to offer an "experience expectant" window for the development of our social and moral brains. Religion appears to provide a highly effective tool for sculpting their sociocultural contours.

NOTES

1. Gera, D. L. (2003). *Ancient Greek ideas on speech, language, and civilization*. Oxford, U.K.: Oxford University Press.

2. Zuckerman, P. (2005). Atheism: Contemporary rates and patterns. In M. Martin (Ed.), *The Cambridge companion to atheism* (pp. 47–68 [59]). Cambridge, U.K.: Cambridge University Press.

3. Pinker, S. (1994). *The language instinct*. New York: William Morrow and Co.

4. Bloch, M. (1989). *Ritual, history and power*. London: The Athlone Press.

5. Alcorta, C., & Sosis, R. (in press). Signals and rituals of humans and animals. In M. Bekoff (Ed.), *Encyclopedia of animal rights and animal welfare*. Westport, CT: Greenwood Publishers.

6. Alcorta, C. (2006). Religion and the life course: Is adolescence an "experience expectant" period for religious transmission? In P. McNamara (Ed.), *Where God and science meet: How brain and evolutionary studies alter our understanding of religion, Vol. II, The neurology of religious experience* (pp. 55–80). Westport, CT: Praeger Press.

7. Lutkehaus, N. C., & Roscoe, P. B. (Eds.). (1995). *Gender rituals: Female initiation in Melanesia*. New York: Routledge.

8. Purzycki, B., & Sosis, R. (2009). The religious system as adaptive: Cognitive flexibility, public displays, and acceptance. In E. Voland and W. Schiefenhöval (Eds.), *The biological evolution of religious mind and behavior*. New York: Springer Publishers.

9. Turner, V. (1967). *The forest of symbols*. New York: Cornell University Press.

10. Ibid.

11. Hublin, J.-J., & Cogqueugniot, H. (2006). Absolute or proportional brain size: That is the question. *Journal of Human Evolution, 50*, 109–113.

12. Kolb, B., & Whishaw, I. Q. (1999). *Fundamentals of human neuropsychology* (4th ed.). New York: W. H. Freeman and Co.

13. Murphy, T. H. (2003). Activity-dependent synapse development: Changing the rules. *Nature Neuroscience, 6*(1), 9–11.

14. Kolb, B., Forgie, M., Gibb, R., Gorny, G., & Rowntree, S. (1998). Age, experience and the changing brain. *Neuroscience and Biobehavioral Reviews, 22*(2), 143–159.

15. Lynch, G., Larson, J., Muller, D., & Granger, R. (1990). Neural networks and networks of neurons. In J. L. McGaugh, N. M. Weinberger, and G. Lynch (Eds.), *Brain organization and memory: Cells, systems, and circuits* (pp. 390–400). New York: Oxford University Press.

16. Moll, J., & de Oliveira-Souza, R. (2007). Moral judgments, emotions and the utilitarian brain. *Trends in Cognitive Science, 11,* 319–321; Beer, J. S. (2006). Orbitofrontal cortex and social regulation. In J. T. Cacioppo, P. S. Visser, & C. L. Pickett (Eds.), *Social neuroscience: People thinking about people* (pp. 153-165). Cambridge, MA: MIT Press; Sebastian, C., Burnett, S., & Blakemore, S.-J. (2008). Development of the self-concept during adolescence. *Trends in Cognitive Sciences, 12*(11), 441–446.

17. Spear, L. P. (2000). The adolescent brain and age-related behavioral manifestations. *Neuroscience and Biobehavioral Reviews, 24*(4), 417–463. Paus, T. (2005). Mapping brain maturation and cognitive development during adolescence. *Trends in Cognitive Science, 9,* 60–68.

18. Daw, N. D. (2007). Dopamine: At the intersection of reward and action. *Nature Neuroscience, 10,* 1505–1507.

19. Dehaene, S., & Changeux, J. P. (2000). Reward-dependent learning in neuronal networks for planning and decision-making. In H. B. M. Uylings, C. G. van Eden, J. P. D. de Bruin et al. (Eds.), *Cognition, emotion, and autonomic responses: The integrative role of the prefrontal cortex and limbic structures* (pp. 219–230). New York: Elsevier.

20. Damasio, A. (1994). *Descartes' error: Emotion, reason and the human brain*. New York: G. P. Putnam's Sons.

21. Wismer Fries, A. B., & Pollak, S. D. (2007). Emotion processing and the developing brain. In D. Coch, G. Dawson, & K. W. Fischer (Eds.), *Human behavior, learning, and the developing brain* (pp. 329–361 [344]). New York: The Guilford Press.

22. Spear, The adolescent brain and age-related behavioral manifestations.

23. Dahl, R. E. (2004). Adolescent brain development: a period of vulnerabilities and opportunities. In R. E. Dahl & L. P. Spear (Eds.), *Adolescent brain development: Vulnerabilities and opportunities* (pp. 1–22 [3]). *Annals of the New York Academy of Sciences*, Vol. 1021. New York: New York Academy of Sciences.

24. Spear, The adolescent brain and age-related behavioral manifestations.

25. Steinberg, L. (2007). Cognitive and affective development in adolescence. *Trends in Cognitive Sciences, 9,* 69–74 [71].

26. Greenough, W. T. (1986). What's special about development? Thoughts on the bases of experience sensitive synaptic plasticity. In W. T. Greenough and J. M. Juraska (Eds.), *Developmental Neuropsychobiology* (pp. 387–408). New York: Academic Press.

27. Blakemore, S.-J. (2008). The social brain in adolescence. *Nature Reviews Neuroscience, 9*(4), 267–277.

28. Moll & de Oliveira-Souza, Moral judgments, emotions and the utilitarian brain.

29. Levitin, D. (2008). *The world in six songs.* New York: Penguin Books.

30. Alcorta, C. S. (2008). Music and the miraculous: The neurophysiology of music's emotive meaning. In J. H. Ellens (Ed.), *Miracles: God, science, and psychology in the paranormal, Vol. 3, Parapsychological perspectives* (pp. 230–252). Westport, CT: Praeger.

31. Glucklich, A. (2001). *Sacred pain.* New York: Oxford University Press.

32. Adolphs, R. (2002). Social cognition and the human brain. In J. T. Cacioppo, G. G. Berntson, & R. Adolphs (Eds.), *Foundations in social neuroscience* (pp. 313–332). Cambridge: MIT Press.

33. Rappaport, R. A. (1999). *Ritual and religion in the making of humanity.* Cambridge, U.K.: Cambridge University Press.

34. Alcorta, C. S. (2006, May). Youth, religion, and resilience. Unpublished Ph.D. thesis, University of Connecticut.

35. Thananart, M., Tori, C.D., & Emavardhana, T. (2000). A longitudinal study of psychosocial changes among Thai adolescents participating in a Buddhist ordination program for novices. *Adolescence, 35*(138), 285–293. Tori, C. (1999). Changes on psychological scales following Buddhist and Roman Catholic retreats. *Psychological Reports, 84,* 125–126.

36. Donahue, M. J., & Benson, P. L. (1995). Religion and the well-being of adolescents. *Journal of Social Issues, 51*(2), 145–160; Smith, C. (2005). *Soul searching: The religious and spiritual lives of american teenagers.* Oxford: Oxford University Press.

37. Regnerus, M., Smith, C., & Fritsch, M. (2003). *Religion in the lives of American adolescents: A review of the literature.* Research Report of the National Study of Youth and Religion, No. 3. Chapel Hill, NC: University of North Carolina at Chapel Hill.

38. Alcorta, Youth, religion, and resilience.

39. Desjarlais, R., Eisenberg, L., Good, B., & Kleinman, A. (1995). *World mental health.* New York: Oxford University Press; Miller, G. (2006). The unseen: Mental illness' global toll. *Science, 311,* 458–461.

40. Sosis, R., Kress, H., & Boster, J. (2007). Scars for war: Evaluating alternative signaling explanations for cross-cultural variance in ritual costs. *Evolution and Human Behavior, 28,* 234–247.

41. Schnittker, J. (2001). When is faith enough? The effects of religious involvement on depression. *Journal for the Scientific Study of Religion, 40*(3), 393–411.

42. Nooney, J. G. (2005). Religion, stress, and mental health in adolescence: Findings from ADD health. *Review of Religious Research, 46,* 341–354 [341].

PART FOUR

Causes of Religious Behavior

In biology contributing causes of behavior can be divided into *proximate* or near causes and *ultimate* or distant causes. Proximate causes are mechanisms that operate only within the lifetime of the individual. Ultimate causes, which also operate within the lifetime of the individual, have adaptively evolved over many generations as a result of the process of Darwinian natural selection. A synonym for ultimate cause is the behavior's adaptiveness, which is covered in Part Five. The two types of causes are related. This part addresses only the proximate causes of religious behavior. Proximate causes of behavior can also be thought of as within and outside of the individual. All proximate causes of behavior are contributory causes. Some may be necessary; none are sufficient. All behavior is a *phenotype*, which is the result of the interaction of a specific genotype (DNA) with a specific environment. Chapter 8 in Part Four addresses how religious beliefs, and the behaviors they predictably cause, may reduce stress in a process the authors call *brainsoothing*. Chapter 9 proposes that some religious behaviors may be "internally guided" and motivated by factors that are not exclusively under the direct influence of Darwinian natural selection. Chapter 10 offers an alternative perspective to the cognitive science view of religious behavior by seeing how aspects of spirituality, a major component of religion, could have evolved through what is known as the mirror neuron system in the brain.

CHAPTER 8

The Brain and Religious Adaptations

Michael T. McGuire and Lionel Tiger

Might there be a characteristic neurophysiological signature among individuals who ascribe to religious beliefs and participate in their rituals and social activities? If the answer is yes, might the signature correlate positively with a reduction of aversive brain-body states, better than average physical and mental health, and extended longevity? This chapter offers answers to these questions for the world's two major religions, Christianity and Islam.

We build from the following points: Everyday life is characterized by random, unexpected, and known sources of stress. Stress initiates unpleasant and undesirable aversive brain-body states. Individuals act to reduce the effects of these states—a process we call *brainsoothing*. Compared to alternative ways of brainsoothing such as relaxing, taking a holiday, or visiting a spa, Christianity and Islam more predictably and effectively brainsoothe. The adaptive outcomes of brainsoothing include improved physical and mental health and extended longevity.

Our primary sources of data are studies of functional areas of the brain which activate during religious-related moments, the influence of these moments on the brain's chemical profile, and health outcome studies. We begin with a discussion of stress.

STRESS

The generic biochemical events of stress are well known. Virtually any stressful event such as an unanticipated flat tire, a disagreement with a spouse, or a moment of uncertainty or ambiguity regarding a personally important matter initiates a series of biochemical reactions that prepare a person to cope. The hypothalamus secretes the hormone Corticotropin-Releasing Factor (CRF), which stimulates the pituitary gland to produce the hormone adrenocortotropic hormone (ACTH), which initiates the release of cortisol, which speeds up the body's metabolism. Simultaneously, the adrenal glands secrete epinephrine and norepinephrine, which prime the body for action and lead to increased heart rate, faster breathing, enhanced alertness, and muscle tension. Should stress be brief, it may serve to motivate and increase alertness. Successful coping may follow. Should it persist, the outcome is an aversive brain-body state that is experienced as a combination of nervousness, irritation, fear, difficulty concentrating and reasoning, sleepiness, and emotional instability.

Less generic are the stress features of environments and the capacity of individuals to manage stress. For example, there are wide differences in what can be called the stress barometer of the work environment. Soldiers in battle, firefighters, air traffic controllers, and policemen live in different stress worlds than librarians and bird watchers. Individuals differ in their capacity to manage stress. Some are adept. Others are less so. Part of this difference has a genetic source. For example, genetic variation affects the amount of neuropeptide Y released during stress and its influence on emotional and stress responses.[1] And part has to do with a person's sex. Brain imaging studies using functional magnetic resonance imaging (fMRI) methodology reveal that males and females respond differently to the same stressful stimuli.[2] Such differences may reflect the expression of selected genes among males and females.

In summary, human beings are vulnerable to stress. Stress is unavoidable. We live in different stress worlds. And we differ in our capacity to manage stress.

COMMON FEATURES OF RELIGION

Religions have their own spatial and historical universes[3,4] that groups define for themselves and that range from the very local as among Zuni and Sioux Indians[5] to the seemingly infinite universes characteristic of Christianity and Islam. They also differ in the beliefs, rituals, and behaviors with which they fill their universes. Nonetheless, repeated patterns of behavior and thought appear among the majority of religions.[6,7] These include: afterlife, beings with special powers, portents, creationism, spirit possession, rituals, sacred text exegesis (interpretation), the sacred, deference, moral obligation, punishment and reward, and revelation. To this list may be added the frequent social clustering of people of the same faith and a type of subordination described as "make-oneself-lower-or-smaller-or-more-vulnerable."[8] Further there is the impressive array of signs and symbols that identify religions and that when worn signal one's religious affiliation to others.[9] They reinforce emotions associated with empathy and friendliness, and initiate attributions of meaning to beliefs and symbols.[10,11,12,13]

From this list we will look at the brainsoothing effects of religious beliefs, socialization, and rituals. They are fundamental, important, and omnipresent features of Islam and Christianity.

BELIEFS–GENERAL FEATURES

Whatever their content or topic—whether religious, political, social, or personal—beliefs are brain-based cognitive-emotion systems that organize and prioritize language, thought, emotion, and behavior. They reduce ambiguity and uncertainty about events both within and outside a believer's control and influence. They give order, direction, purpose, and place to many of the events and complexities of both daily and imaginary life.[14,15,16] Meanings are attributed to symbols, myths, doctrines, and behavior. Selected facts, ideas, feelings, and acts are valued while others fade in importance. Often causal explanations are present—God put humans on earth to carry out his plan. Equally often they provide direction to behavior.

There is more. Beliefs are often treasured as possessions in ways similar to how individuals possess valuable objects.[17] "Possession" perhaps explains the resistance often encountered among those deeply committed to specific religious beliefs to explore the beliefs of other faiths or of no faith at all. And with different types of belief, different areas of the brain are involved. For example, there are neural correlates of true and false belief reasoning[18,19]—religious beliefs are usually true beliefs for believers. Distinct brain regions are activated during belief, disbelief, and uncertainty. There is also evidence of a quest for pleasure and reward in what people believe. Happy thoughts appear to be more congenial to the brain and its chemical equilibrium than unhappy thoughts.[20,21] Few people complain of the stress of happiness.

An intriguing finding comes from fMRI studies of individuals of the same age from the same culture who observe the same stimulus. For example, while two people watch a movie, their fMRI profiles are strikingly similar.[22] But when the movie is over and discussion begins about what was observed and its possible meanings, fMRI profiles differ dramatically. Both culture and upbringing appear to be factors influencing these differences. From another perspective, different interpretation of the same stimulus as well as the need for stimulus repetition to optimize memory storage and retrieval[23,24] invite the speculation that religions have found it necessary to repeat core beliefs more than once in order to narrow the parameters of interpretation among believers.

THE BRAIN AND SOCIALIZATION

Before discussing the brain and its activities during socialization, rituals, and beliefs, we emphasize that we have sampled but a small percentage of the scientific literature. The field of neuroscience is experiencing a period of explosive productivity. The number of research publications each week documents this explosion. While our sample of the scientific literature is small, we have not knowingly excluded any research results that refute the findings and interpretations we discuss. Nonetheless what we discuss and our interpretations will not be the final word. New findings and methods lead to the revision of hypotheses—for example, only in the past two decades has fMRI methodology been available, it changes continually, and results may mislead or invite misinterpretation. Further, for studies of both brain activity (e.g., fMRI, EEG [electroencephalogram], and PET [positive emission tomography]) and within-brain chemical changes the majority of current research methods are indirect. This introduces the possibility of error in measurement and interpretation. Finally, the changes in brain activity and chemistry that we discuss are not limited to religious moments. For example, positive beliefs on any topic appear to activate the brain's prefrontal cortex. On average what is special about religion is its predictable soothing influence on brain activity and chemistry as well as its improbable ubiquity.

Although our primary focus is on religious beliefs, they have proven difficult to separate from socialization and rituals and their effects on the brain.[25] The brainsoothing of each will be considered.

The brainsoothing that results from religious socialization occurs at sites of worship as well as elsewhere. Believers gather at locations they consider sacred, personally meaningful, or defined as important. They see familiar and unfamiliar faces but usually far more of the former. The atmosphere of the site is positive. The experience is rewarding both in anticipation and in act. Emotions are quietly or ebulliently upbeat. Bodies are relaxed. This is in contrast to much of the routine and stress of daily life.

Familiar faces and their emotional expressions are reassuring and invite good thoughts. Other signals such as dress, words, music, and architecture identify that one is among members of our group; for still others it is behavior such as placing a scarf over one's head or drawing a cross in the air with one's hand. The congregants discuss their lives, families, plans, successes and failures, and beliefs. Ambiguity, uncertainty, uneasiness, and hesitancy, which so often accompany encounters among unfamiliar persons, are largely absent. These are moments of social reward. And, of course, the brain is involved; the anterior cingulate cortex encodes expectancy of rewards while neuronal activity related to reward value and motivation occurs in the frontal cortex and the midbrain.[26,27]

The brain begins its activities from the moment of arrival if not before. There is a specific cortical region consisting entirely of face-sensitive cells—cells that inform its owner "I know him or her" or "That is an unfamiliar face." [28,29] Much of this information is processed in the amygdala and the frontal cortex and stored in both the frontal cortex and the hippocampus for subsequent use.[30,31] Other areas of an observer's brain mirror the behavior and expressed emotions of those observed. If a person is viewed as suffering, areas of the observer's brain that activate if the observer is suffering increase their activity.[32,33] Or if an observed person is happy, areas in the observer's brain that activate during moments of happiness mirror what is observed.

Among the brain's key chemicals affected by socialization are serotonin, dopamine, norepinephrine, and oxytocin. These are neurotransmitters/hormones—molecules all—which transmit messages and alter neuronal activity. Serotonin is perhaps the most celebrated member of this group largely because of Prozac and other antidepressant drugs that elevate its levels in the brain and often diminish the effects of depression and anxiety. But long before Prozac was first prescribed it was known among nonhuman primates that brain levels of serotonin increase in relationship to the number of positive signals an animal receives from other members of its group—the details are reviewed elsewhere.[34] The human equivalent of a positive signal, such as an extra-friendly smile with an extended and friendly focus or a hug conveys to the recipient that he is important, a member of our group, respected, and worth attention—religions' social moments can be hotbeds of conviviality. Signals elevate a recipient's sense of status, which is associated with feeling at ease and comfortable physically, mentally, and socially, as well as in charge of one's behavior.[35] Accompanying positive socialization are chemical events that brainsoothe.[36]

Studies of serotonin show that elevated brain levels encourage cooperative behavior and help solidify social bonds by reinforcing the value individuals place in others.[37] Conversely, depletion of serotonin in the prefrontal cortex—one of the thinking parts of the brain—leads to cognitive inflexibility[38] and fosters stubbornness, defensiveness, negativeness, and resistance to changing one's beliefs.[39,40] The administration of the nutrient tryptophan, which is the molecule essential for the synthesis of serotonin and increases its levels in the brain, leads to a decrease in quarrelsome behavior and an increase in dominance behavior among normal humans.[41]

What happens with serotonin happens similarly with changes in the brain's levels of norepinephrine and dopamine. Within limits, norepinephrine elevation leads to increased social engagement and co-operation.[42] As noted, increases in levels of dopamine occur in anticipation of pleasure and reward and their desired effects. And certainly part of religious socialization is the anticipation of the pleasure of desirable social interaction. Is this part of the story of lifelong self-reinforcing religious participation among serious and committed believers?

Then there is oxytocin. It acts as a hormone when it induces labor and lactation in women. It serves as a neurotransmitter in selected brain areas associated with emotion and social behavior such as the amygdala and the nucleus accumbens.[43] It contributes decisively to social attachment and acts of social good—for example, an elevation of brain oxytocin makes one more generous in giving money. Its levels increase in social interactions where people trust one another.[44]

The key ideas here are these. Socializing in a minimally stressful and positive social environment has two major effects. It significantly reduces stress and initiates a reduction in stress-related chemicals such as adrenalin, cortisol, ACTH, CRF, and protein Y. It increases the level of those brain chemicals—serotonin, dopamine, norepinephrine, and oxytocin—associated with pleasure, happiness, and relaxation.

RITUALS

There is nothing unfamiliar about rituals. They are everywhere, every day, every moment. What time school starts, how to manage a four-stop-sign intersection, and how one is seated at weddings. They may be secular in origin, which does not preclude their use in places of worship—individuals shake hands inside and outside of sacred sites the same way. Or they may be religious in origin, which does not preclude their use in public as when both believers and nonbelievers bow their heads in moments of public prayer. And they may be religious in origin but also remain private as when persons at prayer assume specific postures alone in their rooms.

Rituals are behaviors.[45,46,47] They are also behavior rules—usually not formal laws. They are integral parts of everyday behavior. Groups and societies rely on them to function efficiently. They signal a member's savvy about what to do and when. The strong conclusion compels itself that carrying them out usually produces comfort and a sense of safety, at least for the moment.

Every major religion has its rituals that deal with important milestones from birth to death such as biological maturation, marriage, bearing offspring, attaining official membership, and death. So too with behavioral detail. Praying, singing, chanting, moments of silence, who leads in processions, how sacred texts are placed and held, the order of prayers and blessings—all are examples. Rituals focus attention. Thus it is not surprising that studies show that many rituals are accompanied by an increase in cerebral blood flow to the amygdala and prefrontal cortex and enhanced cognitive focus.[48]

An element common to many religious rituals is subordination to a higher authority.[49] From an evolutionary perspective subordinate behavior may reduce the probability of attack as it does among many animal species. For an individual and for a group as a whole there is clear subordination ideologically during prayer, physically and mentally during meditation, mentally and spiritually during confession, and operationally in what one does and does not do. But when such rituals envision or are connected to a higher power it is a special matter predicated on the presence of a deity or higher power. No matter what form it takes, it is a very different type of subordination than, for example, remaining politely quiet during a minister's sermon. The higher authority or power rarely can be visualized, just imagined and inferred. Submission to a higher authority differs in part because real live ministers change, have personalities, and die. But the highest authorities live on, minimally changed and untouchable.

Because many rituals are performed in the religious world, different profiles of brain activity and chemistry are to be expected. That is what is found. For example, transcendental meditation studies show decreased blood pressure,[50] a decline in oxygen consumption,[51] increased galvanic skin response,[52] and reduction (usually) in heart rate.[53] Other studies show that Zen-type meditation increases the activity of the frontal lobe and basal ganglia while it decreases activity in the gyrus occipitalis.[54] And some rituals are associated with an increase in alpha wave activity (associated with alertness) and a decrease in the delta brain waves associated with drowsiness and sleep.[55]

Other studies show that meditation is associated with a significant decrease in brain-body chemicals such as cortisol and ACTH, which are proxy measures for stress.[56] Still other studies find an increase in urinary 5-HIAA, the main metabolic product of serotonin, which suggests that its brain levels are elevated during certain rituals.[57] And there are findings suggesting that cultivating compassion through meditation affects brain regions that lead to greater empathy. Each of these findings is consistent with the brainsoothing hypothesis.

Like many of the positive effects of religious socialization, those of rituals may be short-lived. Sustaining their desired effects requires repetition just as one must exercise vigorously more than once every few weeks to achieve maximum effects or even any at all. Often the short-lived effects result from the fact that when rituals cease people return to stress-filled real life.

RELIGIOUS BELIEF

Religious belief is our third focus. It comprises what is written in sacred texts, what is said by members of the cloth, what is passed on among believers, what one believes oneself whatever its source, and more.

Like religious socialization and rituals, beliefs brainsoothe. They chart the unknown and the future. They answer many of the unanswerable questions that the brain creates. With remarkable, even astonishing, boldness and invention religious beliefs reduce ambiguity and uncertainty about matters of life, death, the soul, and eternity. They provide a menu for the afterlife as the antidote to the cold prospect of complete postlife nothingness. This is apparently unendurable to the majority of human beings. The time-compact present that is so much a mark of everyday life is suddenly extended without end or stress.[58] Religious beliefs may be natural[59,60] as some have claimed, and whatever their origin certainly they counterbalance the symbols of evil[61] and the fear often initiated by reading the likes of *Malleus Maleficarum* and *The Inferno*. It is life after life on earth that is so crucial because, "*It is impossible for us who have been created for eternity to find anything in this world to satisfy our souls fully.*" [62] This is the remarkable message of Christianity and Islam. Not surprisingly, pleasant beliefs of afterlife correlate positively with improved mental health.[63]

Again, the brain is the central player. There is the excitement and reduced stress that comes with arriving at an answer—recall the top-of-the-world feeling of confidence when you aced the answer to a critical college examination question. Emotion and cognition intermix comfortably at such moments.[64] As noted, fMRI studies indicate that different parts of the brain are active in response to belief, disbelief, uncertainty,[65] and the anticipation of reward. Other studies show that contemplation of a religious image enables individuals to detach themselves from the experience of pain.[66] Further, enhanced activation in the amygdala—a feature of positive beliefs—leads to an optimism bias,[67] a finding consistent with the speculation that brains are hardwired to conform to the Golden Rule.[68] A likely result of these events is increased cooperation.[69]

We return to ambiguity and uncertainty. There are ambiguities associated with real life events and there are those that are products of the human imagination dealing with events and forces and personalities that cannot be proven scientifically. Normally the brain avoids ambiguity and uncertainty. It likes answers, concreteness, and predictability. To reduce uncertainty and ambiguity, people read books and newspapers, ask questions, watch the news, pore over the strangely confident accounts of bold astrologers, and adopt religion. Religious behavior may be the external expression of the need for certainty.[70] But there are real life situations that are unavoidably ambiguous with their outcomes uncertain such as the outcome of a serious medical operation or one's fate when going into battle.

How do religious beliefs decrease uncertainty and ambiguity? Brain events are critical. The activity and amount of the chemical actylcholine correlates with the degree of expected uncertainty. Expected uncertainty implies that an outcome is unknown but it will occur by a certain time. For example, at the end of three hours some team will win a football game or by a specific date an election will be held. The activity of the chemical norepinephrine relates sharply to the degree of unexpected uncertainty. Unexpected uncertainty is about events when the outcome is known but its date is unknown—for example, the date and location of one's death.[71] The fate of norepinephrine in unexpected uncertainty is not fully understood, largely because its levels are influenced by a variety of factors (e.g., socialization). But we know that a reduction in uncertainty and ambiguity correlates with diminished actylcholine and norepinephrine levels and diminished cortisol and ACTH release from the pituitary.

Dopamine also is involved. As noted, neuronal activity related to reward value increases dopamine levels.[72,73,74] Furthermore, people with high levels of dopamine are more likely to find significance in coincidences and pick out meaning and patterns where there are none.[75] Perhaps this explains why many believers see the effects of God in even the minute details of everyday life while nonbelievers remain skeptical.

IS THERE AN ADAPTIVE OUTCOME TO BRAINSOOTHING?

The adaptive measures we have selected are reduced aversive brain-body states, above average physical and mental health, and increased longevity. With respect to reduced aversive brain-body states, the overwhelming majority of studies show reductions of stress-related chemicals during positive socialization and rituals. Concerning physical and mental health, the majority of studies indicate that seriously committed believers have better than average physical and mental health.[76] These findings are consistent with the idea that religious moments are low-stress events associated with elevations of serotonin, dopamine, and oxytocin, which occur during these events. Much the same is true for longevity. It is increased[77,78,79] and a likely consequence of better than average physical and mental health. Although there is a scattering of reports that show no adaptive effects among religious participants, we know of no reported results that show the opposite for Christianity or Islam.

WHAT WE HAVE AND HAVE NOT SAID

We have said that available neurophysiological data are consistent with the brainsoothe hypothesis and that we are unaware of reports that refute this hypothesis. We have also said that the hypothesis is consistent with the view that religious beliefs, in conjunction with rituals and socialization, can be viewed as contributing to adaptations as we have defined them. There are, however, alternative views.[80] And we have speculated that the predictable brainsoothing effects of religious participation are significant factors contributing to the high percentage of people who are believers and participants in religious rituals and socialization. A clear implication of these points is that a religion's capacity to facilitate brainsoothing will influence the number of its members.

We have not said or suggested that there is or is not a higher power in the universe, that religion is the only way to brainsoothe, that our hypothesis explains all of religion, or that it applies to other than the world's two major religions. If, as scholars have suggested,[81] religion has gone through progressive changes from more primitive types to the more worldly types we have discussed—Islam and Christianity—our hypothesis may apply only to the worldly types.

There are, of course, many ways of looking at religions and their functions and effects (this entire volume). Evolutionary explanations are particularly interesting. For example, religious belief and behavior may have been selected in the Darwinian sense or they may be by-products of other evolved traits.[82] Or "our ancestors' belief in God may have been what created many parts of the human mind—'gifts' as some would say." [83] While our hypothesis is not inconsistent with these views, we offer two alternatives: that religions have evolved and changed to conform to those evolving capacities of the brain that render brainsoothing more efficient; one's baseline genetic-neurophysiological profile may affect the attractiveness of religious-based brainsoothing and the probability of religious membership.[84]

There is a further implication of our hypothesis: the consistently reported decrease in the number of people participating in religion in Europe and the United States (but apparently not in the world of Islam) invites the view that in the past religions served as a major source of brainsoothing and that they have declined as a key source as alternative ways of soothing such as spas, holidays, media, sports, psychotherapy, professional massages, and gym programs have become perfected. Time should tell. However, even should the importance of religion as a brainsoother decline, this would not imply that the human tendency to submit and to seek ways of offsetting the effects of stress would disappear. It is in any event clear that the resurgence of Christian churches in South Korea, South America, Africa, and parts of the United States does nothing to suggest the power of religion on the brain abates worldwide.

TESTING HYPOTHESES

There are a variety of ways to test our hypothesis.

(1) *Assess the brain and body chemistry of individuals who acquire religion.* This would amount to identifying a group of individuals who have no association with a religion and who subsequently become active members of a religion. There should be detectable brain changes between these two states. After active membership is established, the chemical and brain activation profiles of believers should match the signature profiles we have described above.

(2) *Assess the brain and body chemistry of individuals who leave a religion or who change religions.* One way to view a person leaving a religion is that participation has not been sufficiently brainsoothing. If so, prior to departure the chemical and brain activation profiles should be similar to individuals who have no association with religion and/or who have not developed successful strategies for brainsoothing in nonreligious ways. If they then convert to a new religion, the signature profile should be present.

(3) *Assess moment-to-moment changes in brain neurophysiology.* This would amount to monitoring individuals who are active members of a religion yet still lead an active life outside of religion and who are subject to high degrees of stress. Their brain and body profiles should change as we have outlined.

CONCLUSION

This chapter explores the possibility that there are identifiable neurophysiological events that are features of religious participation despite differences in beliefs, rituals, and events associated with religion. Although we have made a strong case that this is so, clearly we have not proven it. Nonetheless, the approach we have taken along with similar approaches taken by others offers the possibility that the biological contributions to religion—all features—is a critical addition to the study of religion.

NOTES

1. Zhou, Z., *et al.* (2008). Genetic variation in human *NPY* expression affects stress response and emotion. *Nature, 452,* 997–1001.

2. Wang, J. J., *et al.* (2007). Brain imaging shows how men and women cope differently under stress. *Social Cognitive and Affective Neuroscience, 24,* 58–61.

3. Whitehouse, H. (2008). Cognitive evolution and religion; Cognitive and religious evolution. In J. Bulbulia, R. Sosis, E. Harris, R. Genet, C. Genet, & K. Wyman (Eds.), *The evolution of religion* (pp. 31–42). Santa Margarita, CA: Collins Foundation Press.

4. Sanderson, S. K. Chapter 1, this volume.

5. Durkheim, E., & Mauss, M. (1963). *Primitive classification.* Chicago: University of Chicago Press.

6. Steadman, L. B., *et al.* Chapter 2, this volume.

7. Magnusson, M. S. Chapter 4, this volume.

8. Feierman, J. R. Chapter 5, this volume.

9. Ferguson, G. (1954). *Signs and symbols in Christian art.* New York: Oxford University Press.

10. Forsyth, D. R. (1980). The functions of attributions. *Social Psychology Quarterly, 43*(2), 184–189.

11. Taves, A. (2008). "Religious experience" and the brain. In J. Bulbulia, R. Sosis, E. Harris, R. Genet, C. Genet, & K. Wyman (Eds.), *The evolution of religion* (pp. 211–218). Santa Margarita, CA: Collins Foundation Press.

12. Paton, J. J., *et al.* (2006). The primate amygdala represents the positive and negative value of visual stimuli during learning. *Nature, 439,* 865–870.

13. Wilson, B. C. Chapter 10, this volume.

14. Anastas, B. (2007, July 1). The final days. *New York Times Magazine.*

15. Ferguson, *Signs and symbols in Christian art.*

16. Taves, "Religious experience" and the brain.

17. Knutson, B., *et al.* (2008). Neural antecedents of the endowment effect. *Neuron, 58,* 814–822.

18. Sommer, M., *et al.* (2007). Neural correlates of true and false belief reasoning. *Neuroimage, 13,* 1053–1057.

19. Liu, D., *et al.* (2004). Decoupling beliefs from reality in the brain: An ERP study of theory of mind. *Cognitive Neuroscience and Neuropsychology, 15* (6), 991–995.

20. Phillips, H. (2003). The pleasure seekers. *New Scientist, 180,* 36–40.

21. Flannelly, K. J., *et al.* (2008). Beliefs about life-after-death, psychiatric symptomology, and cognitive theories of psychopathology. *Journal Psychology and Theology, 36*(2), 94–103.

22. Pessoa, L. (2004). Seeing the world in the same way. *Science, 303,* 1617–1618.

23. Walker, M. P., *et al.* (2003). Dissociable states of human memory consolidation and reconsolidation. *Nature, 425,* 616–620.

24. Depue, B. E., *et al.* (2007). Frontal regions orchestrate suppression of emotional memories via a two-phase process. *Science, 317,* 215–219.

25. Pegg, M. G. (2008). *A most holy war.* Oxford: Oxford University Press.

26. Roesch, M. R., & Olson, C. R. (2004). Neuronal activity related to reward value and motivation in primate frontal cortex. *Science, 304,* 307–310.

27. Stuber, G. D., *et al.* (2008). Reward-predictive cues enhance excitatory synaptic strength onto midbrain dopamine neurons. *Science, 321,* 1690–1692.

28. Tsao, D. Y., *et al.* (2006). A cortical region consisting entirely of face-selective cells. *Science, 311,* 670–674.

29. George, M. S., *et al.* (1993). Brain regions involved in recognizing facial emotion or identify: An oxygen-15 Pet study. *Journal of Neuropsychiatry, 5,* 384–394.

30. Miller, G. (2006). Probing the social brain. *Science, 312,* 838–839.

31. Wood, J. N., & Grafman, J. (2003). Human prefrontal cortex: Processing and representational perspectives. *Nature Reviews, 4,* 139–147.

32. Rizzolatti, G., & Sinigaglia, C. (2007). *Reflecting on the mind.* Oxford: Oxford University Press.

33. Wilson, B. C. Chapter 10, this volume.

34. Masters, R., & McGuire, M. T. (1994). *The neurotransmitter revolution.* Carbondale: Southern Illinois University Press.

35. McGuire, M. T., & Troisi, A. (1987). Physiological Regulation-deregulation and psychiatric disorders. *Ethology & Sociobiology, 8*(Supplement 3), 95–125.

36. Stuber *et al.*, Reward-predictive cues enhance excitatory synaptic strength onto midbrain dopamine neurons.

37. Knutson, B., *et al.* (1998). Selective alteration of personality and social behavior by serotonergic intervention. *American Journal of Psychiatry, 155*(3), 373–379.

38. Clarke, H. F., *et al.* (2004). Cognitive inflexibility after prefrontal serotonin depletion. *Science, 304,* 878–880.

39. Tse, W. S., & Bond, A. J. (2002). Difference in serotonergic and noradrenergic regulation of human social behaviors. *Psychopharmacology (Berl) 159,* 216–221.

40. Crockett M. J., *et al.* (2008). Serotonin modulates behavioral reactions to unfairness. *Science, 320,* 1739.

41. Moskowitz, D. S., *et al.* (2003). Tryptophan, serotonin and human social behavior. *Advances in Experimental Medicine and Biology, 527*, 215–224.

42. Tse & Bond. Difference in serotonergic and noradrenergic regulation of human social behaviors.

43. Damasio, A. (2005). Brain trust. *Nature, 435*, 571–572.

44. Kosfeld, M., *et al.* (2005). Oxytocin increases trust in humans. *Nature, 435*, 673–676.

45. Feierman, J. R. Chapter 5, this volume.

46. Goldberg, R. Chapter 12, this volume.

47. Magnusson, M. S. Chapter 4, this volume.

48. Lazar, S. W., *et al.* (2000). Functional brain mapping of the relaxation response and meditation. *Neuroreport, 11*(7), 1581–1585.

49. Feierman, J. R. Chapter 5, this volume.

50. Benson, H. (1975). *The relaxation response*. New York: Avon Books.

51. Farrow, J. T., & Herbert, J. R. (1982). Breath suspension during the transcendental meditation technique. *Psychosomatic Medicine, 44*(3), 133–153.

52. Travis, F., & Wallace, R. K. (1999). Autonomic and EEG patterns during eye-closed rest and transcendental meditation (TM) practice: The basis for a neural model of TM practice. *Conscious Cognition, 8*(3), 302–318.

53. Holmes, D. J., *et al.* 1980. Effects of TM and resting on physiological and subjective arousal. *Journal of Personality and Social Psychology, 44*, 245–252.

54. Ritskes, R., *et al.* (2003). MRI scanning during Zen meditation: The picture of enlightenment. *Constructivism in the Human Sciences, 8*, 85–89.

55. Lazar *et al.*, Functional brain mapping of the relaxation response and meditation.

56. Kamei, T., *et al.* (2000). Decrease in serum cortisol during yoga exercise correlated with alpha wave activation. *Perceptual Motor Skills, 90*, 1027–1032.

57. Bujatti, M., & Riederer, P. (1976). Serotonin, noradrenaline, and dopamine metabolites in the transcendental meditation technique. *Journal of Neural Transmission, 39*, 257–267.

58. Frazer, J. T. (1999). *Time, conflict, and human values*. Urbana: University of Illinois Press.

59. Bloom, P. (2007). Religion is natural. *Developmental Science, 10*(1), 147–154.

60. Boyer, P. (2008). Being human: Religion: Bound to believe? *Nature, 455*, 1038–1039.

61. Ricoeur, P. (1967). *The symbolism of evil*. Boston: Beacon Press.

62. Graham, B. (2007). *Decision, 48*(9), 2–5 [4].

63. Flannelly, K. J., *et al.* (2007). Beliefs, mental health, and evolutionary threat assessment systems of the brain. *Journal of Nervous and Mental Disease, 195*, 996–1003.

64. Dolan, R. J. (2002). Emotion, cognition, and behavior. *Science, 298*, 1191–1192.

65. Goel, V., & Dolan, R. J. (2003). Explaining modulation of reasoning by belief. *Cognition, 87*, B11–B22.

66. Wiech, K., *et al.* (2008). An fMRI study measuring analgesia enhanced by religion as a belief system. *Pain, 139*(2), 467–476.

67. Sharot, T., *et al.* (2007). Neural mechanisms mediating optimism bias. *Nature, 450,* 102–105.

68. Tiger, L. (1979). *Optimism: The biology of hope.* New York: Simon & Schuster.

69. Yamamoto, M. E., *et al.* Chapter 14, this volume.

70. Oviedo, L. Chapter 9, this volume.

71. Cohen, J. D., & Aston-Jones, G. (2005). Decision and uncertainty. *Nature, 436,* 471.

72. Roesch & Olson, Neuronal activity related to reward value and motivation in primate frontal cortex.

73. McNamara, P. (2002). The motivational origins of religious practices. *Zygon, 37*(1), 143–160.

74. Burke, K. A., *et al.* (2008). The role of the orbitofrontal cortex in the pursuit of happiness and more specific rewards. *Nature, 454,* 340–344.

75. Brugger, P. (2002, July). Paranormal beliefs linked to brain chemistry. *New Scientist Print Edition,* 22.

76. Flannelly, Beliefs about life-after-death, psychiatric symptomology, and cognitive theories of psychopathology.

77. Williams, D. R., & Sternthal, M. J. (2007). Spirituality, religion and health: Evidence and research directions. *The Medical Journal of Australia, 186,* 47–50.

78. Merril, R. M. (2004). Life expectancy among LDS and Non-LDS in Utah. *Demographic Research, 10,* 1–2.

79. Rogers, R., *et al.* (1999, May 17). Life expectancy and religion. *Science Daily.*

80. Kirkpatrick, L. A. (2008). Religion is not an adaptation: Some fundamental issues and arguments. In J. Bulbulia, R. Sosis, E. Harris, R. Genet, C. Genet, & K. Wyman (Eds.), *The evolution of religion* (pp. 61–66). Santa Margarita, CA: Collins Foundation Press.

81. Sanderson, S. K. Chapter 1, this volume.

82. Wilson, D. S. (2008). Evolution and religion: Theoretical formation of the obvious. In J. Bulbulia, R. Sosis, E. Harris, R. Genet, C. Genet, & K. Wyman (Eds.), *The evolution of religion* (pp. 23–29). Santa Margarita, CA: Collins Foundation Press.

83. Feierman, J. R. (2009). How some major components of religion *could* have evolved by natural selection. In E. Voland and W. Schiefenhövel (Eds.), *The biological evolution of religious mind and behavior.* New York: Springer-Verlag.

84. Oxley, D. R., *et al.* (2008). Political attitudes vary with physiological traits. *Science, 321,* 1667–1669.

CHAPTER 9

Is Religious Behavior "Internally Guided" by Religious Feelings and Needs?

Lluis Oviedo

This chapter has two goals. The first goal is to show how religious emotional feelings can be contributing causes of religious behavior. In this respect the chapter is a companion to the previous chapter, which showed how religious beliefs can be a contributing cause of religious behavior. The second goal, which is more ambitious, is to show that at least some cognitive religious beliefs, emotional religious feelings, and the religious behaviors they motivate exist because they are "internally guided." As such, they are not wholly dependent on Darwinian evolution by natural selection for their existence. As has been developed in Chapter 1, religious behavior has certainly evolved. However, natural selection is not the only mechanism by which it might have done so. At times in this chapter the discussion of these two interrelated topics—emotional feelings as contributing causes of religious behavior and religious beliefs, feelings, and behavior being inner-guided outside of the realm of natural selection—will become interwoven. When the term "religious experience" is used in the chapter it means a perception, feeling, and communication with a sphere beyond the actual empirical reality (*transcendence*). This is distinct from what is fully present in the empirical world (*immanence*). Religious experience proclaims the existence of a reality distinct from the empirical reality that can constrain or inspire specific human behaviors.

The evolutionary study of religion in general and religious behavior in particular is itself "evolving," as is every intellectual endeavor. Currently, some of the basic presumptions used to interpret evolutionary studies are now being questioned. The problem has been outlined recently by several critics from different fields.[1] Their writings show dissatisfaction with the adequacy of natural selection as the primary mechanism of evolutionary change. As a result, the evolution of species, individuals, social forms, behaviors, and even the theory of natural selection itself are now subject to more than one interpretation.[2] Therefore, the evolutionary study of religion in general and religious behavior in particular is more open and richer than before, even if in this wake some of the simplicity and predictability of the former unitary theories may have been lost.

What does this all mean for the evolutionary study of religious behavior? First, it brings a sense of liberation from the old boundaries and former ways of looking at religious behavior, which were constraining its evolution into the narrow mold of natural selection. The freed space allows for more creative and richer pathways and prompts new perspectives. Nevertheless, these newer perspectives need to develop methods to achieve scientific verification through refutability. Second, it engages with a broader understanding of the factors weighing in human behavior, taking into account a more *emergentist* (belief in emergence, particularly as it involves consciousness) view, avoiding a too *reductionist* stance, but keeping, nevertheless, the scientific standard.[3]

A recent assessment from within the field of cognitive science states that its theories are not simply a rewording of folk-psychology explanations,[4] as has been claimed by some critics of the field. So-called folk-psychology explanations of human behavior that resort to beliefs, desires, or simple planning do not become replaced by the cognitive approach. Rather, they become enlarged, deepened, and complemented with the available scientific means. Transferring this assessment into the scientific study of religion, the traditional understanding of religious experience as a set of conscious cognitive beliefs and emotional feelings in transcendent beings that motivate religious behavior is not undermined by a cognitivist understanding. Also, the more traditional theological ways of understanding religious behavior and its motivation can be expanded and better understood by some of the new research in biology and cognitive science.

DISSATISFACTION WITH THE PRESENT STATE OF AFFAIRS

Much of the literature concerning the scientific study of religious behavior and its motivation has inadequately addressed the complex interaction of human cognitive and emotional operations. The reductive approach that often is required in science risks leaving out some dimensions that are central to the religious experience. The high complexity gets overlooked. It is not that some of these new research programs into the scientific study of religious behavior and its motivations are wrong or misleading; they are just incomplete. They cover only a partial aspect of the total religious experience, often leaving aside the entire realm of consciousness. Nevertheless, these reductive programs should be pursued, as we still know too little about the possible adaptive nature of religion.[5] Also, does natural selection act on religious behavior per se or on its underlying motivations? Does it act at the level of the individual or the social in-group or both? Furthermore, it is unclear what kinds of religious behaviors become adaptive or counteradaptive in what specific environments.

The ethologist Robert Hinde, trying to explain the persistence of religion, could not avoid referring to the conscious dimensions and needs that religious beliefs seem to serve. Indeed, one of his strongest claims is the existence of a "self" that guides one's own life. That self becomes an unavoidable constituent of human life that is required to explain to itself its own behavior and to understand its own evolution. As a result, "for the firm believer, the religious system becomes part of the self."[6] Various religious beliefs are integrated into the concept of self in different degrees for specific individuals and situations. It is therefore not strange that religion is associated with very conscious functions related to the essential needs of the assumed self-system:

> Belief in a deity is related to a number of human propensities, especially understanding the causes of events, feeling in control of one's life, seeking for security in adversity, coping with fear of death, the desire for relationships and other aspects of social life, and the search for a coherent meaning of life.[7]

Appreciate that the book from which the above humanistic quotation is extracted carries the subtitle *A Scientific Approach to Religion*. Similar humanistic elements are also found in the historical reconstruction of ethology by Paul Griffiths.[8] This chapter will therefore take into account these humanistic dimensions in following this alternative path and hopefully provide the theoretical grounds for its further development.

COGNITIVE BELIEFS, EMOTIONAL FEELINGS, AND THEIR RELATIONSHIP

It has been stated, although not everyone has been in agreement, that religious behavior results from the confluence of cognition and emotions. One of the authors who has stressed this point most clearly is—again—the well-known ethologist Robert Hinde. In his own words:

> in discussing beliefs it is difficult not to give the impression that belief is a solely intellectual matter. Nothing could be farther from the truth. We now know that the cognitive and emotional aspects of human psychological functioning are much more closely interwoven than was formerly thought to be the case [e.g., Damasio, 1994] and this is especially important for religiosity.[9]

There has been much discussion in the literature of the overall relationship between cognition and emotion and how this relationship can be modeled.[10] The distinct approaches cover the broad range among psychology, neurology, and biology. Summarizing the discussion, emotions (which are self-perceived as feelings) can operate at the conscious and the unconscious level and can precede or follow cognition. Emotions can also have effects at the level of the individual and the in-group. A growing list of authors has proposed that emotion and cognition need to be well integrated for optimal functioning of the individual.[11] After all, humans frequently think about how they feel and are consciously aware of their feelings about what they think.

IMPLICATIONS OF COGNITIVE-EMOTIONAL INTERRELATIONSHIP FOR THE EVOLUTION OF RELIGIOUS BEHAVIOR

The preceding summary of the relationship between cognition and emotion gives an introduction for a more balanced view of the causes of religious behavior that go beyond the reductive approaches. One of the simplest ways to address the relationship between cognition and emotion as causes of religious behavior is the "emotional priming" theory of religion.[12] Some students of religion have applied the theoretical model of well-known neuroscientist Antonio R. Damasio: emotions are "somatic markers," in a positive and negative fashion, which become conscious as feelings, helping in the process of decision making or facilitating quick reaction.[13] Ilkka Pyysiäinen, a scholar engaged in the cognitive study of religion, also acknowledges the effect of emotion on cognition in causing religious behavior and points to their role in learning process as well. For him "Religious reasoning is guided by emotion as a negative 'gut feeling.'"[14] Being that fear is an essential negative emotion that can potentially prevent dangerous consequences of behavior, religious behavior would be influenced by the basic fears associated with submissiveness and predation but now transferred to fear of supernatural agents.

In a similar fashion Harvey Whitehouse, another specialist in the cognitive study of religion, addresses "emotionally arousing memories"[15] associated with religious behavioral rituals. An example given is the initiation rites that are often associated with traumatic events. In this way the religious behavioral rituals bring up strong association memories when executed. However, in other contexts like religious narratives the emotional somatic markers can generate positive associations as well.[16] Furthermore, it is easy to imagine a "strong positive feeling" arising in connection with newfound answers to some of life's great questions that religious narratives provide.[17] These theories link religious behaviors with "positive somatic markers," thereby associating the behavior with positive emotions that can in turn have a positive influence on religious beliefs.

There are also theories of religious behavior pointing to its "byproduct" character on natural selection. These theories explain religious beliefs and feelings as traits derived from the selection of other nonreligious functions. One example shows aspects of religion "parasitizing" the attachment system.[18] In other cases it has been proposed that religiously motivated cognitive beliefs and emotional feelings enhance learning directly, thereby influencing individuals to behave in adaptive ways in social settings.[19] Similar attempts have been made to explore the deep link between religious behavior and the emotional feeling of gratitude and to point to the social utility of both the feeling and the behavior. Showing gratitude through ritualized religious behaviors is often a form of "costly signaling" that is intended to detect cheaters and implement in-group cooperation.[20] However, interpretation of the survival value of ritualistic religious behavior in such studies may not be enough. They often stop short at this simplest level without seeing any more than that by just concentrating on the behavior's survival value.

Another approach to integrating cognitive beliefs and emotional feelings as causes of religious behavior is offered by a recent study on the emotion of "wonder" as one of the bases of spiritual experience.[21] Within this framework emotions exert "leverage" on perception and cognition, allowing for an expansion of these capacities. Building on Robert Plutchik's ideas,[22] emotions help to "restore harmonious relationship with the environment."[23] Wonder is clearly associated with this dynamic, as it reacts to some unexpected event and prompts a reordering of patterns to make a place for the new perception. Robert Fuller, professor of Religious Studies, also critically questions cognitive anthropologist Scott Atran[24] and his reduction of the concept of wonder to explain false supernatural agents. Moving beyond this narrow path is the issue of the social value of such "moral emotions" as "wonder and awe." These emotions both enhance and expand vision and attention.[25] Fuller proposes two distinctive functions of wonder that are applicable to understanding the role of this emotional feeling as a proximate cause of religious behavior:

> Wonder motivates attention and motivates a quest for increased connection and belongingness with the putative [supposed] source of unexpected displays of life, beauty, or truth. Wonder is thus somewhat rare among the emotions in its functional capacity to motivate persons to venture outward into increased rapport with the environment. Second, wonder awakens our mental capacity for abstract, higher-order thought. Indeed, wonder seems to direct our cognitive activities to identify causality, agency, and purpose in ways that are not directly connected with our biological survival.[26]

These expansive features associated with the emotional feeling of wonder offer a different way to examine the evolution of religious behavior that helps to develop cognitive beliefs beyond their actual boundaries. The emotional feeling of wonder thus prompts a continuous challenge to increase knowledge and to transcend present limits. Fuller, relying on other authors as well, proposes how wonder helps to create a "higher order" of meaning and purpose and provide moral guidance in addition to influencing cognitive openness and balance. A similar evaluation can be carried out with other spiritual emotions both positive and negative, such as hope, mystical love, guilt, and religious fear. All of this is evidence that religious behaviors coevolve with and are influenced in a causal way by emotional feelings. Cognition also provides ways to understand and give meaning to these emotional feelings. Thus a much broader view emerges as to how cognitive beliefs and emotional feelings are intertwined causes of religious behavior.

The relationship between brain structures, which have evolved, and higher cognitive functions involved in human consciousness is complex and poorly understood. The two levels of analysis therefore must be kept separate with the presumption that there is an "emergence" of properties from the physical realm of brain operations to human consciousness. Whereas the brain can be understood in mechanistic terms, consciousness appears to exhibit some level of autonomy and its own yet-to-be-understood pattern or regulation.

THE INNER-GUIDED PERSPECTIVE AND THE EMERGENCE OF HUMAN SPIRITUALITY

At this point two perspectives have been suggested with which to understand the evolution and causes of religious behavior. First is the reductive perspective that stresses the biological survival value of religious behavior and the beliefs and feelings that motivate it within the context of natural selection. Second is the more autonomous inner-guided path that pursues a more complex form of coevolution having more to do with religious feelings and satisfying inner needs. This more autonomous, inner-guided path would not be so *directly* constrained by natural selection.

In addition to the writings of Fuller, which have been discussed previously, another recent author, Paul Thagard, also addresses this other-than-natural-selection perspective by explicitly stating the "evolutionary irrelevance" of the emotional dimension. He argues that religion cannot be considered as an adaptation. Even if "emotional cognition" can be a contributing cause of religious behavior, there is no evidence that evolutionary pressures are involved in originating and guiding this process. He states, "Our evolved cognitive-emotional capacities make human beings susceptible to religion, but they make us susceptible to myriad other cultural developments; so the explanatory connection between evolution and religion is very weak." [27] For Thagard, religious cognitive beliefs are the result of integration between cognitive and emotional aspects "incorporating both explanatory reasoning and the satisfaction of desires," a mix he calls "emotional coherence." Among these desires he points to "avoiding anxiety, maintaining social connections with other religious people, having a basis for distinguishing right from wrong, and hoping for a blissful afterlife." [28]

As can be seen, Fuller and Thagard address the non-natural-selection causes of religious behavior in different ways. Taking into account their ideas, the evolution of religious behavior would occur as a result of a balance between both: external influences of natural selection and internal pressures having to do with religious feelings and inner needs, both being involved in the final outcome.

To further develop and extend this inner-guided theory of the evolution of religious behavior, the following are its basic tenets: (1) religious behavior coevolved within the process of an increasing integration between cognitive beliefs and emotional feelings during human evolution; (2) this integration may have a survival value, which has been explained in diverse terms, mostly as contributing to the improvement of in-group functioning; (3) religious behavior and the cognitive beliefs and emotional feelings that are its causes also serve personal emotional needs and feelings beyond sheer biological demands of an increase in survival, which, nevertheless, may indirectly be achieved as a result of personal satisfaction and well-being; and (4) it is possible to reconstruct the development of many historical religious behaviors as well as their determining cognitive beliefs and emotional feelings following the previously described pattern. This process would obviously be distinctively human and may be similar to the appeal of aesthetics in which some of what is beautiful and motivates behavior, as in arts, transcends and is sought out by its beholders beyond its survival value or reproductive success.

Another consideration is that humans evolved the capacity for symbolization and with it symbolic language that allows for greater communication within the in-group. Symbolic language also allows foreseeing and anticipation of both life and death. These new higher cognitive faculties would then be reacted to by an evolved emotional system. Following the emergence of these new cognitive and emotional capacities the spiritual dimension would have a foundation upon which to emerge along with religious codification that creates a culture-specific, systematic order. The religious codification would have enlarged symbolic realms, focused and balanced emotions, and brought human expectations beyond their actual limits. As several authors have proposed, this type of coevolutionary process within which religious behavior could have evolved is very similar to what has been called "emotional imprinting." [29]

As the cognitive system expanded with the development of various new cultural forms, new requirements and conditions would have been added. Religious cognitive beliefs and emotional feelings, which are causes of religious behavior, constitute a major part of this complex system. The result of all of the above is the distinct anthropological and social pattern of religious behavior, cognitive beliefs, and emotional feelings that now is recognized collectively as religion.

ADDITIONAL FUNCTIONS OF RELIGIOUS-SPECIFIC COGNITIVE BELIEFS AND EMOTIONAL FEELINGS

In addition to being *proximate* (immediate or near) causes of religious behavior, religious-specific cognitive beliefs and emotional feelings appear to have other functions as well. There are two well-known published theories on these other functions of religious-specific cognitive beliefs. The first is by the eminent ethologist Robert Hinde; the second is by the cognitive scientist Paul Thagard. In the opinion of Hinde, religious beliefs also address the need for deeper understanding and meaning, control and security in uncertain events, coping with fear of death, and the improvement of social life.[30] For Thagard the functions of religious beliefs are to cope with anxiety, the facilitation of social connections, moral foundation, and hope beyond death.[31] Summarizing, in addition to being contributing causes of religious behavior, religious beliefs also are associated with the management of anxiety and uncertainty through attribution of meaning; the improvement of social relationships, including the moral codification; and the management of the fear of death.

The psychologist Robert A. Emmons proposes additional functions of "specific sacred emotions": gratitude, awe and reverence, wonder, and hope.[32] He shows how religion "regulates emotions" through forgiveness and mindfulness. Religious behavior may be identified as the external expression of these internally guided human needs for meaning and certainty, the quest for transcendence, hope beyond death, universal harmony, internal peace, forgiveness before intense guilt, and quest for greater love. It would be the external expressions of religious behavior that would subject the individual executing such behavior to natural selection. Yet, the "internally guided" needs for such things as meaning, certainty, transcendence, hope, internal peace, forgiveness, love, and so forth, can be ends in themselves, meaning they can be their own rewards apart from any behavior they might motivate.

MECHANISMS OF RELIGIOUS-SPECIFIC COGNITIVE BELIEFS, EMOTIONAL FEELINGS, AND BEHAVIOR

It is beyond the scope of this chapter to fully explore the actual bio-behavioral mechanisms by which cognitive beliefs and emotional feelings could generate religious behavior. Presumably the mixture of positive and negative emotional feelings combined with cognitive elaborations results in outward behaviors that become aspects of a particular religion. The interplay of these behavioral motivating factors is rather complex, often resulting in a mixture of the emotional feelings of fear and joy as well as worry and calm as part of the subjective religious experience. An example of such complexity is the classical account of philosopher of religion Rudolf Otto.[33] He described the combination of rational and nonrational (feelings and emotions) as "the constitutive religious elements." Then among the emotions Otto distinguished two sorts: negative, linked to fear before the tremendous dimension of the sacred, and positive, as the fascination or attraction it triggers.

A deeper study of this topic needs to take into account the different means used to manage and better integrate religious cognitive beliefs and emotional religious feelings within organized religions. Religious institutions have the need to improve communication through their behaviorally mediated oral traditions as well as behaviorally generated texts and rituals, a process reconstructed in the histories of religion in an exemplary way by the classic phenomenologist Mircea Eliade.[34] Organized religions also have the need to strengthen religious commitment, which they do through law, prophecy, and sometimes warnings linked to "apocalyptic" scenarios. They also establish and nourish moral codes as a condition of sociality. Some cognitive religious beliefs may also have evolved as a result of a complex entanglement between the practical needs of a social group and the means at their disposal, a process that can be termed rationalization.

The preceding thought shows how culturally transmitted, cognitive religious beliefs could have coevolved with emotional feelings and behaviors to meet basic needs, some of which were and still are outside the direct influences of natural selection. This integrated perspective is also more compatible with many theological traditions by which sacred texts and narratives are interpreted across different religions. This perspective is also more compatible with modern studies on religion that provide theological interpretation of complex religious experiences. Of course, the weak component in the above is that such a perspective risks being of limited scientific value if it cannot furnish refutable means through hypothesis testing. Nevertheless, it is possible to scientifically test some of what has been said above.

TESTING IF RELIGIOUS BEHAVIOR IS ALSO INNER-GUIDED BY RELIGIOUS FEELINGS AND NEEDS

First, the empirical studies on emotional intelligence (EI), reviewed by psychologist John D. Mayer and colleagues,[35] can be used to test the role of the coevolution and interrelationship of religious cognitive beliefs and emotional feelings in facilitating in-group cooperative social behavior. It would be predicted that EI scores would correlate positively with scores that measure spirituality and institutional religiosity. Another way of testing would be to explore whether religious behavior is affected by impairments in the emotional system. It would be predicted that individuals who have difficulty being in touch with their emotional feelings would be less inclined to engage in religious behavior. There are a number of personality disorders, such as Antisocial Personality Disorder and Borderline Personality Disorder, in which this occurs.

In addition, if feelings are self-perception of mood, individuals with mood disorders (too much = mania and too little = depression) should be over-religious when manic and under-religious when depressed. That is actually what is found clinically, as "having a special relationship to God" is one of the more common manifestations of grandiose manic delusions.[36] Also, a correlation between depressive states and questioning or even loss of religious faith is widely known. Evidence for this can even be found in the writings of Mother Teresa.[37]

Another way of testing this relationship is in the neurological studies that have shown some involvement of the emotional-generating and processing parts of the brain in a number of different religious experiences.[38] There also have been studies on the impairment of religiously motivated feelings, such as gratitude, in patients with neurological conditions, such as Parkinson's disease.[39]

Finally, as evidence of the interdependence of religious cognitive beliefs, emotional feelings, and behaviors, one finds that an overabundance of religious cognitive beliefs and feelings of fear and anxiety leads to the pathological conditions called "scrupulosity." In this condition one finds an obsessive-compulsive type of cognitive, ruminative worrying and emotional feelings of anxiety over sometimes seemingly trivial religious matters.[40]

DISCUSSION, APPLICATION, AND FURTHER RESEARCH

Before concluding this review and in order to advance the complementary theory that religious behavior is also being internally guided by religious feelings and needs somewhat freed from evolution by natural selection, a discussion of the foreseeable criticisms of this internally guided theory is warranted. The internally guided theory could be perceived by some as too complex because there are too many variables being considered. Even if the initial attempt were to reflect on religious behavior as a coevolved result of the integration of cognitive beliefs and emotional feelings, the theory "grows by its sides." As it does, it takes into account more and more social factors and collateral phenomena, such as our knowledge of our own morality and other aspects generated through consciousness. Admittedly, conscious reasons, desires, and motivations are difficult variables to study. The theory therefore needs to specify its first order core elements and then later add the more complex dynamics involved in the interplay between cognitive belief and emotional feelings as causes of religious behavior. Only much later should the theory expand to account for some of the more complex variables related to human consciousness.

There also are some issues regarding the internally guided theory's practical usefulness even before its predictive scientific usefulness is tested fully. First is the relationship between the psychology of religion and spiritual states, where the interplay between cognitive beliefs and emotional feelings are more apparent and available for analysis.

Take as an example the case of Mother Teresa of Calcutta. One of the most recent texts on her spiritual journey[41] clearly identifies through her letters a long stage in her mature life where she could not feel the positive emotions she was used to experiencing in the former stages, resulting in much puzzlement and psychological pain. This case shows the complexity in the relationship between religious cognitive beliefs and emotional feelings. It also shows that religiously motivated emotional feelings become a true variable, as they can even fade away, leaving a sense of struggling belief in which an important part of its felt reference feels missing.

A second area in which the potential practical usefulness of this internally guided theory can be demonstrated resides in its application to social trends in the global religious landscape. The resurgence of religious fundamentalism and its future can be better understood within this theory. Both, secularization and religious "fanatization" are susceptible to analysis within this framework, where emotional feelings play an important role as a variable. One can also use the theory to better understand the processes in technologically advanced societies subjected to the shock of fast modernization.

Future research on the role of cognitive beliefs and emotional feelings in the generation of religious behavior should not be restricted in direction. Religious behavior and its causes through both external means and internal needs have to be viewed within the field of human development, where changes in religious beliefs, feelings, and behavior vary over the lifetime. This offers a good case for testing and extending such theories. Some studies have already been made[42] but there is still a lot to be done. Furthermore, better and more sophisticated theories may be needed if we want to understand the complexity of sacred religious narratives and how such narratives emerged and were written through the interaction of cognitive beliefs and emotional feelings.

A final need is to somehow connect the present scientific studies of religion with sacred theological traditions. Otherwise, the scientific endeavor risks missing its point and developing theories and ways of understanding religious behaviors, cognitive beliefs, and emotional feelings of very little value from the perspective of practitioners of the real religious world experience. For example, a scientific theory of religious behavior in which reflective contemplative discernment and free will are not considered as determinants of behavior will be unable to understand some of religion's meaning and deep dynamics. The scientific study of religion also needs to address the human person as someone able to anticipate future scenarios and who uses religious behavior, cognitive beliefs, and emotional feelings to cope with high levels of uncertainty. The reductive format of many scientific approaches may not be able to accomplish these requirements alone, which calls for the cooperative and mutually respectful interchange between religion and science.

NOTES

1. The most recent and vocal has been Jerry Fodor: Fodor, J. (2008). Against Darwinism. *Mind and Language, 23*, 1–24; Roughgarden, J., Oisho, M., & Akçay, E. (2006). Reproductive social behaviour: Cooperative games to replace sexual selection. *Science, 311*, 965–969; Brakefield, P. M. (2006). Evo-Devo and constrains on selection. *Trends in Ecology and Evolution, 21*, 362–368. See also Dupré, J. (2001). *Human nature and the limits of science* (pp. 82ff). Oxford: Clarendon; O'Hear, A. (1997). *Beyond evolution: Human nature and the limits of evolutionary explanation.* Oxford: Clarendon.

2. Waskan, J. A. (2006). *Models of cognition* (pp. 53ff). Cambridge, MA, London, U.K.: MIT Press.

3. Brown, W. S. (2007). The emergence of causally efficacious mental function. In N. Murphy & W. R. Stoeger (Eds.), *Evolution and emergence: Systems, organisms, persons* (pp. 198–226). Oxford, New York: Oxford University Press.

4. Waskan, *Models of cognition*, pp. 58–76.

5. Richerson, P. J., & Boyd, R. (2007). *Not by genes alone. How culture transformed human evolution.* Chicago, London: University of Chicago Press.

6. Hinde, R. (1999). *Why gods persist: A scientific approach to religion* (p. 32). London, New York: Routledge.

7. Ibid., p. 67.

8. Griffiths P. E. (2008). History of ethology comes of age. *Biology and Philosophy, 23*, 129–134 [131].

9. Hinde, *Why gods persist*, p. 65.

10. Strongman, K. T. (2003). *The psychology of emotion: From everyday life to theory* (pp. 90–95). Chichester: Wiley; Lazarus, R. S. (1999). The cognitive-emotion debate: A bit of history. In T. Dalgleish & M. Power (Eds.), *Handbook of cognition and emotion* (pp. 3–19). Chichester: Wiley.

11. Haidt, J. (2006). *The happiness hypothesis: Finding modern truth in ancient wisdom* (p. 16). New York: Basic Books.

12. Atran, S., & Norenzayan, A. (2004). Religion's evolutionary landscape: Counterintuition, commitment, compassion, communion. *Behavioral and Brain Sciences, 27*, 713–70 [720].

13. Damasio, A. R. (1994). *Descartes' error: Emotion, reason, and the human brain.* New York: G. P. Putnam Sons.

14. Pyysiäinen, Y. (2004). *Magic, miracles, and religion: A scientist's perspective* (p. 130). Walnut Creek, CA; Lanham, MD: Altamira Press.

15. Whitehouse, H. (2004). *Modes of religiosity: A cognitive theory of religious transmission* (p. 106). Walnut Creek, CA; Lanham, MD: Altamira Press.

16. Pyysiäinen, *Magic, miracles, and religion*, p. 128.

17. Clément, F. (2003). The pleasure of believing: Toward a naturalistic explanation of religious conversion. *Journal of Cognition and Culture*, *3*, 69–87 [69].

18. Kirkpatrick, L. A. (2005). *Attachment, evolution, and the psychology of religion* (pp. 232ff). New York: The Guilford Press.

19. Alcorta, C. S., & Sosis, R. (2005). Ritual, emotions, and sacred symbols: The evolution of religion as an adaptive complex. *Human Nature*, *16*, 323–352.

20. Emmons, R. A., & McNamara, P. (2006). Sacred emotions and affective neuroscience: Gratitude, costly signaling, and the brain. In P. McNamara (Ed.), *Where God and Science Meet I* (pp. 11–30). Westport, CT; London, U.K.: Praeger.

21. Fuller, R. (2006). Wonder and the religious sensibility: A study in religion and emotion. *Journal of Religion*, *86*, 364–384.

22. Plutchik, R. (2002). *Emotions and life: Perspectives from psychology, biology, and evolution*. Washington DC: American Psychological Association.

23. Fuller, R. (2006). Wonder and the religious sensibility: A study in religion and emotion. *Journal of Religion*, *86*, 366.

24. Atran, S. (2002). *In God we trust: The evolutionary landscape of religion* (p. 57). New York: Oxford University Press.

25. Haidt, *The happiness hypothesis*.

26. Fuller, R. (2006). Wonder and the religious sensibility: A study in religion and emotion. *Journal of Religion*, *86*, 370.

27. Thagard, P. (2006). *Hot thought: Mechanisms and applications of emotional cognition* (p. 249). Cambridge, MA; London: MIT Press.

28. Ibid., p. 240.

29. Atran, *In God we trust*, pp. 176–179, for the emotional imprinting related to religious conversion. Furthermore: Deacon, T. W. (2006). The aesthetic faculty. In M. Turner (Ed.), *The artful mind: Cognitive science and the riddle of human creativity*. Oxford and New York: Oxford University Press. See pp. 21–53 for an analogical development in the aesthetic perception.

30. Hinde, *Why gods persist*, p. 67.

31. Thagard, *Hot thought*, p. 240.

32. Emmons, R. A. (2005). Emotion and religion. In R. F. Paloutzian & C. L. Park (Eds.), *Handbook of the psychology of religion and spirituality* (pp. 233–252). New York: Guilford Press.

33. Otto, R. (1950 [1917]). *The idea of the holy*. Oxford: Oxford University Press.

34. Eliade, M. (1987 [1959]). *The sacred and the profane: The nature of religion*. Orlando, FL: Harcourt.

35. Mayer, J. D., Roberts, R. D., & Barsade, S. G. (2008). Human abilities: Emotional intelligence. *Annual Review of Psychology, 59*, 507–536.

36. American Psychiatric Association. (1995). *Diagnostic and Statistical manual of mental disorders, fourth edition* (p. 357). Washington, DC: American Psychiatric Association.

37. Kolodiejchuck, B., & Mother Teresa. (2007). *Come be my light*. New York: Doubleday.

38. Azari, N. P., Missimer, J., & Seitz, R. J. (2005). Religious experience and emotion: Evidence for distinctive cognitive neural patterns. *The International Journal for the Psychology of Religion, 15*, 263–281; Newberg, A., d'Aquili, E., & Rause, V. (2002). *Why God won't go away*. New York: Ballantine.

39. Emmons & McNamara, Sacred emotions and affective neuroscience, pp. 11–30.

40. Spilka, B., Jr., Hood, R. W., Hunsberger, B., & Gorsuch, R. (2003). *The psychology of religion: An empirical approach* (3rd ed.; pp. 511, 529). New York: Guilford Press.

41. Kolodiejchuck & Mother Teresa, *Come be my light*.

42. Reich, K. H. (1997). Integrating differing theories. The case of religious development. In B. Spilka & D. N. McIntosh (Eds.), *The psychology of religion: Theoretical approaches* (pp. 105–113). Boulder, CO: Westview Press.

CHAPTER 10

Mirror Neurons, Culture, and Spirit: Causes of Religious Behavior

Burgess C. Wilson

Many respected theories of religion today are based on the cognitive model. That model, of which there are numerous variations, hypothesizes that the brain is composed of multiple domain-specific modules, each of which is specialized to automatically produce a specific set of nonreflective beliefs. These beliefs are conjectured to be unconscious, to form the basis for an intuitive knowledge of the world, and to underpin reflective thought.

The theories of religion offered by Justin Barrett[1] and Scott Atran[2] are two such examples. Each of these theories is based on a cognitive model of brain function and views religion as the evolutionarily unintended by-product of interacting cognitive modules. In particular, these modules are what give rise to *animism*, which is defined as the attribution of conscious life to inanimate objects. According to Barrett and Atran, animism originates by way of a module dedicated to the automatic and unconscious detection of animate beings in the physical environment. Survival in times past, they suggest, was dependent on the detection of predators and prey; and for this reason the module evolved a hypersensitivity to fragmentary information and motion. This hypersensitivity though, while making detection more likely, also results in more of these positive detections being in error—which are known as false positives. Barrett refers to this module as the "hypersensitive agency detecting device." Once an animate being is detected, according to these authors, the information is subsequently passed on to a module commonly referred to as "Theory of Mind." This module is hypothesized to utilize a naïve psychological theory to infer mental states in detected agents, which occasionally include false positives; and it is these false positives attributed to mind that are theorized to be the neurological basis for animism, and that secondarily promote religion.

The validity of the cognitive model, however, which underpins these biologically based theories of religion, is being challenged by an alternative theory regarding how the brain normally detects and represents animate beings.[3] Simulation theory, versions of which are accepted by many neuroscientists today, argues that an attributor arrives at a mental attribution by simulating or reproducing in his or her own mind the same state as the target's—and not exclusively through, as cognitive theories suggest, inferential reasoning ultimately based on a naïve psychological theory. This latter conceptualization offers the basis for an alternative model by which to understand the neurological basis for animism and, by extension, religion and religious behavior. Specifically, it is hypothesized that:

> *First, simulation,* which is proposed to be the neurological basis for an automatic and unconscious capacity to understand others, is similarly involved in the implicit attribution of consciousness and mental states to nonhuman form.
>
> *Second, belief systems and culture* influence the capacity for these implicit attributions to be understood explicitly as spirit; and these explicit attributions are the biological basis for animism.
>
> *Third, nonhuman forms in nature,* to which agency has been attributed, function as innate releasing stimuli that elicit prosocial behavior; and these behaviors influence the management of natural resources by small-scale societies, to promote survival.

THE IMPLICIT BASIS FOR ANIMISM: MIRROR NEURONS

Simulation theory, in a form advanced by an increasing number of neuroscientists today, hypothesizes that the neural substrate central to an automatic and unconscious capacity to understand others is the mirror neuron. These neurons, which were first discovered in the macaque monkey in the 1990s, were initially observed to discharge during the execution and observation of goal-directed actions such as eating.[4,5] Later, these neurons were discovered to discharge when an observed goal-directed action was partly obscured from view, as well as when the action was heard but not seen. In one study, for example, a monkey was shown an entire hand-grasping action; and in a subsequent condition, the monkey observed the same hand-grasping action partly obscured from view. In the subsequent condition, in which the concluding part of the action was hidden from view, more than half the recorded mirror neurons responded.[6] And in a separate study, a monkey saw and heard an action that generated a sound unique to that action; and when it heard the sound of the action alone, about 15 percent of the originally activated mirror neurons responded. These neurons are referred to as audiovisual mirror neurons.[7] Given that mirror neurons discharge before the completion of an observed action, and in response to sound alone, some of these researchers suggest that the mirror neuron system provides advance knowledge regarding the end result of an action—which is to say, the capacity to anticipate the end result of a motor action before it is completed.

Evidence that the mirror neuron system underlies a capacity to predict the end result of a motor action before completion is further supported by several studies examining the effect of context on mirror neuron activation. In one study, a monkey observed, in the first condition, an initial grasping action that was followed by a second motor action appropriate to its given context; and in the second condition, the same initial grasping action was presented, but the context and second motor action were changed.[8] The results showed mirror neuron discharge in advance of the second motor act, but only in one of the two conditions. Another study, but this time done on human subjects using functional magnetic resonance imaging (fMRI), had similar results.[9] In that study, the observation of actions embedded in a context, as compared to the same actions observed without a context, yielded greater signal strength in premotor mirror neuron areas. These findings indicate that mirror neuron systems are not simply responding to action but also to context—suggesting that mirror neurons are involved in the capacity not only to accurately anticipate second motor actions but also to understand their contextual meaning.

These processes, in addition to their involvement with action, are activated in both the experience and observation of emotion. A study in a monkey, for example, indicated that mouth-related mirror neurons discharge in the observation of communicative facial gestures.[10] Studies involving human subjects show similar results. In one study, subjects passively observed emotionally expressive faces, and fMRI results showed neural activation in the premotor cortex and nearby regions typically activated in the production of facial movements; and it is these same areas that are conjectured to contain the action mirroring system in humans.[11] Another study, using electromyography, had human subjects observe emotionally expressive faces, the results of which showed a rapid, covert activation of their facial musculature that reflected the facial patterns of the observed faces.[12,13] Imaging studies too indicate that in the observation and experience of emotions, such as disgust, the identical neural structures are activated.[14] These findings, which show equivalence between the observation and experience of emotion, suggest that a shared neural substrate, utilizing the mirror neuron system, underlies an experience-based capacity to comprehend observed emotion.

This expanding body of research has led Vittorio Gallese and others to propose that, while we use both implicit and explicit belief and knowledge-based strategies to understand others, mirror neuron systems constitute a fundamental basis for an automatic and unconscious capacity to understand others, based on simulation research findings. As discussed above, he and others argue that since context-dependent mirror neuron activation occurs in advance of an observed action's completion, that neural output is a prediction regarding the end result of a goal-directed motor action. Moreover, since the same neural structures are activated in the execution and observation of goal-related action and emotion, Gallese argues that just as we understand our own actions as directed by way of intentions, goals, and agency, presumably so too, by default, do we infer these same attributes in the agent whose actions and emotions we observe. Thus, when we observe a cup being gripped in the context of drinking tea and there is subsequent mirror neuron discharge, the activation presumably enables us not only to anticipate the cup will be brought to the observee's mouth, but to infer agency and intentionality—which is to say, understand the anticipated action of drinking as the volitional motor act of an intentional agent motivated by desire. Moreover, when these mechanisms are activated, according to Gallese and colleagues, they automatically establish a "phenomenal state of 'intentional attunement'" with the observee, in which there is "a sense of connectedness to the other," which contributes to a feeling of "self-integrity."[15] This simulation process is empathy according to Gallese, if its definition includes the capacity to experience the motor and affective states of another person.

Thus far, simulation has been discussed regarding actual movement performed by human beings. A study of human subjects observing static images of a reaching hand, however, showed mirror neuron activity,[16] as did another study utilizing static images of a grasping action.[17] Based on these and other results, and the fact that the observation of art sometimes elicits physical sensations in people, David Freedberg and Gallese hypothesize that art, including abstract art, also activates the mirror neuron system.[18] Art, they suggest, contains "visible traces of goal-directed movement," and it is these traces that are capable of activating the relevant motor areas in the observer's brain. These traces though, while essential to the experience of art, are not unique to it; and it is suggested here that form in general can contain them—and as such, expressive forms in nature, like trees or mountains, can activate the mirror neuron system as well.

Regarding emotion, as discussed above, static images of faces can also activate the mirror neuron system; and Freedberg and Gallese further hypothesize that art, given its capacity to elicit feelings of emotion, has a similar capability. They suggest that art utilizes "implicit suggestion" to infer emotion, thereby activating the mirror neuron system. This is consonant with the view of the gestalt psychologist Rudolph Arnheim who argues that "expression," while fundamental to our emotional experience of people, is not unique to them; however, unlike Freedberg and Gallese who discuss these factors in relationship to art, Arnheim discusses them in relationship to all objects. He writes: "a flame, a tumbling leaf, the wailing of a siren, a willow tree, a steep rock...all convey expression through the various senses."[19] And if Arnheim is right, they all have the capacity to activate the mirror neuron system, thereby eliciting an emotional and motor response within the observer.

These findings suggest the mirror neuron system is not uniquely sensitive to human beings, but to particular visual and motor patterns; and in accord with this conclusion, studies indicate both infants[20] and adults[21] automatically attribute agency to featureless objects mimicking goal-directed behavior; and infants spontaneously attribute emotions to objects that move in certain patterns.[22] As such, it is suggested that while human beings typically manifest a large number of these patterns, so do other forms in nature to a lesser extent. This presumably results, given that the mirror neuron system operates automatically and unconsciously, in motor and emotional responses to expressive form in general; the implicit attribution of intentionality, emotion, and agency to that form; and the establishment of a "phenomenal state of 'intentional attunement,'" which may give rise to feelings of interpersonal connectedness and self-integrity. These findings and conjectures are the basis for the hypothesis presented here that the mirror neuron system and simulation, which is to say empathy, are the implicit basis for animism.

THE EXPLICIT BASIS FOR ANIMISM: CULTURAL BELIEF SYSTEMS

The output of this neuronal activation is in the form of bodily states, sensations, and feelings. This output may in turn be explicitly interpreted by way of brain processes that involve inferential reasoning, knowledge, culture, and belief—the influences of which may result in explicit interpretations being made, regarding this output, that differ between those living in the West and small-scale societies.

In the West, cultural beliefs are dominated by an empirical worldview, monotheistic religion, and consumerism—all of which reject, explicitly and/or implicitly, the capacity for inanimate form to have consciousness or mind. As such, these beliefs are suggested to conflict with the experiential knowledge evoked by expressive form; and under these conditions, the brain seeks out cognitive consistency. There is a tendency to reject evidence or ideas that undermine central beliefs, for example, known as the principle of conservatism; and internal discord arises when one's ideas or beliefs are contrary to each other, known as cognitive dissonance. The suggested result is a tendency to reject or disregard bodily inference related to nonhuman agency, i.e., animism. Moreover, mental attitudes and culture have been demonstrated to have an effect on the activity of the mirror neuron system itself. A review of studies done on pain and empathy by Tania Singer and Chris Frith concludes that an observer's capacity to activate muscle groups at the site of observed pain, which is indicative of mirror neuron activity, is dependent on his or her mental attitude and, in particular, attention.[23] Consonant with this conclusion is a study in which participants observed identical communicative gestures performed by in-group and out-group members. Results showed increased corticospinal (a spinal tract that originates in the motor cortex) excitability in the observation of in-group versus out-group members—suggesting to the authors that motor resonance mechanisms are modulated by cultural factors.[24] These results suggest that Western attitudes, which may decrease the attention paid to inanimate form on the one hand and which views animism as foreign or illogical on the other, may reduce or inhibit inanimate form's capacity to activate the mirror neuron system.

These findings do not necessarily imply, however, that the observer is completely insensitive to, or unaffected by, nonhuman form—particularly when that form strongly and consistently mimics goal-directed behavior and emotion. Studies show that adults will often ascribe mental states, personality, and even gender to geometric shapes that illustrate goal-directed behavior, despite their conscious understanding that such ascriptions are illogical.[25] In addition, since the activation of these neurons may result in feelings of attunement and connectedness, which can provide feelings of self-integrity, this system may underlie and explain aspects of many of our most important cultural and aesthetic experiences—like that of art and nature. The experience of a gothic cathedral, for example, which may give rise to feelings of spiritual connectedness, is suggested to be due to mirror neuron activation; and so too is the experience of personally meaningful art, in which feelings of attunement and connectedness may arise, but not an overt sense of the spiritual. There is presumably an activation of these processes in the experience of nature as well, according to many a feeling of tranquility and self-integrity; and it may be in the summation of these experiences, elicited by water and cloud and tree and church, there arises the felt experience of an all-powerful ever-present spiritual being, underpinning and promoting monotheistic religion.

In contrast to Western culture, small-scale societies interpret these bodily experiences differently. This difference may be due to at least three factors. First, research in Western children indicates that these subjects have a tendency toward viewing both living and nonliving things as purposeful and intentional;[26] and whereas this tendency is lost by adulthood in Western people, indigenous people seemingly retain it. This latter perspective presumably makes animism intuitive. Second, the natural environment in which small-scale societies reside is more organic and kinetic than the typically stolid rectangularity of urban landscapes. This presumably results in relatively greater mirror neuron activation, the increased propensity and intensity of which may contribute to a belief in animism. Third, indigenous people lack a Western worldview, which rejects inanimate form's capacity for consciousness or mind; and for this reason, small-scale societies may not view animism as *a priori* (i.e., derived by deduction) counterintuitive. Given these three factors, it is hypothesized that the feeling

experiences of motor intentionality, emotion, and attentional attunement, which arise in the observation of expressive form and/or the
audition of sounds associated therewith, are attributed to that form
by small-scale cultures—giving rise to the explicit understanding of
nonhuman form as both animate and mindful. These attributions are
not suggested to be inherently religious, however. Robert Lowrie
writes, for example, when a Crow Indian states rocks can reproduce
he or she is placing it "into the organic kingdom, but it no more follows that he attributes spirit to it than that we ascribe a soul to a cat
when we describe it as animate." [27] He goes on to say, "both animism
and animatism are essentially non-religious, or only potentially religious." [28] That said, if the experience of nonhuman form is processed
by way of simulation, that form is not only "like me" [29] and thus
attributed human-like characteristics like mind and emotion; but
because "like-me" does not mean the same as me, additional thoughts
and fantasies and biases can be attributed to that form, including
powers and qualities associated with spirit and religion.

These findings are the basis for the following hypothesis: animism
is the interdependent product of implicit feeling-based processes on
the one hand, and culture and inferential knowledge-based systems
on the other. This proposal views belief, inference, and knowledge as
essential to animism, but places at its center processes of simulation
and felt experience; and, as such, this is an *empathic theory of animism*.
This theory, however, is not meant to, nor able to, explain all of animism or religion; but rather to suggest, on a more limited basis, a
basic biological mechanism around which the greater complexity of
spirituality and religion may scaffold.

THE EVOLUTIONARY BASIS FOR ANIMISM: GROUP SURVIVAL

From an evolutionary perspective, what is the relationship between
animism and the mirror neuron system? Presumably, the mirror neuron system did not evolve in the direct service of animism itself; and,
moreover, if "religion costs resources that rarely are fully repaid," [30]
as Atran has suggested, religion would not have had selective value,
typically. If this point of view is correct, mirror neuron activation by
nonhuman form could be an evolutionarily unintended by-product,
known as a spandrel. This latter hypothesis, however, is perplexing.
Given religion's apparent cost, why has not an inhibiting mechanism

evolved to prevent this phenomenon from occurring? The answer may lie in the biological difficulties involved in such work; but it is also possible that animism actually enhances survival and is adaptive. The cost of religion is typically measured in regard to its effects within and between groups of people; animism, however, influences behavior regarding how natural resources and the environment are related to and treated, as well as how species are understood to interrelate— and these influences may have had selective value during the majority of evolutionary history, during which our ancestors lived in small-scale societies.

The management of environmental resources is crucial to the survival of any society; and without social mechanisms to manage these resources they can be devastated in the face of unrestrained individual self-interest.[31,32] One solution is the use of institutional measures, which small-scale societies lack; and another solution, which is available to these groups, is animism.[33,34] Research in support of this latter hypothesis has been conducted by researchers including Doug Medin and Atran, who have examined land-use patterns amongst two groups of Maya indigenous to Guatemala—the Itza' and Q'eqchi.[35] They write that the Itza' Maya, who live in their native ecosystem, treat their natural resources as volitional beings; and they believe they will be revenged if they violate spirit preferences regarding the treatment of nature. The Q'eqchi Maya, in contrast, are displaced from their native Highland origin; and while these people hold to a similar animistic worldview, their spirit beliefs are no longer attached to environmental practice. This difference in the attachment of spirit to ecology is suggested by these authors to result in significant differences in land use patterns between the two groups: the Itza' destroy five times less land than the Q'eqchi. A similar phenomenon, they write, is observed in the Menominee: an American Indian tribe living on their native tribal lands, for whom spirit remains attached to their local ecology. This culture, like the Itza' Maya, exhibits a sustainable forestry use, and believes if a person treats nature in a greedy or wasteful manner spirit beings will harm them. In both cultures, the use of natural resources is negotiated with spirits who stand in as proxies for the common good; and as such, individual decision making is in accord with good environmental practice and group survival.

Animism influences how individuals behave toward, and relate to, nature, as just discussed; and it may also influence the way in which species are understood to behave toward, and relate to, each other. Medin and Atran have observed that the Itza' and Menominee have extensive knowledge of how species, including those from different domains like plants and animals, harm and hurt each other. They see this knowledge as evidence of a "bias" toward understanding species in terms of their "reciprocal" relationships to one other. This is in marked contrast to the Q'eqchi and Ladinos (Spanish-speaking immigrants to the Mayan Lowlands) who do not link spirit belief to their ecological practice, and who have a decreased propensity toward understanding species in terms of how they interrelate to each other.[36] How can we understand the origin of this bias? It is conjectured here to be a result of animism, so long as it remains attached to the local ecology. Animism places nature within a social frame, which introduces into nature the fundamental assumption that (social) interactions are bidirectional. The result is a presumed sensitivity to, and propensity toward seeking out, evidence in favor of bidirectional relations amongst species. This may lead to a more sophisticated and nuanced understanding of nature, and secondarily enhance group survival.

Given these findings and speculations, it is hypothesized that mirror neuron sensitivity to nonhuman form, both animate and inanimate, serves as a phylogenetic (evolutionary) adaptation to promote ecological stability in the face of unrestrained individual self-interest, and secondarily promote individual and group survival. It is further hypothesized that nonhuman form, experienced as spirit, functions as an "innate releasing mechanism" [37] to initiate coordinated motor patterns associated with social behaviors, such as approach and avoidance, cooperation, dominance and submission, sacrifice, and prostration. These behaviors are presumed to be mostly nonspecific and extend to the full panoply of interpersonal behavior; and the particular behaviors chosen by any group result from their own particular cultural practice and environmental needs. These behaviors though, despite their lack of specificity, are presumed to always include those related to empathy, since it arises as a consequence of mirror neuron activation. Consonant with this expectation, Medin and Atran[38] have observed small-scale cultures interacting with nature by way of indirect reciprocity[39]—where we help those who help us—as exemplified by helping the trees that provide food for the animals we eat. Also seen is reciprocal altruism[40]—where we help those who will help us in the future—as exemplified by limiting the number of fish we eat today so fish will still be available tomorrow.

These behaviors though, given their potentially high cost, are not necessarily adaptive if they are broadly dispersed over the panoply of expressive form that is nature. And, in fact, small-scale groups seem to concentrate their behavioral expenditures on those natural resources most necessary for survival, like the food supply. How does this focusing occur? One set of mechanisms may have to do with an interacting dynamic between human attitudes, the mirror neuron system, and behavior. As mentioned above, Singer and Frith suggest mental attitudes and, in particular, attention influence whether or not mirror neurons fire during the observation of pain.[41] In similar fashion, because small-scale societies pay particular attention to their natural resources insofar as they are sought out and utilized, these resources are more likely to activate this system. This presumably increases the likelihood these resources will be experienced as spirit and responded to empathically.

Other research has shown increased proficiency at a prescribed set of movements by a dancer increases the activation of premotor mirror neuron areas during their observation in others.[42] Thus it may be that one function of animal-mimicking dance, common in small-scale cultures, is to increase mirror neuron activation, and hence empathy, during the observation of these animals. In addition, empathy can also be modulated through reward. Atran[43] has written that small-scale societies utilize the tit-for-tat strategy when interacting with spirits, wherein cooperative behavior is made dependent on reciprocation;[44] and as such, empathic behavior, which is typically cooperative, when not reciprocated by way of its effect on the natural resource base, is presumably not reinforced, and vice versa. This leads, presumably, to a decrease in empathic behavior directed toward those resources, which is adaptive; and when these behaviors are considered collectively, regarding all the natural resources available to a society, it suggests that small-scale societies who live in disruption resistant ecosystems may engage in fewer of these empathic behaviors than those living in more disruption prone environments.

These mirror neuron-related mechanisms, while suggested here to be essential to animism's effect on behavior, are not presumed to be the only ones responsible for how small-scale societies relate to their natural environments. Behavior is highly complex and influenced by a multiplicity of neurologically based processes and environmental influences; that said, however, it is suggested that mirror neuron processes provide an important and unique influence regarding the elicitation of prosocial behavior directed toward the natural environment, which is adaptive.

CONCLUSION

Cognitive theories of religion place modular processes, utilizing belief and inferential reasoning, center stage. And of particular centrality, according to Barrett and Atran, are those modular processes that give rise to animism, which they see as essential to religion. In fact, they do not see religion as arising except by way of those processes. The *empathic theory of animism*, which is offered here, takes a different stand. It suggests that animism is a product of empathy and involves simulation and cognition. In addition, this chapter takes a less certain view of how animism, and the neurological mechanisms underlying it, is involved in the biology of religion. Animism and religion are closely related in small-scale societies and are to some extent indistinguishable, according to Mircea Eliade;[45] and in that way, it is difficult to imagine these religions arising except by way of expressive form and mirror neuron activation. The role of expressive form and mirror neuron activation, however, is less obvious regarding monotheistic religion. It may be that there is no necessary link; but it is not unreasonable to imagine that the activation of mirror neuron processes by inanimate form results, in its totality, in an implicit sense of energy and/or life emanating from the natural world. And, in turn, this energy makes the felt concept of God intuitive, underpinning and promoting monotheistic religion; and in the absence of this energy, due to failures in the mechanisms of empathy, God is not felt and hence counterintuitive.

In order to elevate these cognitive and empathic theories of animism above speculation, empirical validation is required. At the most general level, empirical research looking at how the brain normally detects and represents animate beings is relevant. As those processes are better understood, they will likely help validate or invalidate some of the fundamental assumptions that each of these theories make; and by so doing, help validate or invalidate them. At a more specific level, the capacity for inanimate form to activate the mirror neuron system can be studied. The empathic theory predicts that art and expressive forms in nature, for example, can activate motor programs and emotion via the mirror neuron system; and that these forms can likewise, under some conditions, activate social processing areas of the right brain associated with empathic interpersonal attunement and reward.

This theory does not predict, however, that all forms have an equal capacity to activate the mirror neuron system; and neither does it predict that all people, or cultures, have an equal capacity to empathize. There may be innate biological factors involved, as well as cultural ones, that influence the capacity for any particular form, or any particular individual, to activate the mirror neuron system; and these factors can be studied. In addition, differences in brain activity regarding how the brain processes inanimate form, as seen in art and nature, for example, versus human beings can be studied; and these differences may help elucidate the role of simulation regarding animism and religion.

The outcome of these proposed studies, positive results from which are not predicted by the cognitive theories of religion, could help validate or invalidate aspects of these cognitive and empathic theories of animism and religion. Validation for these theories can also occur at the psychosocial/behavioral level; however, insofar as these theories instigate specific neurological structures in the etiology of religion, these specific structures require empirical validation regarding their hypothesized activity during religious experience. The results of this work, to the extent that empirical validation is even possible, will help further our understanding of the biology of animism and religion; and anthropological research further examining the relationship among animism, resource management, and survival, will help clarify the hypothesized evolutionary basis for these phenomena.

NOTES

1. Barrett, J. (2004). *Why would anyone believe in God?* Walnut Creek, CA: AltaMira Press.

2. Atran, S. (2002). *In gods we trust: The evolutionary landscape of religion.* New York: Oxford University Press.

3. Goldman, A., & Sripada, C. (2005). Simulationist models of face-based emotion recognition. *Cognition, 94*, 93–213.

4. Rizzolatti, G., Fadiga, L., Gallese, V., & Fogassi, L. (1996). Premotor cortex and the recognition of motor actions. *Cognitive & Brain Research, 3*, 131–141.

5. Gallese, V., Fadiga, L., Fogassi, L., & Rizzolatti, G. (1996). Action recognition in the premotor cortex. *Brain, 119*, 593–609.

6. Umilta, M. A., Kohler, E., Gallese, V., Fogassi, L., Fadiga, L., Keysers, C., & Rizzolatti, G. (2001). "I know what you are doing": A neurophysiological study. *Neuron, 32*, 91–101.

7. Kohler, E., Keysers, C., Umilta, M. A., Fogassi, L., Gallese, V., & Rizzolatti, G. (2002). Hearing sounds, understanding actions: Action representation in mirror neurons. *Science, 297*, 846–848.

8. Fogassi, L., Ferrari, P. F., Gesierich, B., Rozzi, S., Chersi, F., & Rizzolatti, G. (2005). Parietal lobe: From action organization to intention understanding. *Science, 302,* 662–667.

9. Iacoboni, M., Molnar-Szakacs, I., Gallese, V., Buccino, G., Mazziotta, J., & Rizzolatti, G. (2005). Grasping the intentions of others with one's own mirror neuron system. *PLOS Biology, 3,* 529–535.

10. Ferrari, P. F., Gallese, V., Rizzolatti, G., & Fogassi, L. (2003). Mirror neurons responding to the observation of ingestive and communicative mouth actions in the monkey ventral premotor cortex. *European Journal of Neuroscience, 17,* 703–1714.

11. Carr, L., Iacoboni, M., Dubeau, M. C., Mazziotta, J. C., & Lenzi, G. L. (2003). Neural mechanisms of empathy in humans: A relay from neural systems for imitation to limbic areas. *Proceedings of the National Academy of Sciences U.S.A., 100,* 5497–5502.

12. Lundqvist, L., & Dimberg, U. (1995). Facial expressions are contagious. *Journal of Psychophysiology, 9,* 203–211.

13. Dimberg, U., & Thunberg, M. (1998). Rapid facial reactions to emotionally relevant stimuli. *Scandinavian Journal of Psychology, 39,* 39–46.

14. Wicker, B., Keysers, C., Plailly, J., Royet, J. P., Gallese, V., & Rizzolatti, G. (2003). Both of us disgusted in my insula: The common neural basis of seeing and feeling disgust. *Neuron, 40,* 655–664.

15. Gallese, V., Eagle, M. E., & Migone, P. (2007). Intentional attunement: Mirror neurons and the neural underpinnings of interpersonal relations. *Journal of the American Psychoanalytic Association, 55,* 131–176.

16. Urgesi, C., Moro, V., Candidi, M., & Aglioti, S. M. (2006). Mapping implied body actions in the human motor system. *Journal of Neuroscience, 26,* 7942–7949.

17. Johnson-Frey, S., Maloof, F., Newman-Norlund, R., Farrer, C., Inati, S., & Grafton, S. (2003). Actions or hand-object interactions? Human inferior frontal cortex and action observation. *Neuron, 39,* 1053–1058.

18. Freedberg, D., & Gallese, V. (2007). Motion, emotion and empathy in esthetic experience. *Trends in Cognitive Sciences, 11,* 197–203.

19. Arnheim, R. (1949/1966). *Toward a psychology of art* (p. 64). Berkeley and Los Angeles: University of California Press.

20. Csibra, G., Gergely, G., Bíró, G., Koos, O., & Brockbank, M. (1999). Goal attribution without agency cues: The perception of "Pure Reason" in infancy. *Cognition, 72*(3), 237–267.

21. Heider, F., & Simmel, M. (1944). An experimental study of apparent behavior. *American Journal of Psychology, 57,* 243–249.

22. Premack, D. (1995). The infant's theory of self-propelled objects. *Cognition, 36,* 1–16.

23. Singer, T., & Frith, C. (2005). The painful side of empathy. *Nature Neuroscience, 8,* 845–846.

24. Molnar-Szakacs, I., Wu, A. D., Robles, J. F., & Iacoboni, M. (2007). Do you see what I mean? Corticospinal excitability during observation of culture-specific gestures. *Public Library of Science ONE*, *2*(7), e626. doi:10.1371/journal.pone.0000626.

25. Heider & Simmel, An experimental study of apparent behavior.

26. Kelmen, D. (1999). Functions, goals, and intentions: Children's teleological reasoning about objects. *Trends in Cognitive Sciences*, *12*, 461–468.

27. Lowrie, R. (1948). *Primitive religion* (p. 134). New York: Liveright.

28. Ibid., p. 134.

29. Gallese, Eagle, & Migone, Intentional attunement.

30. Atran, *In gods we trust*, p. 6.

31. Hardin, G. (1968). The tragedy of the commons. *Science*, *162*, 1243–1248.

32. Berkes, F., Feeny, D., McCay, B., & Acheson, J. (1989). The benefit of the commons. *Nature*, *340*, 91–93.

33. Ingold, T. (1996). The optimal forager and economic man. In P. Descola and G. Palsson (Eds.), *Nature and Society*. London: Routledge.

34. Bird-David, N. (1999). "Animism" revisited: Personhood, environment, and relational epistemology. *Current Anthropology* (supplement) *40*, S67–S92.

35. Medin, D. L., & Atran, S. (2004). The native mind: Biological categorization, reasoning and decision making in development across cultures. *Psychological Review*, *111*(4), 960–983.

36. Ibid.

37. Tinbergen, N. (1951). *The study of instinct*. Oxford: Clarendon Press.

38. Medin & Atran, The native mind.

39. Alexander, R. (1987). *The biology of moral systems*. New York: Aldine de Gruyter.

40. Trivers, R. (1971). The evolution of reciprocal altruism. *Quarterly Review of Biology*, *46*, 35–57.

41. Singer & Frith, The painful side of empathy.

42. Cross, E. S., Hamilton, A. F., & Grafton, S. T. (2006). Building a motor simulation de novo: Observation of dance by dancers. *NeuroImage*, *31*, 1257–1267.

43. Atran, *In gods we trust.*

44. Axelrod, R. (1984). *The evolution of cooperation*. New York: Basic Books.

45. Eliade, M. (1959). *The sacred and the profane: The nature of religion*. London: Harcourt Brace Jovanovich.

PART FIVE

The Adaptiveness of Religious Behavior

When behavior leads to increased survival or an increase in reproductive success, it is said to have adaptiveness. Determining if a behavior has adaptiveness is a process. It starts with theoretical propositions regarding how the behavior in question might have led to or may currently lead to an increase in survival or reproductive success. Next, testable hypotheses are generated to assess the potential relevance of the hypotheses. Theoretical propositions have a life cycle of their own, starting with their initial proposal through their testing. The four chapters in this part represent four different theoretical propositions regarding the adaptiveness of religious behaviors. They are at different stages in this cycle. The first two are still at the theoretically plausible stage, the third is being tested with a computer simulation, and the fourth is being tested by actually measuring the behavior of individuals.

CHAPTER **11**

The Adaptiveness of Changing Religious Belief Systems

John S. Price

For many years as a psychiatrist I treated patients who had undergone a change of belief system. In some cases the new belief system had a religious theme, such as that the patient was the Son of God or the Virgin Mary. What was most impressive was the utter conviction with which the new beliefs were held. No amount of argument could achieve any lessening of the new beliefs. Unfortunately for the patient, the new belief system was incompatible with continuing life in his or her previous social world; hence there was a referral to the psychiatric service. Often the new belief system was associated with highly prosocial aspirations, such as to "make the desert bloom," and a sense of mission to persuade others to go to "a land without evil."

One such patient was brought in by the police. He had been proclaiming himself as the Second Coming of Christ. I pointed out to the police that the second coming was widely anticipated by a large proportion of the population and that it was therefore not unreasonable for anyone to think they might have been selected. The police replied that he was clearly insane because he had been giving away his money to passersby. They said that he had even given away his credit card, and, to clinch the proof of his insanity, he had shouted out his personal identification number (PIN). There was little else wrong with this young man apart from his conviction of his sacred destiny. He was due to come before a judge to review his compulsory detention. I argued with him that he should tone down his claim a little. I suggested that if he told the judge that he might spend some time in a theological college in order to prepare himself for his new role, he might be released from the section of the Mental Health Act under which he was detained. But his sense of mission was too strong. He told the judge that he intended to continue preaching. The judge, without the slightest hesitation, made an order for continued compulsory detention.

About this same period, Boston anthropologist Charles Lindholm[1] produced his book *Charisma*, which described similar experiences in a range of individuals who were labeled gurus, cult leaders, prophets, and inspirers of New Religious Movements. (When used in this chapter, a *cult* means a group of people who follow a leader and proclaim a revolutionary ideology; over time a cult may develop into a religion.) This was followed by *Feet of Clay* in which Oxford psychiatrist Anthony Storr[2] lucidly equated the revelatory experiences of these gurus with the delusions of psychotic patients. What distinguished the guru from the patient was his ability to persuade other people to share his new beliefs. As Storr put it, "some gurus avoid the stigma of being labelled insane or even being confined in a mental hospital because they have acquired a group of disciples who accept them as prophets rather than perceiving them as deluded."[3]

Perhaps there was a biological advantage in being a guru and leading a group of disciples to a "promised land." When successful this advantage might be great enough to balance those many cases in which a new sect died out for some reason, or committed mass suicide, or practiced celibacy, or those other cases in which the guru failed to recruit followers and ended up in a hospital. Perhaps this might account for the persistence of the genetic predisposition to psychosis in spite of the reduced reproduction that is typical of such patients.[4] It may also help us to understand the social deficits of future patients, who are destined to relate only to followers and not to peers.[5] Finally, it might also help us to understand the negative features of schizophrenia such as apathy and withdrawal, since the prospective guru has failed to have his new belief system validated by followers, has missed the "ecstatic merger of leader and follower which seems so central to the charismatic experience,"[6] and receives only negative responses from those to whom he communicates his message.

BELIEF SYSTEMS (MAZEWAYS)

Human beings have a set of beliefs about themselves and the world they live in. Following the lead of anthropologist Anthony Wallace, this set of beliefs will be called a "mazeway." [7] The *mazeway* contains beliefs about the relationship of the individual to his group, his ancestry, his gods, his purpose in the world, and his moral code. Most of the mazeway is shared with members of the same group and is learned during childhood. Learning about specific beliefs depends on language. Therefore, the development of mazeways must have begun after our hominid ancestors split off from the chimpanzee line and we began to develop a symbolic vocal language. Then each group could get one or more unique symbols to define it—a name, a unique language or dialect, a myth of its origins, and maybe a flag or even a national anthem.

This development of group symbols must have greatly enhanced the cohesiveness of groups and as a result encouraged group competition. Group efficiency and solidarity were further enhanced by the adoption of a unique concept of God, together with a myth of origin and a prescription for moral behavior. Most writers on religion agree that such a group should have an advantage to outcompete any group lacking such beliefs. [8]

Anthropologists have found that each human group or tribe has such a system of shared beliefs about the world and its origins and the relation of each individual to the ancestors and the gods. The bulk of this mazeway is common to all members of the group, but differs from the mazeway of every other group. The elements of a mazeway —e.g., beliefs about God, purpose, moral code—are neither false nor true. They are unverifiable. They consist of what the late University of Michigan anthropologist Roy Rappaport[9] has called sacred knowledge, to distinguish it from ordinary practical (profane) knowledge. The late Harvard evolutionary biologist Stephen Jay Gould[10] spoke of two nonoverlapping "magisteria" of sacred and profane discourse, while Karen Armstrong,[11] former Roman Catholic nun and author of several books on comparative religion, distinguished between the sacred "mythos" and the profane "logos."

The existence of sacred knowledge makes it possible for every group to have a different mazeway. Each child learns the mazeway of his/her group, which then appears self-evident. One has no insight into the irrationality of one's own belief system, which can get compartmentalized away from other aspects of one's reasoning process. People who subscribe to different mazeways from one's own are regarded as infidels or heathen. The ubiquity of mazeways suggests that over the past few million years groups whose members lacked the capacity to develop a mazeway must have died out. [12]

CHANGE OF BELIEF SYSTEM (MAZEWAY RESYNTHESIS)

Even more remarkable than the development of unique sacred belief systems is the capacity for change of belief system. This has been observed over and over again by anthropologists in the formation of cults and New Religious Movements. The future prophet or cult leader undergoes an intense experience, sometimes accompanied by apparent physical illness and often by auditory hallucinations. As a result, a new mazeway is formed. It is as if the elements of the old mazeway were shaken in a kaleidoscope and a new and meaningful pattern emerges. There is a sense of mission and a compulsion to share the new mazeway with others. The reaction of those others is sharply divided between those who reject the new ideas, which are regarded as heresy, and those who accept them and regard them as being of supernatural origin. These latter undergo "conversion" to the new ideas of the prophet in what has been called "secondary mazeway resynthesis" (to distinguish it from the "primary mazeway resynthesis" of the prophet). They then become followers or cult members, and a new social unit with a new and unique mazeway has been formed.[13]

CHANGE OF BELIEF SYSTEM (PSYCHOTIC DELUSION)

In psychiatry one deals with situations where something has gone wrong, otherwise patients would not come or be brought to psychiatrists. Seeing something going wrong sometimes enables one to visualize how things would be if things went right. Changes of belief are common in psychiatric patients. When they are counterintuitive and counterfactual, we call them delusions. In psychiatry a delusion is a fixed false idea not shared by members of one's social group. For those who are not familiar with delusion formation, the description by Sir Martin Roth (former president of the British Royal College of Psychiatrists) may give the feel of what it is like for the delusional schizophrenic patient:

> The patient may have already begun to see the outside world as transfigured by elements of threat, mystery, danger and unreality, the "delusional atmosphere" common in this disorder. It is at this

stage that an overwhelming idea of wide-ranging significance often erupts out of a clear sky in the minds of schizophrenic patients and leaves an indelible impression. It arrives direct and unmediated by any relevant or understandable antecedent even of experience. Such a "primary delusion" instils in the patient the total conviction that he is the new Messiah or the reincarnation of St John the Baptist or Mohammed or a delusion of similar character. The fear-laden perplexity and confusion of the patient abates for a period. The world is once again perceived as whole and authentic. The delusion explains it all. This symptom marks perhaps the most clear break in the continuity of psychic life of the schizophrenic patient.[14]

Melvin R. Lansky[15] describes the reconstruction of reality and the change in world design that may be experienced by the psychotic patient. He observes that a delusion confers a sense of specialness on the holder. According to Los Angeles psychiatrist M. Goldwert, the patient may come to "consider himself as a specially ordained pillar of God, the messianic center around which all world phenomena are organised."[16] The City of Jerusalem attracts patients with messianic delusions.[17] It is reported to have induced such delusions in seemingly stable tourists.[18]

This experience is very similar to the mazeway resynthesis described by anthropologists in the prophets who start New Religious Movements. The new beliefs are held with utter conviction. They are not amenable to discussion or modification. In the case of the psychotic patient, this leads to management problems because the world views of the patient and doctor are different. In the case of the prophet, the strength of his conviction is attractive to followers and leads to the formation of a charismatic relationship between prophet and followers in which everybody attributes the new belief system to supernatural origin. Strength of conviction also makes the prophet and his followers unacceptable to the parent group, and tends to result in the prophet leading his followers to a "promised land."

A delusion has been defined as a fixed false belief that the social group as a whole does not share.[19] What makes someone "ill" is the failure to persuade others of the truth of the belief. All the prophet is doing is asking potential converts to exchange one arbitrary belief system for another. Bigelow noted that "each group requires something intimate, unique to itself, around which its members can cohere. Irrational beliefs serve this purpose far better than rational ones: they are not only easier to produce, but also less likely to be confused with enemy beliefs." [20] It is the arbitrary character of the new belief system, like the arbitrary shapes and colors of a flag, that make it such a good "in-group marker."

VIEWS FROM ANTHROPOLOGY

Many anthropologists have reported on New Religious Movements from around the world.[21] They emphasize that they all begin in the revelatory experience of a single individual. According to H. B. M. Murphy, "It is noteworthy that many Messianic movements, both in Africa and the Pacific, are best interpreted as the cultural extension of individual delusions and that they arise in religious settings which emphasise the emotional or non-rational interchange of beliefs between members." [22] Contrary to what one might expect, new belief systems do not emerge as a consensus from group discussion. They arise in a single individual in what has been called "primary mazeway resynthesis."

Roland Littlewood,[23] professor of anthropology and psychiatry at University College, London, argues that "individual delusions may be converted into a shared public culture by the manipulation of previously accepted symbolism." In his study of "charisma," the late Oxford sociologist Bryan Wilson points out that "If a man runs naked down the street proclaiming that he alone can save others from impending doom, and if he immediately wins a following, then he is a charismatic leader: a social relationship has come into being. If he does not win a following, then he is simply a lunatic." [24] The late Dennison University cultural anthropologist Felicitas D. Goodman and colleagues conclude:

> Not infrequently in primitive societies the code, or the core of it, is formulated by one individual in the course of a hallucinatory revelation: such prophetic experiences are apt to launch religiously oriented movements, since the source of the revelation is apt to be regarded as a supernatural being.[25]

Many studies of cults and revitalization movements have noted that the leaders are liable both to auditory hallucinations and to sudden changes in beliefs. Jungian psychiatrist Anthony Stevens and I have argued that the various features seen in psychosis are just what is needed to produce the reversal of belief that is seen in the formation of a new religion.[26] In particular, we refer to the tendency to form well-articulated belief systems that are at odds with the beliefs of the majority and that are held with utter conviction. It is this unshakableness of belief that lends charisma to the prophet and unmanageability to the psychotic patient.

THE CHOICE BETWEEN PROPHESY AND MADNESS

What decides whether a person becomes a prophet or a psychotic? In some cases the new belief system is too bizarre or too unappealing to potential followers. However, commentators have pointed out that very bizarre belief systems have attracted a following. As Aldous Huxley put it, "There is no dogma so queer, no behaviour so eccentric or even outrageous, but a group of people can be found to think it divinely inspired." [27] However, it may be that the pool of potential followers may be too satisfied with life to desire change. Or they may be competing with another group and so be fully occupied with another main group process. If followers are obtained, the prophet becomes a cult leader, if they are not, he or she is likely to be labeled a psychotic patient. It is interesting to note the similar role of cult followers and psychiatric nurses: while the prophet or patient is preoccupied with supernatural matters, it is up to the followers or nurses to "chivvy" (remind or harass) him or her about the daily mundane matters of life such as washing and eating—the difference being that the followers work within the delusional system and the nurses outside it.

The Religious Experience Research Centre in Lampeter University (in Wales, United Kingdom) has documented many examples of people who have had supernatural experiences and are neither cult leaders nor psychiatric patients. They could go either way according to their social reception.[28] They are at a choice point, which leads either to religious behavior or to psychotic behavior. Religious behavior has been defined as "the communicated acceptance of a supernatural claim." [29] If person A says, "I am the Messiah," he is manifesting psychotic behavior; but if person B then says, "Yes, you are the Messiah," not only is this second statement in the category of religious behavior, but also it converts the statement of person A from psychotic behavior to religious behavior.

GROUP COMPETITION AND GROUP SELECTION

I pointed out above that group efficiency and solidarity are enhanced by the adoption of a unique God together with a myth of origin and a prescription for moral behavior. Such a group should out-compete any group lacking such beliefs. Other adaptations favor group cohesiveness. For instance, we have suggested that affective disorders are part of an appeasement system that reduces within-group conflict and permits a harmonious distribution of leader and follower roles within the group.[30] Cooperation within groups and aggression between groups appears to have been the rule during hominid evolution.[31]

Like the amoeba, a group needs to split in order to succeed in evolutionary terms. Therefore, in addition to the capacity to develop belief systems, human groups had to evolve the capacity for a change of belief system, expressed in a small proportion of individuals. They also needed to have the capacity to be converted to someone else's new belief system as expressed in a rather larger proportion of individuals.

Of course, a human social group can split without a new mazeway, as when colonization occurs. We have called this *homopistic* splitting (from the Greek for "same" and "belief"). But the *heteropistic* splitting associated with mazeway resynthesis must greatly enhance the rate of splitting. Rapid group splitting favors selection between groups as opposed to selection within groups. This is important for the evolution of group processes and for the coevolution of genes and culture.[32] Most important of all, it selects for the capacity of a group to decide which of its members shall be fittest in terms of reproduction, and so to select people who put the interests of the group (i.e., the common good) before their own selfish interests. Such a capacity cannot evolve by means of within-group selection. Thus in the delusion formation of our psychotic patients we see the malfunction of a capacity that has very likely played a significant part in humankind becoming what it is.

THE CAPACITY TO BE CONVERTED TO A NEW BELIEF SYSTEM

In the formation of a cult, it is necessary to have not only a leader who has generated a new belief system but also a pool of potential followers who have the capacity to be converted to this new system.

The vast majority of human beings grow up with a belief system inculcated into them by parents and teachers—the human child appears designed to take for granted what it is told. We have an innate quality of indoctrinability.[33] What is surprising is that our firmly indoctrinated belief systems can be changed radically in what is known as religious conversion.

This conversion of the followers to the mazeway of the prophet has been called "secondary mazeway resynthesis" to distinguish it from the primary mazeway resynthesis undergone by the prophet. For one thing it is reversible. Those who have been converted often revert back to their original beliefs, whereas the new beliefs of the prophet and the madman are relatively permanent. This means that in the convert the new belief system is held together with the original belief system, which is split off or dissociated from conscious awareness. Also, the new belief system is swallowed whole and is not altered or added to. As a result, all the members of the cult share the belief system generated by the prophet. The converts or followers have the capacity for various dissociative behaviors like speaking with tongues, seizures, and possession by spirits. These characteristics are similar to the dissociation seen clinically in hysterical disorders such as fugues, paralyses, and sensory impairments.

Felicitas D. Goodman and colleagues[34] have given good descriptions of the information produced by the spirit guides of cults in Trinidad. These guides are followers rather than prophets. However, they have high standing in the social group. They are constantly sought to answer questions the answers to which are not available to the group. They provide answers from various spirits. The information they give is quite different from the revelatory experience of the prophet. It tends to be personal, and somewhat lacking in imagination; nor is it emotive or accompanied by a sense of mission. It is elicited, whereas the delusions and hallucinations of the prophet are spontaneous. It is similar to the material produced by Western mediums in séances. The shamans or magicoreligious practitioners who have been found in most primitive human groups are probably similar; they tend to increase group cohesion rather than cause fission. Canadian psychiatrists Joseph Polimeni and Jeffrey Reiss have suggested that shamanism may have a genetic relation to schizophrenia.[35] It seems likely that shamans, prophets, and cult followers all have a tendency to mystical and numinous experiences, described by English psychologist Michael Jackson as benign schizotypy.[36]

What is clear is that the capacities for primary and secondary maze-way resynthesis are complementary. Both are required for the formation of new groups with new belief systems. We need both the prophet to generate the new belief and the convert to transform the prophet and potential madman into a cult leader. The splitting of a human group is more complex than the cell division of the amoeba. However, both are required for the rapid dispersion of the species over the available habitat.

ESCAPE FROM BOREDOM

Two groups of people have been noted to have escaped from boredom. They view most other people and also themselves in their previous lives as only half alive or half asleep, and not fully activated and functional. One such group is composed of fighting men, who are actively competing with another group. Anthony Stevens[37] has described the experience of such men who feel really alive for the first time in their lives. William Butler Yeats has written a poem about a similar experience in a fighter pilot.[38]

The other group of escapees from boredom are cult members, both leaders and followers. They feel fully engaged in a divine mission. The female members, when they have sex with the cult leader, describe a transcendental experience, like mating with the Holy Ghost. The followers of the Russian mystic Georges Ivanovitch Gurdjieff are a good example, regarding the bulk of humanity as being like machines, or half asleep, while they themselves can be awakened by carrying out "the work."[39]

This sense of wakefulness and mission in these two groups (fighters and cult members) may very well be due to the mobilization of one of the two great archetypal processes of group expansion and group splitting. Over the past few million years we, as individuals, have been selected to devote much of our individual energy to group functions. If we do not engage in them, we feel empty, bored, and unfulfilled.

DISPERSAL

Dispersal is important in biology. Many amazing biological devices have evolved to ensure it, such as the production of fruits and nectar by plants and the provision of tasty protuberances called elaiosomes by seeds to attract insects. Often a species will produce two forms:

(1) a maintenance *phenotype* (the outcome of genes and the structures they produce interacting with a specific environment) that is adapted to the environment in which it is born, and (2) a dispersal phenotype that is programmed to move to a new area and that often has the capacity to adapt to a new environment.[40]

According to the present theory, humans have developed two dispersal phenotypes in the forms of the prophet and the follower. The coordinated action of these two phenotypes would serve to disperse us over the available habitat. This dispersal must have been aided by the major climatic changes over the past few million years in which vast areas of potential human habitat have repeatedly become available because of melting of ice sheets.

The dispersal phenotypes might have evolved through selection at the individual level, since the reproductive advantage of colonizing a new habitat would have been enormous. They would also promote selection between groups. This is important because selection at the group level can achieve results not possible at the level of selection between individuals. One result of the dispersal phenotype includes *ethnocentrism* (the tendency to favor one's own ethnic group over another) and the tendency to use "ethnic cleansing." The other result, as previously noted, is selection for cooperation, self-sacrifice, and a devotion to group rather than individual goals. Factors that promote selection at the group level are rapid splitting of groups, small size of daughter groups, heterogeneity (differences) of culture between groups, and reduction in gene flow between groups. These factors are all promoted by the breaking away of prophet-led groups with new belief systems.

One of the problems of selection at the group level is that of free-riders. These are people who take more than their share and contribute to the common good of the group less than their proper share.[41] Selection at the group level gives free-riders their free ride. They potentially could increase until they destroy the cooperative fabric of the group.

However, the psychology of the free-rider, which is one of self-aggrandizement and neglect of group goals, is not likely to be indoctrinated with the mazeway of the group. Nor is it likely to be converted to the new belief system of the prophet. Therefore, theoretically one would predict that cults and New Religious Movements should be relatively free of free-riders. Such an absence of free-riders would further enhance selection at the group level. Moreover, this is a testable theoretical proposition.

Cult followers have been studied and found to be high on schizotypal traits, such as abnormal experiences and beliefs.[42] They have not yet been tested for the sort of selfish attitudes and behavior that characterize free-riders. If a large cohort of people were tested for some measure of selfishness, it is predicted that those who subsequently joined cults would be low on such a measure. Predictions could also be made about future cult leaders. They would be likely to be ambitious males who were not at the top of the social hierarchy of their original group. If part of why human groups split in general is to give more reproductive opportunities to males in the new group, it can also be predicted that leaders of new religious movements would be males of reproductive age. Female cult leaders are not likely to be more fertile as a result of having many sexual partners, but their sons might be in an advantageous position for increased reproduction.

CONCLUSION

The biobehavioral science of ethology is about the movement of individuals. We have seen that change of belief system has been responsible for massive movements of individuals over the face of the earth. Religious belief systems appear to have manifest advantages both for the groups that espouse them and the individuals who share them. It is still controversial whether belief systems are adaptations or by-products of other evolutionary adaptive processes. Regardless of the answer to this question, the capacity for change of belief system, both that seen in the prophet and also that seen in the follower, may be adaptations because they have fostered the alternative life history strategies of dispersal from the natal habitat.

Moreover, change of belief system, when it is successful in the formation of a new social group and transfer of that group to a "promised land," accelerates many of the parameters that have been thought in the past to be too slow for significant selection at the group level, such as eliminating free-riders, rapid group splitting, heterogeneity between groups and reduction of gene transfer between groups. Natural selection at the group level would also favor the evolution of the capacity for change of belief system, so that during the past few million years we may have seen a positive feedback system leading to enhanced cult formation and accelerated splitting of groups. This may have contributed to the rapid development of language and culture in our lineage.

NOTES

1. Lindholm, C. (1990). *Charisma*. Oxford: Blackwell.

2. Storr, A. (1996). *Feet of clay: A study of gurus*. London: Harper Collins.

3. Ibid., p. xv.

4. Crow, T. J. (1995). A Darwinian approach to the origins of psychosis. *British Journal of Psychiatry, 167*, 12–25.

5. Burns, J. (2007). *The descent of madness: Evolutionary origins of psychosis and the social brain*. Hove: Routledge.

6. Lindholm, *Charisma*, p. 63.

7. Wallace, A. F. C. (1956). Mazeway resynthesis: A biocultural theory of religious inspiration. *Transactions of the New York Academy of Sciences, 18*, 626–638; Wallace, A. F. C. (1970). *Culture and Personality* (2nd ed.). New York: Random House.

8. Wilson, D. S. (2002). *Darwin's cathedral: Evolution, religion, and the nature of society*. Chicago: University of Chicago Press.

9. Rappaport, R. A. (1999). *Ritual and religion in the making of humanity*. Cambridge, U.K.: Cambridge University Press.

10. Gould, S. J. (2001). *Rock of ages: Science and religion in the fullness of life*. London: Cape.

11. Armstrong, K. (2000). *The battle for God: Fundamentalism in Judaism, Christianity and Islam*. London: Harper.

12. Hinde, R. A. (1999). *Why gods persist: A scientific approach to religion*. London: Routledge.

13. Galanter, M. (1989). Cults and new religious movements. In M. Galanter (Ed.), *Cults and new religious movements*. Washington, DC: American Psychiatric Association; Wallace, Mazeway resynthesis.

14. Roth, M. (1996). Commentary on "audible thoughts" and "speech defect" in schizophrenia. *British Journal of Psychiatry, 168*, 536–538 [237].

15. Lansky, M. R. (1977). Schizophrenic delusional phenomena. *Comprehensive Psychiatry, 55*, 157–168.

16. Goldwert, M. (1990). Religio-eccentricity in reactive schizophrenia. *Psychological Reports, 67*, 955–959.

17. Perez, L. (1978). The messianic idea and messianic delusion. *Mental Health and Society, 5*, 266–274.

18. Bar-El, I., Witztum, E., Kalian, M., & Brom, D. (1991). Psychiatric hospitalisation of tourists in Jerusalem. *Comprehensive Psychiatry, 32*, 238–244.

19. Garety, P. A. & Hemsley, D. (1994). *Delusions: Investigations into the Psychology of delusional reasoning*. Oxford: Oxford University Press.

20. Bigelow, R. (1969). *The dawn warriors: Man's evolution towards peace* (p. 246). Boston: Little, Brown.

21. Lanternari, V. (1963). *The religions of the oppressed: A study of modern messianic cults*. Trans. from Italian by L. Sergio. London: Macgibbon &

Kee; Ribeiro, R. (1970). Brazilian messianic movements. In S. L. Thrupp (Ed.), *Millennial dreams in action: Studies in revolutionary religious movements.* New York: Shocken Books; Wallis, R. (1984). *The elementary forms of the new religious life.* London: Routledge.

22. Murphy, H. B. M. (1967). Cultural aspects of the delusion. *Studium Generale,* 20, 684–691.

23. Littlewood, R. (1984). The imitation of madness: The influence of psychopathology upon culture. *Social Science and Medicine, 19,* 705–715 [705].

24. Wilson, B. (1975). *The noble savages: The primitive origins of charisma and its contemporary survival* (p. 7). Berkeley CA: University of California Press.

25. Goodman, F. D., Henney, J. & Pressel, E. (1974). *Trance, healing and hallucination: Three field studies of religious experience* (p. 192). London: Wiley.

26. Stevens, A., & Price, J. (2000). *Evolutionary psychiatry: A new beginning* (2nd ed.). London: Routledge; Stevens, A., & Price, J. (2000). *Prophets, cults and madness.* London: Duckworth.

27. Huxley, A. (1936). Justifications. *The olive tree* (p. 159). London: Chatto and Windus.

28. Jackson, M., & Fulford, K. (1997). Spiritual experience and psychopathology. *Philosophy, Psychiatry, Psychology, 4,* 41–65.

29. Steadman, L. B., Palmer, C. T., & Ellsworth, R. M., Chapter 2, this volume.

30. Price, J. S., Gardner, R., Jr., Wilson, D., Sloman, L., Rohde, P., & Erickson, M. (2007). Territory, rank and mental health: The history of an idea. *Evolutionary Psychology, 5*(3), 531.

31. Alexander, R. D. (1979). *Darwinism and human affairs* (pp. 228–229). Seattle: University of Washington Press.

32. Boyd, R., & Richerson, P. (1985). *Culture and the evolutionary process.* Chicago, IL: University of Chicago Press.

33. Eibl-Eibesfeldt, I. (1982). Warfare, man's indoctrinability and group selection. *Zeitschrift für Tierpsychologie, 60,* 177–198.

34. Goodman et al., *Trance, healing and hallucination.*

35. Polimeni, J., & Reiss, J. (2002). How shamanism and group selection may reveal the origins of schizophrenia. *Medical Hypotheses, 65,* 655–664.

36. Jackson, M. (1997). Benign schizotypy? The case of spiritual experience. In G. Claridge (Ed.), *Schizotypy: Relations to illness and health* (pp. 227–250). Oxford: Oxford University Press.

37. Stevens, A. (2004). *The roots of war and terror.* London: Continuum.

38. Price, J. S. (2007). A creativity myth: Madness and the creation of new belief systems. In R. Pine (Ed.), *Creativity, madness and civilisation* (pp. 21–32). Cambridge, U.K.: Cambridge Scholars Publishing.

39. Ouspensky, P. D. (1950). *In search of the miraculous: Fragments of an unknown teaching.* London: Routledge and Kegan Paul.

40. Krebs, J. R., & Davies, N. (1993). *An Introduction to behavioural ecology* (3rd ed.). Oxford: Blackwell Scientific Publications; Hewitt, G. M., & Butlin, R. (1997). Causes and consequences of population structure. In J. R. Krebs & N. Davies (Eds.), *Behavioural ecology: An evolutionary approach* (4th ed.; pp. 350–372). Oxford: Blackwell; Geist, V. (1971). *Mountain sheep.* Chicago: University of Chicago Press; Geist, V. (1989). Environmentally guided phenotype plasticity in mammals and some of its consequences to theoretical and applied biology. In M. N. Bruton (Ed.), *Alternative life-history styles of animals* (pp. 153–176). Dordrecht: Kluwer Academic Publishers.

41. Wilson, D. S., & Wilson, E. (2007). Rethinking the theoretical foundation of sociobiology. *Quarterly Revue of Biology, 82*(4), 327–348.

42. Day, S., & Peters, E. (1999). The incidence of schizotypy in new religious movements. *Personality and Individual Differences, 27,* 55–67; Peters, E., Day, S., McKenna, J., & Orbach, G. (1999). Delusional ideation in religious and psychotic populations. *British Journal of Clinical Psychology, 38,* 83–96.

CHAPTER 12

The Adaptiveness of Fasting and Feasting Rituals: Costly Adaptive Signals?

Rick Goldberg

THE THEORY OF COSTLY SIGNALING

At the heart of biological communication theory is the assumption that specific organisms will, under certain circumstances, benefit by signaling one another.[1] These circumstances occur when the communication contains information helpful for the survival and/or reproduction of both senders and receivers of signals. When males compete with other males, females with other females, or either of them for the attention of the opposite sex, individuals send and receive signals and thus "size each other up." The central premise of costly signaling theory is that signals are perceived as reliable (and not deceptive) only if the costs to develop and transmit them are recognizably high.

Those who practice fasts or provision feasts bear a high cost— respectively, the endurance of discomfort or even pain and/or the expenditure of their valuable resources. Though secularists often dismiss the stringencies of religious observances as primitive and irrational stubbornness, my task here is to show how these costly, ubiquitous behaviors can make good biological sense. Costly signals may be exaggerated even to the point of egregious wastefulness. The famous "poster boy" for wasteful biological signals is the peacock, whose strutting sexual display of iridescent tail feathers is so striking.

Religious feasting and fasting, widespread phenomena in human populations, are well-fitted into the dynamic of costly biological signaling. Folkways of traditional eating behaviors are heritable, socially coordinated motor patterns that take on a variety of functions other than nourishment. The need for cooperation in hunting, gathering, and other communal endeavors gave rise to the widespread social consumption of food that, at designated times, achieved sacramental status. This chapter will explore from an evolutionary perspective why the behavior called fasting, an act of apparent denigration, and food donation, an act of exaggerated food consumption called communal feasting, can elevate the status of some individuals. In layman's terms, I will describe how costly elements of fasting and feasting serve the human desire to be well thought of by those who matter. To flesh-out these sacrificial behaviors, diverse examples of religious feasting and fasting will illustrate the characteristics most amenable to biological interpretation.

My theme is that fasting and feasting may be characterized as costly, and therefore reliable, signals that enable individuals to display reproductive value within the sexual selection process. By engaging in communally sanctioned religious fasts and feasts, people demonstrate a willingness to cooperate with others, but also to "show off" sacrificially by competing for prestige and its rewards. Costly signaling theory demonstrates how these food-related, culturally sanctioned, ritualized behaviors provide selection advantages for individuals who participate.

Why should we think of fasting and feasting as both sacrificial and competitive? In religious fasting, the self-denial of desirable food allows an individual to elevate his social rank by demonstrating food discipline in ways that are socially admired. When people fast simultaneously, the experience of communion through deprivation can enhance group cohesiveness; thus, highly motivated and disciplined populations gain competitive advantages over those that are less cohesive.

The rigors of food denial are much easier for those of highest rank who tend to be better nourished. If well-fed, prestigious individuals hold the advantage in fasting over the undernourished, then under what circumstances can the well-endowed be expected to sacrifice in ways that those of low status cannot? The answer is apparent at the time of a communal feast: when a feast is planned, someone has to donate the food for mass consumption, usually in exorbitant quantities. That donor is rewarded with the highest prestige for his sacrificial generosity.

FASTING AND FEASTING AS COOPERATIVE AND COMPETITIVE SACRIFICIAL DISPLAY

> In the religious life, surrender and sacrifice are positively espoused; even unnecessary givings-up are added in order that the happiness may increase.
>
> —William James, *The Varieties of Religious Experience*

Food acquisition by hunting was often a collective action in which cooperation was rewarded by success for all, but with greater relative success for the prominent hunters. The leader of the hunt was entitled, if the hunt proved successful, to eat and distribute a disproportionate share of the meat.[2] As a result, he would reward family members and friends according to his own preferences. The power of highly regarded hunters notwithstanding, food scarcity has dominated our history, and communal rules for sharing at least some of the available food are found in all human and most primate communities.[3] The functional benefit of food sharing by generous individuals could be in part a reduction of the costs associated with group living. In all probability, our species evolved in closely knit, small bands in which the ability of high ranking individuals and their subordinates to cooperate and live in sufficient harmony was necessary for survival.

There are few behaviors about which people are more aware than the eating patterns of family and neighbors. Slander, gossip, and ridicule, the age-old weapons of social denigration, often concern themselves with the eating habits of their targets.[4] Additionally, we seem to have evolved an inhibition against eating in the presence of others who are not themselves eating. Therefore, when a person wishes to eat in public, he must be willing to share his food with the others present. Communal feasting is not affected by this natural inhibition against eating in public because everyone has access to as much food as he or she can stomach, often over a period of many hours or even days. A common ingredient of festive food sharing has been the mutual communication of a religious claim referencing the supernatural agents through whose beneficence, according to the claim, the food has been provided in such abundance.[5]

Like food sharing, abstaining from eating reliably signals a willingness to sacrifice over the short term. When individuals share the sacrificial fast, submitting to the discipline of temporary food denial communicates honestly a willingness to cooperate with the genetic and metaphorical co-descendants of common ancestors. Also, the ability to withstand the rigor (handicap) of fasting displays an individual's healthfulness and vigor to both potential mates and competitors for mates. To amplify an individual's sacrificial display, the fast may include proscriptions against bathing, shaving, wearing jewelry, attractive clothing or shoes, and working to earn money. The self-abnegating refusal to eat a fair share of the food will also enhance one's social standing. As an added benefit, a fasting individual will exempt himself temporarily from any obligation to supply food to others. One is seldom expected to engage in two separate acts of sacrificing (fasting and providing food for feasting) at the same time.

CHARACTERISTICS OF FASTS

In medieval Catholicism, deliberate and extreme renunciation of food and drink were examples of the "courageous" asceticism that marked the saints. These practices were considered among the highest Christian values, features of the ideal life admired by the masses.[6] Monastic orders used fasts to decrease sexual desire, to promote celibacy, to elevate austerity in opposition to indulgence, and to mortify their own flesh.[7]

Individual fasts were considered saintly and were undertaken as a form of self-discipline, expiation of one's own sins, or public mortification for the sins of society. Money saved from meals not eaten was delivered to the needy. While fasts for spiritual improvement were viewed as saintly, fasting for the sake of improving health or beauty was thought to be nothing but a mockery.[8] Interestingly, women who were later canonized as saints used fasting as a means of austerity more so than saintly men. Although women were only about 18 percent of those canonized by the Church from A.D. 1000 to 1700, they represented over 50 percent of those in whose lives illness, often brought about by penitential fasting, was the major factor in attaining sainthood.[9]

In Hinduism, fasting is characterized by a wide range of food abstention, from specific foods to no food at all.[10] Most fasts require not eating certain foods, such as cooked rice, while permitting others, such as fruit. Fasts are performed to fulfill a vow, on certain days of the week or month, or at certain times of the year.[11] Whereas Hindu men fast to gain personal merit, the more frequent fasts by women are usually undertaken on behalf of their husbands or extended families.[12]

Mahatma Gandhi was highly successful in exploiting fasts to promote his political agenda. Gandhi strategically calculated his ability to unite the Indian people with the publicity of his premeditated fasting. As a journalist, Gandhi knew well the power that could flow from publicly orchestrated self-denial; he used that technique to help rid his country of British rule and later to prevent intercommunal fighting. For Gandhi, fasts were a subcategory of religious vows. As he wrote, "A person unbound by vows can never be absolutely relied upon." [13]

In the Koran, fasting is considered a pillar of Islam, a regimen of subordinated piety. Fasts may be imposed as penance for transgression or for ritual purification. Sufis practiced fasting as a mantra for systematic destruction of the ego resulting in "fana," the state of self-annihilation.[14] During the month-long fast of Ramadan, Muslims collectively eat nothing during daylight hours and feast abundantly after dark. In a recent French survey, while only 36 percent of Muslims said they were strictly observant of Islamic law, 70 percent reported strict observance of the Ramadan fast.[15] Though only a small minority of American Jews observes Jewish Law to any extent, a much larger percentage nonetheless assumes the obligation of the fast of Yom Kippur.

Jews may fast individually to expiate sin or remediate the effect of bad dreams.[16] Collectively, Jews fast in pleading for God's help in battle, evoke God's pity to relieve distressful conditions such as drought, recall historical catastrophes, or induce individual and communal soul searching (as on Yom Kippur).[17] Jewish law punishes those who do not participate in communal fasting with the threat of becoming "cut off from their people." [18] Moses is said to have fasted for 40 days prior to receiving revelation on Mount Sinai. In the Bible, fasting is seen as preparation for prophecy by, in some instances, inducing susceptibility to visions. Anecdotally, the only time the Nazis served decent food in the concentration camps was on Jewish fast days, in an attempt to mock Judaism and break Jewish solidarity.[19]

In China, it was customary in anticipation of a significant ceremony for the chief celebrant to engage in a fast of purification. For example, the priestess of the minor cult based on care of silk-producing worms prepared for her annual rite by periods of fasting.[20] In the Ethiopian Orthodox Church, rules of fasting are a principal element of Christian identity. For common Ethiopians, the number of fast days observed annually totals 110–150, while for priests and monks the total can reach 220 days.[21] Mormons set aside one day a month for total abstinence fasting, the main purpose of which is to contribute the food saved (or its money equivalent) to the poor.[22] The World Council of Churches recommended in 1974 that one day per month be set aside as a fast day to save food for those in need. Their various member denominations were asked to use the saved funds for charitable purposes.[23] Practicing food denial was used during certain New York City political and charitable fundraising events: despite paying the price for a full dinner, attendees were served only beans and rice. Other examples of fasting include puberty fasts among the Ojibwa people,[24] occupational fasting among the Island Carib,[25] and the Irish fast to notify a debtor of impending collateral seizure or to coerce an enemy.[26]

While the communalist religions all evidence traditional fasting, Buddhists and most Protestant sects practice fasting to a lesser extent. One possible interpretation of this distinction is that community-centered religions are "tribal brotherhoods" that institutionalize mutual sacrifice, whereas noncommunalist Buddhism and Protestantism, "universal otherhoods," seldom promote sacrificing.

PHYSIOLOGY OF FASTING

Religious fasts may be undertaken by individuals acting alone (private fasts) or in concert with others (public fasts). During these fasts, the food most commonly eliminated is meat *because* it is the most highly valued. Religious fasting may require traditional abstention from all or certain foods for a period of time, *especially* when hungry.[27] Voluntary religious fasting may mimic illness fasting, because sickness often causes an involuntary loss of appetite. Most people and animals instinctively stop eating when they feel sick and continue to avoid food until they feel better. As a result, food abstention long ago became associated with curing illness.[28] In voluntary religious fasting, preventive maintenance of spiritual health is the objective. It is no coincidence that the fast for *religious purification* has today been copied by the secular health-conscious as the cleansing fast to *purify the body*.

Since human populations have historically suffered periodic food shortages, the custom of religious fasting may have developed to make virtue out of necessity—fasts of up to three days have been used to diminish the hunger drive. There are abundant examples of herbs functioning as aids in hunger suppression. Coca leaves are chewed by Andean Indians to inhibit hunger and fatigue. Peyote, tobacco, coffee, and tea have likewise been used to blunt appetite.[29] In addition, herbs inducing odor and tactile sensitivity divert attention away from hunger. Prolonged, semi-isolated fasts were often used to lead practitioners on journeys of spiritual connection.[30] The delirium that accompanies prolonged fasting, though viewed fearfully, may elevate the self-denier to the status of community visionary. Among the Algonquin tribes, long and rigorous fasting was required of boys and girls from an early age. These fasts were expected to induce dreams and other visionary impressions, stamping the character of each youngster for life.[31]

Physiologically, there are reasons why fasting can be beneficial. During the initial phase, the body subsists on its stored substances. But body tissue is not burned indiscriminately; rather, dying, damaged, and diseased cells are metabolized first. Additionally, the organs of elimination detoxify the body more efficiently during a fast because they do not have to deal with an influx of new food containing toxic material. Thus the systems that digest, process, and eliminate food are allowed time to rest and recuperate.[32] Motor skill performance, including sexual function, declines while fasting but accelerates rapidly when eating is resumed.[33] As a result, periodic fasting by men could function as a strategy to increase the likelihood of conception if a man were to resume eating in synchrony with his mate's ovulation.

In 1964, five psychiatrists did a study of controlled fasting that lasted several days. The participants were a dozen men who, prior to the study, had never met one another. The individuals focused more on themselves and less on each other at the beginning. But after the fast was over, they agreed that going through the experience together made the ordeal easier and created a sense of mutual bonding.[34] Though this coordinated group fast physically weakened each individual, the participants' submission to mutual sacrifice created an enduring bond. Historically speaking, coalitional solidarity in human populations brought great advantages, especially during times of internal tension caused by food scarcity, or due to the sacrifices required of warriors in battle.

FEASTING AS DISPLAY

> When a great man gives, it is a sign of magnanimity;
> when a poor man gives, it is a sign of his bondage.
>
> —Arab historian *Ibn Khaldun*

In the ancient world, feasting was a periodic activity of those members of the upper classes who could afford to compete in resource generosity and wastefulness.[35] In Egypt, the public meal became an aesthetic experience. Roman governments recognized the importance of sponsoring celebratory public feasts on religious occasions, providing entertainment and plentiful food distribution to large parts of the population.[36] In private venues, Homeric feasts served to display the prestige of the host and to curry favor with high-ranking guests of honor. Adult males typically reclined as much as possible on couches while eating, and the floor was purposefully littered with food tossed aside by ostentatiously wasteful diners. Lavish dinner parties in ancient Rome were excessive to the point of vulgarity; at imperial banquets splendor and extravagance knew no bounds. Dandies could go through several changes of brilliantly colored and elaborately embroidered clothes during the course of a single dinner.[37] Who was invited and who was overlooked was a topic of great interest; the seating arrangements at the affair rigidly displayed the social hierarchy of the guests. To emphasize the point of segregated seating, those of higher rank were served better food in plain sight of their lesser peers.[38]

Who can forget film maker Federico Fellini's hilarious treatment of the dining and drinking excesses of Petronius's Satyricon? Sixteenth-century banquets in Italian courts were extravagant multimedia events given to astound and overwhelm the senses of guests. The feast preceding Lent could consist of five separate courses of between 15 and 19 dishes each. A management guide for organizing and conducting such affairs, *Dello Scalco*, was used extensively by aristocratic banquet planners of the time.[39]

In Rome, the ritualized sacrificing of animals was often followed by communal consumption of their meat.[40] Early on, wealthy Romans were leery of the Greek preference to serve fish rather than meat at banquets; they somewhat changed their mind once they realized that, because certain kinds of fish were very expensive, fish dishes could be just as effective in the conspicuous display and consumption necessary for a successful feast. Later, in the Christian world, serving fish would become emblematic of the spirituality of Jesus. Unlike meat, which was thought to stimulate lust, fish was considered conducive to piety because its "cooling effect" helped subdue passions and overcome temptation.[41] In feudal Europe, three activities were seen as binding together a king and his magnates: joint Christian worship, the hunt, and the feast. The banquet thus became a means by which kings maintained ties with those from whom fealty was expected.[42] In addition, the spread of Christianity initiated the practice of regulating what, when, and how people ate. The sinfulness of gluttony inevitably gave rise to the attainment of prestige through knowledge of and conformity to a complex set of table manners.[43] Coping with place settings, knowing which fork to use, and swallowing before talking all became powerful signals of social rank.

The prime examples of exorbitant feasting in the Americas were the potlatches of indigenous peoples on the Northwest Coast. Centered in religious ceremonialism, a potlatch was characterized by the giving away of enormous quantities of food and other valuables. This occasion served to validate the host's succession to a position of high rank, and it took place when the claimant succeeded in accumulating enough goods to give away extravagantly and wastefully to justify his newly acquired standing.[44] The earliest imperial banquets in China were in part religious rituals designed to display authority, with 2,000 servants needed to run the food service.[45]

One of the most effective ways of acquiring social standing is to be a net provider of food for others. Food generosity has been judged traditionally as a sign of good character; additionally, the rationing of food to their subordinates by those in power has been, like generosity, an effective means of establishing and maintaining control and prestige.[46] Writing of wedding celebrations, Pat Caplan comments on the reason why ostentatious feasting persists. He observes that feasts are a gastro-political arena for promoting status, a leveling mechanism whereby those who have the good fortune to be marrying off a child are obliged to display their generosity by feeding others.[47] From an ethological (i.e., behavioral biology) perspective, prestige can be defined as an individual's social standing that determines his or her ability to gain personal benefits by influencing the behavior of others. In addition to proximate (near term) benefits for those with prestige during their lifetimes, there are also longer-lasting benefits for descendants who inherit high rank from their forebears, an inheritance called "hereditary privilege." In any generation, and for whatever reason, those individuals with the highest social standing have had the best access to reproductive and other resources and have therefore achieved, on average, the greatest reproductive success.

In community hierarchies, there is a direct relationship between status and a history of having donated food to others.[48] Feasting to commemorate religious occasions therefore depended on the manifest generosity of food donors. When donors provide food (usually to excess) for communal festivity, relatively honest signals are sent to the grateful beneficiaries that elevated prestige for the donors is fully justified.

CONCLUSIONS

Though fasting and food provisioning might at first glance appear to be self-sacrificial, from a costly signaling perspective they may be seen as just the opposite.[49] Individuals who display socially sanctioned, conspicuous fasting earn esteem through food denial. Since people readily notice the visible cues of eating habits, religious fasting is always done traditionally to ensure public approval. "Unapproved" food deprivation is viewed with suspicion if not contempt, so fasting must be done according to public standards (and not in total secrecy).[50] Public fasts can be seen as "competitive asceticism," increasing an individual's long-term stature even as short-term fitness is decreased from the lessening or elimination of food. In other words, fasting gives opportunities to community members for holier-than-thou, ostentatious piety.[51]

Fasting to influence the opinion of others should be understood within the context of an individual's hunger due to food insufficiency. In our evolutionary history, it must have been important to detect who was starving and who was bluffing to get more than his fair share. Though all individuals can enhance esteem by disciplined fasting, those with more resources have the most to gain because their sacrifice is greater than that of resource-poor individuals.

From a modern perspective, some might ask if a fast or feast should be considered religious or secular behavior. But until recently in human history, there was no distinction made between the categories *religious* and *secular*. In Western cultural thinking, heavily influenced by modern Protestant Christian individualism, projecting the religious-secular bifurcation backwards into history often results in a distorted understanding of early religious behavior. In antiquity, virtually all private and communal activities were traditional, copied from previous generations, and infused with ancestral/supernatural authenticity.[52] Religious fasting and feasting are therefore ritual expressions reflecting submission to ancestral influence. Why would common descendants sustain traditions that emulate and therefore "please" their genetic and metaphorical ancestors? Perhaps the answer lies in appreciating the potentially adaptive value of traditions that reference, characterize or petition "supernatural" ancestors thought to be capable of intervening beneficially or malevolently in the lives of their descendants. If ancestral influence were so perceived, it would likely select for mutual cooperation among descendants while downplaying their ever-present, competitive antagonisms.

My goal in this chapter has been to explore, from an evolutionary perspective, how fasting, an act of apparent self-denigration, and feasting, which requires the donation of large quantities of food, function as status enhancers. By understanding the biological dynamic of religious fasting and feasting, we can see how selection favored those who traditionally both cooperated and displayed competitively. High social standing is always a scarce commodity—there is never enough to go around. For our social species, commonly shared experiences like fasting and feasting gave selection advantages to those most able to create and sustain the bonds of cohesion during hard times. From a sexual selection perspective, those individuals perceived as most successful in activities of competitive cooperation were accorded the highest prestige and, consequently, achieved the highest reproductive success.

NOTES

1. Hauser, M. D. (1997). *The evolution of communication*. Cambridge, MA: The MIT Press.

2. Historically, providing meat was necessary when hosts wanted to impress guests. Note the anti-veggie attitude of the Lele of Kasai: "The Lele have a craving for meat. To offer a vegetable meal to a guest is regarded as a grave insult. Much of their conversation about social events dwells on the amount and kind of meat provided" (from a study by anthropologist Mary Douglas, quoted in Canetti, E. [1973]. *Crowds and power* [p. 129]. New York: Continuum).

3. Following the lead of seminal anthropologist Levi-Strauss, many anthropologists see eating as a social experience as central to human behavior as language.

4. Grimm, V. E. (1996). *From feasting to fasting, the evolution of sin* (p. 196). London: Routledge.

5. Note, for example, the sacrificing-feasting required by Deuteronomy 14:23.

6. Bynum, C. W. (1997). Fast, feast, and flesh. In C. Counihan et al. (Eds.), *Food and culture* (p. 139). New York: Routledge; Montanari, M. (1994). *The culture of food* (p. 24). Oxford: Blackwell.

7. The recalcitrant body had to be forced into submission by periodic fasting. Toward that same goal, priestly celibacy was used to deny the body its sexual needs. For women, the link between regular fasting that weakens the body and the maintenance of virginity was duly recognized (Grimm, *From feasting to fasting, the evolution of sin*, pp. 194, 195).

8. Henisch, B. A. (1976). *Fast and feast* (pp. 28–29). University Park: Penn State University Press.

9. Bynum, Fast, feast, and flesh, p. 139; Montanari, *The culture of food*, p. 140.

10. Hassan, K. A. (1971). Hindu fasting and related rituals in a north Indian village (p. 43). Presented at 70th Annual Meeting of the American Anthropological Association, New York.

11. Kaushik, J. N. (n.d.). *Fasts of the Hindus around the year* (p. 35). Delhi: Books for All.

12. Caplan, P. (1992). *Feasts, fasts, famine: Food for thought* (p. 12). Providence: Berg.

13. Gandhi, M. K. (1944). *Ethics of fasting* (p. 55). Delhi: Indian Printing Works.

14. Armstrong, K. (1993). *A history of God* (p. 227). New York: Ballantine Books.

15. Laqueur, W. (2007). *The last days of Europe* (p. 39). New York: St. Martin's Press.

16. After a Jew completes an individual fast, his prayer is as follows: "when the Holy Temple existed, if someone sinned, he brought an offering of [animal] fat and blood for the altar. May it be Your will that the diminution of my fat and blood today [by my fast] should be [favorable to You] as if I had offered it upon the altar" (Taken from Scherman, R. N., & Zlotowitz, M. [Eds.]. [2006]. *Artscroll Sidur Kol Ya'akov* [prayer book; p. 249]. Brooklyn, NY: Mesorah Publications.) Co-editors were Rabbi Nosson Scherman and Rabbi Meir Zlotowitz.

17. Johnson, P. (1987). *A history of the Jews* (p. 155). New York: Harper & Rowe; the Hebrew name of the Talmudic tractate on fasting is *Ta'anit*, from a root that also means "self-affliction" or "self-impoverishment."

18. Leviticus 23:27–30.

19. Telushkin, Rabbi J. (1991). *Jewish literacy* (p. 362). New York: William Morrow.

20. Schafer, E. H. (1977). *T'ang—Food in Chinese culture* (p. 133). New Haven, CT: Yale University Press.

21. Knutsson, K. E., & Selinus, R. (1970). Fasting in Ethopia. *American Journal of Clinical Nutrition, 23*(7), 958.

22. Eckstein, E. F. (1980). *Food, people and nutrition* (p. 255). Westport, CT: AVI.

23. Ibid., p. 252.

24. Radin, P. (1914). *Canadian Geological Museum Bulletin 2*, 69–78.

25. Taylor, D. (1950). The meaning of dietary and occupational restrictions among the Island Carib. *American Anthropologist, 52*(3), 343–349.

26. Robinson, F. N. (1909). Notes on the Irish practice of fasting as a means of distraint. *Anthropological essays presented to Frederick Ward Putnam.* New York: Stechert.

27. Obligated fasting despite hunger certainly has its limits. Chasidism gained a following in eighteenth-century European Jewry because of their leniency regarding the fasting obligations of malnourished Jews.

28. Sheinkin, D., Schachter, M., et al. (1979). *Food, mind and mood* (p. 70). New York: Warner Books; as is the case during illness, fasting is necessarily accompanied by lessening of the normal level of muscular movement.

29. Fieldhouse, P. (1986). *Food & nutrition: Customs & culture* (pp. 59–60). Dover: C. Helm.

30. Benedict, F. G. (1915). *A study of prolonged fasting* (Pub. No. 203; p. 48). Washington: Carnegie Institute.

31. Tylor, Sir E. B. (1958). *Religion in primitive culture—Part II* (p. 497). New York: Harper & Brothers.

32. Sheinkin, Schachter, et al., *Food, mind and mood*, p. 72.

33. Glaze, J. A. (1928). *Psychological effects of fasting* (p. 39). Dissertation, University of Michigan, Ann Arbor.

34. Kollar, E. J., Slater, G. R., et al. (1964). Measurement of stress in fasting man. *Archives of General Psychiatry III* (p. 115).

35. A word for "feast" in the Judaic liturgy is *s'udah*, whose root means to support or sustain. Hence, a feast can be seen as the means by which a wealthy and generous food donor supports/sustains others.

36. Rawson, B. (2007). Banquets in ancient Rome: Participation, presentation and perception. In D. Kirby & T. Luckins (Eds.), *Dining on turtles: Food feasts and drinking in history* (p. 29). New York: Palgrave MacMillan.

37. Strong, R. (2002). *Feast: A history of grand eating* (p. 25). Orlando: Harcourt.

38. Ibid., p. 26; today we see the same protocol on airplanes when first class passengers receive better food than those in tourist class. However, our etiquette requires that the curtain separating the two classes remain closed.

39. Albana, K. (2007). Food and feast as propaganda in late Renaissance Italy. In D. Kirby & T. Luckins (Eds.), *Dining on turtles: Food feasts and drinking in history* (pp. 33, 41). New York: Palgrave MacMillan.

40. Berkert, W. (1996). *Creation of the sacred* (p. 153). Cambridge, MA: Harvard University Press.

41. Fletcher, N. (2004). *Charlemagne's Tablecloth* (pp. 48, 51). New York: St. Martin's Press.

42. Strong, R. (2002). *Feast: A history of grand eating* (p. 63). Orlando: Harcourt.

43. Ibid., pp. 50, 67; strict enforcement of table etiquette, like wasteful flamboyance, its predecessor, can be interpreted biologically as a "handicap."

44. Rosman, A., & Rubel, P. G. (1971). *Feasting with mine enemy: Rank an exchange among northwest coast societies* (pp. 5, 6, 201, 203). New York: Columbia University Press.

45. Fletcher, N. (2004). *Charlemagne's tablecloth* (p. 57). New York, St. Martin's Press.

46. Banquet hosts were typically seated on raised platforms—the spectacle of his or her dining was considered a public event to be witnessed by the privileged guests. As an added entertainment, the host had a designated assayer to publicly taste each dish before he or she would eat it. This ritual reinforced the implicit claim that the host was so prominent that someone might want to poison him (Strong, *Feast: A history of grand eating*, p. 93).

47. Caplan, P. (1992). *Feasts, fasts, famine: Food for thought* (p. 11). Providence, RI: Berg. Even though sponsoring a feast after a Jewish wedding is not required, it has become, nonetheless, a very old custom. In the Talmud, a wedding is referred to as a "house of feasting" (Ket. 71b3).

48. In cultures where the monarch is considered divine, he is expected to be provided with the best of everything to excess. Failure of the people to provide the king with sufficient luxury might anger the gods and lead to a famine. Recall the opulent international feast hosted by Reza Pahlevi to legitimize his status as Shah of Iran or the extravagant coronation of Bokasa of the Central African Republic (Fletcher, *Charlemagne's tablecloth*, p. 4).

49. Fasting may also play an integral and opposite role to feasting since any experience is better appreciated through an encounter with its opposite. For this reason, many feasts are preceded by fasts—the abundance of food after dark on Ramadan is all the more appreciated after a day's total abstention. The Church's great spiritual feast of Easter is preceded by Lent, the longest period of partial fasting (Fletcher, *Charlemagne's tablecloth*, pp. 90–92).

50. Many eating disorders characterized by food-denial are secretive, tainted by shame and deceit.

51. Grimm, *From feasting to fasting, the evolution of sin*, p. 32.

52. Using this line of inquiry, should Thanksgiving be considered a Christian religious holiday or merely an historic American commemoration of the amity between Pilgrims and Indians? While traditional blessings thanking God for abundant food are typically included at Thanksgiving, blessings are also included by the religiously observant at every other meal during the year. Though modern holidays like Thanksgiving present this dilemma, the problem will disappear when scholars of religion can view pre-modern religion *as it really was* rather than *as they think it must have been*.

CHAPTER 13

Cooperative Punishment and Religion's Role in the Evolution of Prosocial Altruism

Klaus Jaffe and Luis Zaballa

Historically, human social behavior has been studied by sociologists. However, in the past several decades biologists, who had been studying the social behavior of nonhuman animals for centuries, began to look at human social behavior as well. Their initial reception into this field was hostile due to the concern expressed by many sociologists that biology was going to cannibalize sociology and that human social behavior was going to be conceptualized as being completely genetically determined. This fear, which was ill-conceived, was never realized. Whereas genes have been shown to contribute to human behavior in terms of congenital (present at birth) predispositions, virtually no human behavior is completely genetically determined. Yet two important concepts emerged that help explain many aspects of human social behavior.

One is kin selection, as devised by the eminent British evolutionary biologist William Hamilton.[1] It means that the frequency of a gene in a population will be influenced not only by the effect the gene has on a particular individual's survival but also on the survival of individuals who are close relatives (kin). There are more of one's genes in one's close relatives than there are in oneself. As a result, even if genes "act" selfishly,[2] there are still more of them in one's relatives than in oneself, which results in human behavior being influenced by kin selection in ways that predispose people to do things that benefit one's close relatives even at a cost to self. Kin-selected acts are therefore not really altruistic, as genes are just benefiting themselves in the various bodies of relatives in which they reside.

A more general definition of altruistic behavior, according to Rutgers University Anthropology Professor Robert Trivers, is "a behavior that benefits another organism, not closely related, while being apparently detrimental to the organism performing the behavior, benefit and detriment being defined in terms of inclusive fitness."[3] The term "inclusive fitness" is just another way of addressing the result or outcome of kin selection in which the reproductive benefit is calculated across all close relatives.

Here we want to apply these concepts to human social behavior, specifically to the issue of the relationship between the individual and the social group. We define prosocial behavior on the part of an individual as behavior that benefits the social group. Volunteering to do community service is an example. Altruistic behavior is behavior that costs the doer and benefits the other. Putting these two terms together, prosocial altruism, which is the word used in the title of this chapter, is behavior in which the "other" is the social group in which the doer is a member.

The evolution of prosocial altruism (i.e., behavior of an individual that favors the group at a cost to the actor) has been commonly approached as an instance of the public goods problem. This problem is how to manage goods or resources that belong to and are used by everybody in the social group and yet where the individual user has no incentive to spend his or her resources to supply or replenish the goods. There is also the free-rider problem. This problem is where everybody has to contribute some resources for a common group enterprise, but where some free ride, benefiting from the communal goods without participating in the expenses of contributing goods. This predicament is often referred to as the social dilemma,[4,5,6] and is the modern version of the centuries old quest for philosophical and political ideas that may lead to a better society.[7]

The essential problem in a social dilemma is that each group member is tempted to act socially and be a member of the group in order to reap the fruits of the social welfare resulting from the concurrent prosocial efforts of other group members. However, individual group members are more strongly tempted to spare the altruistic costs of prosocial behavior while still enjoying those fruits. As a result, the predictable outcome is the disappearance, or nonappearance, of prosocial behavior among individuals in a social group. There is a presumption in this last statement, which is that the predisposition to behave in a prosocial altruistic way, versus a freeloading way, has genetic determinants. Although humans have flexibility in their behavior, there are genes, which, when possessed, predispose someone to take more than they give back to their social group.[8] We know that being an unfair reciprocator is one of the hallmarks of Antisocial Personality Disorder and that this disorder does have genetic determinants.[9] That finding does not mean that genes completely determine if one behaves antisocially. Rather, there are genes, which, when congenitally possessed, tend to bias behavior in this direction. In the rest of this chapter we will discuss selfish behavior and prosocial altruism as that which needs to be understood rather than address the genes that may predispose to these behaviors. However, in order for what we say to make sense, one has to presume that there are congenitally acquired genes that predispose individuals to prosocial altruistic and free-riding behaviors.

Different features in this competition between selfish behavior and prosocial altruism might tilt the balance toward prosocial behavior.[10] The most important feature has to do with degree of relatedness. It is expressed in what is called *Hamilton's rule*. This rule states that prosocial behavior is favored by genetic relatedness and states that what looks like altruism is much more likely to occur between related individuals than between nonrelated ones. That is, the behavior will favor the passage to the next generations of the genes eliciting it, as they are likely to occur in closely related individuals. The rule is that a costly action should be performed if $c < r \times b$. In this simple inequality c is the cost in fitness to the actor, r the genetic relatedness between the actor and the recipient (between 0 and 1), and b is the fitness benefit to the recipient. Fitness benefit is measured in the reproductive success of the actor. Hamilton's rule is the basis of kin selection theory. It is used to explain the majority of social behaviors in diverse species found in nature. Yet many prosocial behaviors and altruistic acts are performed among genetically unrelated individuals. This is especially true as human social groups became larger throughout human evolution. Thus, Hamilton's rule cannot be used to explain all types of prosocial behaviors within human social groups.

Another feature that might tilt the balance in favor of prosocial behavior beside genetic relatedness is the *social synergy* achieved by social cooperation.[11] Social synergy means that the effectiveness and efficiency of action by a group is more than the sum of the individual actions of the group members. As an example, the cooperative group effort of a football team can advance a ball down the playing field in a more effective and efficient manner than if the individual members of the team each tried to do this individually and not in a coordinated and planned way. As another example, the cooperative effort of the crew of a large sailing ship can get the ship to sail in the desired direction more effectively and efficiently than the sum of the individual actions of the different crew members if they were not coordinated. That is, social cooperation can be achieved and maintained even among unrelated individuals if the collective benefit of the prosocial behavior is very big, so as to eventually benefit also the altruist. Computer simulations[12] and empirical evidence, for example, evidence from interspecies interaction in insects,[13] suggest that when the synergy or benefits achieved by a given prosocial behavior is very large, social behavior is evolutionarily stable. In other words, when the benefits of being part of society are very high, compliance to social norms is easier.

Not always are the benefits to the individual of being part of a social group evident from the very beginning to the individual. When the individuals are not related or the eventual long-term benefits of sociality are not very large, prosocial behavior could be stabilized through punishment of the free-riders. When punishment of a free-rider is done by another individual group member, such punishment could incur an individual cost to the punishing individual. The cost could be in resources or time or by retribution to the individual or the individual's family from the person who is punished. Therefore, because there are individual costs involved, when an individual punishes a free-rider in the group, this is called altruistic punishment. The entire group benefits from punishing the free-rider but only the punishing individual bears the cost of being the punisher. Nevertheless, the occurrence of altruistic punishment, through which individuals punish other individuals for failing to act prosocially, increases the costs of free-riding for the free-rider. It thereby improves the option of individuals in the group engaging in prosocial behavior.[14,15] The problem is that because altruistic punishment is also costly to the individual who is doing the punishment, rational individuals would, again, be more inclined to let others assume the costs of punishing the free-rider individually, while still enjoying the fruits of prosocial behavior by being a member of the social group.

If human ancestral groups were, on the contrary, able to display cooperative punishment, and sustain the capacity for cooperative punishment for long periods of time, they would be curbing the biological fitness of congenital free-riders, while raising the biological fitness of congenital altruists.[16] A "congenital" free-rider or altruist is someone who has the genetic predisposition to be a nonfair or fair reciprocator in reference to his or her social group.[17] By "cooperative punishment" we mean punishment that is carried out by rule or law or order of the social group, even though individuals in the social group may be actually giving the punishment as agents of the social group. Birds, for example, commonly engage in a communal behavior called mobbing,[18] which serves to defend themselves or their offspring from predators. An analogous example of cooperative punishment in humans in modern societies is incarceration in prison for persons found guilty of serious crimes, or paying specialists (i.e., policemen and prison guards) to punish efficiently.[19] In other words, cooperative versus individual altruistic punishment creates the perfect environment for the biological evolution of prosocial altruism.[20] As we will develop in this chapter, religion could have played and may still play such a role as the substrate for dispensing cooperative punishment. We also will present what we believe are good reasons, at least from a biological perspective, why some religion can do this in some circumstances better than a form of secular governance.

The next question is, how can one go about showing scientifically that this could be the case—that cooperative punishment could have played a role in the emergence of prosocial altruism in human social groups of unrelated individuals? It is not possible to go back in time when human social groups were getting larger than small hunter-gatherer bands and becoming composed of unrelated individuals. That change may have occurred on a large scale sometime around 10,000 or so years ago when agriculture and animal husbandry began to replace the hunter-gatherer band. Humans could then live in larger groups of unrelated individuals by having domesticated animals and growing cereal grains and rice outside of and around the population centers. There are only two ways of showing what the role of cooperative punishment may have been in the evolution of prosocial altruism. One way is by what are called computer simulations. The other way is by setting up a game scenario for modern humans that looks at the degree to which people engage in prosocial altruism versus selfish free-riding as a function of their religious affiliation or nonaffiliation. That way is covered in the next chapter. In this chapter we will address the question by computer simulations.

COMPUTER SIMULATIONS

To show scientifically that cooperative punishment could facilitate the evolution of prosocial altruism in human populations of unrelated individuals, we have modeled through computer simulation the evolution of a virtual population of 500 hunter-gatherers by means of a computer program called SOCIODYNAMICA,[21] previously used to model economic aspects of altruistic cooperation,[22] altruistic punishment,[23] and the role of shame in stabilizing cooperation.[24]

All 500 individuals in the virtual population agree to contribute part of their hunting and gathering efforts in order to form a common pile of food every economic period that would ensure the diversity of nutrients they need. Such diverse nutrients could hardly be obtained individually, which creates the social synergy previously discussed. In the simulation each individual collects 3 food units in each economic period. The prosocial individuals ($s = 1$) contribute with 1 unit of food to the common food pile each period. The resulting common food pile is periodically distributed evenly among all group members, independently of their individual contribution. A fixed expense for each individual is survival, which is simulated here by a cost of 0.5 food units each period. When the accumulated wealth of an individual is larger than 2 units, it will use its excess wealth for self-reproduction, at a cost of 2 units per clone. A lifetime of an individual consists of only 10 periods, and random death is constantly introduced to keep the population steady at 500. Every new clone will be identical genetically to its parent except for an occasional mutation, which occurs on average at a rate that affects 10 percent of all new genes.

We set up the simulation so that at first, half of the actors are congenital prosocial altruists in the sense that they always honor their commitments of contributing 1 food unit to the common food pile, while the other half of the actors are congenital free-riders that never do so. The free-riders keep all of their food for themselves. Later on, gene frequencies in the simulation will vary according to reproductive success of each type of agent, which in turn affects the size of the common pile gathered each period. The gene frequencies change because of the congenital aspect of being either a prosocial altruist or a selfish free-rider. Figure 13.1 reflects at each moment in time the percentage of prosocial genes within the population over a period of 50 periods in three different social scenarios—No Punishment, Altruistic Punishment, and Cooperative Punishment. Note that because the lifetime of the individual is only 10 periods, 50 periods represents several generations. The simulation could just as well have been made making the average lifetime of an individual 50 periods and looking at changes in gene frequencies in the population over 250 periods.

The following three different situations or social scenarios were explored with our simulations:

- *No Punishment (NP).* It is initially agreed that the collecting system will rely entirely on people's good will, with no monitoring and enforcement of the social contract.

- *Altruistic Punishment (AP).* To tackle the free-riders problem, group members are allowed to enforce the social contract by punishing individually those who fail to contribute, which involves a detraction of food units. Since free-riders will presumably resist being punished, altruistic punishers will also incur certain costs.

- *Cooperative Punishment (CP).* Here, group members apply punishment cooperatively, meaning that the costs of punishing free-riders are not assumed by a few freelance punishers, but distributed among all society members (operationally implemented by detracting the aggregate costs of punishment from the common pile).

The summary of the different variables used in the simulations is given in Table 13.1.

RESULTS

The simulations showed that the successful enforcement of social norms, required as a precondition for the evolution of prosocial altruism, is highly dependent on keeping punishment costs low, on the one hand, and punishment effectiveness high, on the other, thereby increasing the cost-effectiveness of punishment (K/C). This can be clearly seen from Figure 13.1.

In Figure 13.1, the NP curve reflects the situation of a zero percent effectiveness in punishment ($E = 0$). The AP curve, for its part, always remains below the CP line. The CP curve shows that the social system begins to work when the cost/benefit ratio is below a threshold of 0.5.

In Figure 13.2 we show the number of agents that show prosocial behavior at equilibrium for systems with different punishment

Table 13.1
Variables defining the rules of the game in the simulations.

Society	Defined by the use of the social contribution *C*. Societies simulated were: No Punishment (*NP*), Altruistic Punishment (*AP*) or Cooperative (Collective) Punishment (*CP*).
C	Contribution. Was paid as a proportion of the wealth accumulated by the agent. All agents with $s = 1$ paid their contribution.
Y	Cost to the punisher. In the present simulations $Y = C$.
K	Cost of the fine extracted to the punished agents.
E	Efficiency in punishing free-riders (agents with $s = 0$). This efficiency is given as the percentage of free-riders punished. In the NP social scenario, $E = 0$.
P	Proportion of prosocial agents in the particular social scenario: $100 \times$ Agents with $s = 1$ / agent with $s = 0$.

efficiencies (*E*). The figure shows that prosocial behavior can be sustained if more than *half* of the infractions are punished (that is, $E > 60$).

The findings can be summarized by saying that the cost of punishment to the punisher times the probability of having to pay the cost of punishment by the punisher is less than the cost of punishment paid by the free-rider times the probability of the free-rider having to pay the cost. For those readers who like to think about such relationships symbolically the following inequality summarizes our findings analytically:

$$C \times p_c < K \times p_k$$

where *C* is the punishment cost, *K* is the cost of the punishment paid by the free-rider if caught, and p_c and p_k are the probability of having to pay the cost *C* or the cost *K*, respectively.

What the preceding analytic inequality shows is that social behavior is evolutionarily stable if the cost of punishment times the probability of having to pay a cost for punishing is much less than the cost the punished individual has to pay times the likelihood that he is caught

Figure 13.1.   Average of *P* reached when simulating three different societies (NP, AP, CP) at different ratios of the costs to the punished *K* and the cost to the punishers *C*. The efficiency of reaching free-riders for punishment *E* = 60%.

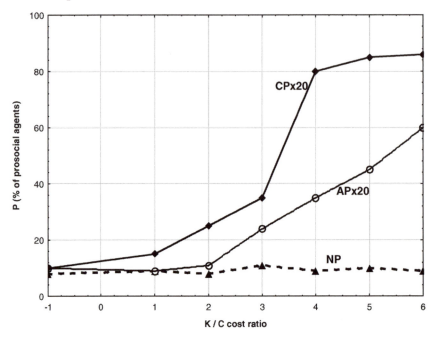

and has to pay a fine. Recent experimental evidence from economic games confirms that the *K/C* ratio and p_k are fundamental in triggering altruistic punishment.[25]

DISCUSSION

Our results show that cooperative punishment has a critical quality of dividing the costs of punishment among society members, and has the potential to enhance the cost-effectiveness of punishment significantly, by both reducing its costs and increasing its effectiveness.

Cooperative punishment eventually achieves a reduction in the costs of punishment as a consequence of the synergy that typically results from cooperation.[26] Strong resistance may be expected when one individual tries to punish another individual, leading potentially to considerable damage to the punisher. But when various individuals punish someone cooperatively, resistance may be expected to fall

Figure 13.2. **Average values for *P* derived from simulations in the three different scenarios (NP, AP, CP), where *c* = *p* = 1 and *p*´ = 2. *E* varies from 0 to 100, as indicated in the horizontal axis. Data points represent the average of 200 simulations, each consisting of 200 time steps.**

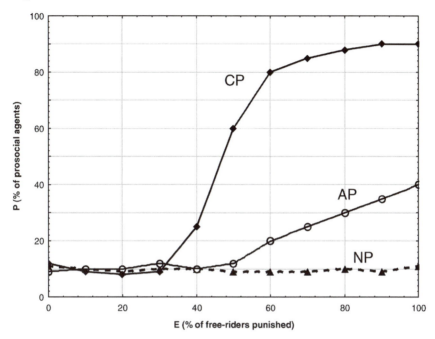

dramatically. When a large group of individuals decide to engage in punishment, a simple sign of their willingness may be sufficient to convince the violator to follow the rules, which means that the costs of punishment would be virtually reduced to zero.

Another benefit of cooperative punishment is that it may increase the effectiveness of punishment as a result of the combined capacities of all society members in monitoring individual behavior, making it possible to detect infractions in a way that noncooperative freelance punishers could not.

Certainly, cooperative punishment involves additional costs in terms of the observations, evaluations, and discussions required to reach agreement and to maintain a cohesive flux of information. In constituted societies punishment costs may actually lay for the most part in these necessary proceedings rather than in execution of punishment itself. We believe, however, that in the end all these factors add up to the cost-effectiveness of cooperative punishment, reinforcing its power to exert a consistent selective pressure leading to the evolution of prosocial altruism.

Forming a group or maintaining a religion, of course, has a cost, which might be quite high. Historically, not all religions necessarily aimed at improving harmony among humans.[27] Some religions might develop important social functions, such as promoting prosocial behavior,[28] and thus guarantee their long-term survival, but others might not and eventually go extinct.[29] But once a group exists, excluding a member from the group (banning, isolating, excommunicating, shaming, lowering his or her reputation, etc.) is a very cheap way of applying a large punishment (K) at a low additional cost to punishers (C). Moral punishment is a very ancient human practice and may be common in many social institutions, including most religions. Based on the simulation results, we propose then that the prosocial effect of religions is mainly through cooperative punishment.

Our simulations showed the importance of the K/C ratio in achieving evolutionarily stable prosocial behavior. The K/C ratio is the cost of the fine extracted to the punisher divided by the prosocial contribution made by the agent. A way to maximize inequality $C < K$ is to make $C = 0$, $K = \infty$ (and $p_k = 1$). This is achieved by religions where God is the one who punishes[30] so that for humans $C = 0$, and where the punishment is hell for eternity ($K = \infty$). Superhuman gods, of course, find free-riders with $p = 1$.

This means that the prosocial effect achieved by cooperative punishment might be an evolutionary driver for those religions that favor prosocial behavior, making them adaptive in evolutionary terms and favoring their maintenance. This effect, however, does not explain the evolutionary origins of religion.

An empirical way to falsify the propositions made here involves finding a way to quantify the costs of being punished or excluded from social groups and to compare them with the costs of participation. If such costs can be quantified, it should then be feasible to measure the effect religions have on each of these costs. Intuitively, it seems obvious that religion makes exclusion from a group much easier, which in turn elevates the costs to free-riders, without increasing the cost of participation in the religion. Many a modern social structure seems to draw on this strength, exploited by all religions, to enhance their performance.

Recent work by the researchers Dominic Johnson and Oliver Kruger[31] seems to confirm that there exists a robust relationship between God's punishment and public goods. They tested the supernatural punishment hypothesis in 186 world cultures. This work was based on the fact that cooperation toward public goods relies on credible threats of punishment to deter cheats. However, punishing is costly, so it remains unclear who incurred the costs of enforcement in our evolutionary past. The theoretical work presented here suggests that human cooperation is promoted if people believe in supernatural punishment for moral transgressions. Using the data from 186 societies around the globe, Johnson showed that the likelihood of supernatural punishment—indexed by the importance of moralizing "high gods"—is associated with cooperation. These studies, however, do not consider the ratio between the cost of punishment (K) and the cost to punish (C). Further studies including these insights could prove to increase our understanding of the adaptive values of religions.

SUMMARY

Punishment is often required to enforce prosocial behavior. Using the agent-based computer simulation model SOCIODYNAMICA, we show that the cost/benefit ratio of punishment is critical for its evolutionary establishment and maintenance. One way to reduce this ratio is to distribute the costs of punishment evenly among all group members such as in mobbing. This solution, however, is sensitive to the ability of the group to reach most free-riders for eventual punishment. The simulations show that if punishment costs can be distributed among group members and punishment reaches over 60 percent of the individuals, the establishment of prosocial behavior can be assured. We propose that religions allow the implementation of cooperative punishment among human societies, stabilizing prosocial behavior. Religions have a cost of establishment and maintenance, but once in existence they can implement supernatural punishment that achieves infinitely large punishment at zero cost to humans. Religions exploit cooperative punishments by banning noncompliers from their protective benefits and condemning them to eternal sufferings, maximizing punishment while minimizing the cost for punishment. The simulations show that any institution able to reduce the cost for punishment while increasing punishment is likely to become an evolutionarily adaptive strategy, but that only religions are able to maximize the cost-benefit ratio by promising hell forever to noncompliers at no additional cost to the remaining religious practitioners.

APPENDIX
MATHEMATICAL FORMULATION OF THE MODEL

The model emulates a widely used experimental economics game in which each member of a group is provided an endowment, b, that increases every time step in 3 units, which can be kept or invested in a public good. The combined investment in the public good is multiplied by a factor, s, and distributed equally to everyone in the group. The total payoff of each individual (the proportion of the endowment kept for oneself plus one's share of the public good) is related to fitness as excess food is used to produce offspring. In the present set of experiments, $s = 1$. Increasing "s" will increase the odds for cooperative strategies to invade the population.[32] Thus, $s = 1$ is a very stringent condition for cooperators to survive.

The accumulated wealth-fitness (W) of either cooperators (c) or free-riders (f) is as follows:

$$W_c = \Sigma_c \, b + s - c$$

$$W_f = \Sigma_f \, b + s - p$$

Where:

  b = amount of resources received through feeding (constant)
  c = cost of cooperation (constant)
  p = cost of punishment × probability of being punished

The benefit received through social cooperation (s) is defined as follows:

$$s = (n_c \times c \times \alpha - \Sigma p') \, / \, (n_c + n_f)$$

Where:
  α = synergy achieved trough social cooperation
  p' = cost to punish the captured free-riders
  n_c = total number of cooperators
  n_f = total number of free-riders

NOTES

1. Hamilton, W. D. (1964). The genetical theory of social behavior I, II. *Journal of Theoretical Biology*, 7, 1–52.

2. Dawkins, R. (1976). *The selfish gene*. Oxford: Oxford University Press.

3. Trivers, R. L. (1971). The evolution of reciprocal altruism. *Quarterly Review of Biology, 46*, 35–57.

4. Axelrod, R. (1984). *The evolution of cooperation*. New York: Basic Books.

5. Bowles, S., & Gintis, H. (2004). The evolutionary basis of collective action. *Santa Fe Working Papers* (pp. 1–20). Santa Fe, NM: Santa Fe Institute.

6. Fehr, E., & Gächter, S. (2002). Altruistic punishment in humans. *Nature, 415*, 137–140.

7. Hobbes, T. (1994 [1652]). *Leviathan*. Indianapolis, Cambridge: Hackett Publishing Company.

8. Gintis, H. (2003). The hitchhikers guide to altruism: Genes and culture, and the internalization of norms. *Journal of Theoretical Biology, 220*, 407–418.

9. Mealey, L. (1995). The sociobiology of sociopathy: An integrated evolutionary model. *Behavioral and Brain Sciences, 18*(3), 523–599.

10. Zaballa, L. (2006). *Polis: A natural history of society*. Kiev: Dukh i Litera, Mohyla Academy—National University of Kiev.

11. Jaffe, K. (2001). On the relative importance of haplo-diploidy, assortative mating and social synergy on the evolutionary emergence of social behavior. *Acta Biotheoretica, 49*, 29–42.

12. Jaffe, K. (2002). An economic analysis of altruism: Who benefits from altruistic acts?" *Journal of Artificial Societies and Social Simulations, 5*(3).

13. Osborn, F., & Jaffe, K. (1997). Cooperation vs. exploitation: Interactions between Lycaenid (Lepidoptera: Lycaenidae) larvae and ants. *Journal of Research on the Lepidoptera, 34*, 69–82.

14. Boyd, R., Gintis, H., Bowles, S., & Richerson, P. J. (2003). The evolution of altruistic punishment. *Proceedings of the National Academy of Sciences, 100*(6), 3531–3535.

15. Fehr, E. (2000). Cooperation and punishment. *American Economic Review, 90*, 980–994.

16. Sober, E., & Wilson, D. S. (1998). *Unto others: The evolution and psychology of unselfish behavior*. Cambridge, MA: Harvard University Press.

17. Quervain D., Fischbacher, U., Treyer, V., Schellhammer, M., Schnyder, U., Buck, A., & Fehr, E. (2004). The neural basis of altruistic punishment. *Science, 305*, 1254–1258.

18. Lorenz, K. (2002). *On aggression*. London: Routledge Classics. (Also available at Google Books.)

19. O'Gorman, R., Henrich, J., & Van Vugt, M. (2008). Constraining free riding in public goods games: Designated solitary punishers can sustain human cooperation. *Proceedings of the Royal Society B*, DOI 10.1098/rspb.2008.1082.

20. Hauser, M. D. (2006). *Moral minds: How nature designed our universal sense of right and wrong*. New York: HarperCollins.

21. SOCIODYNAMICA, written by Klaus Jaffe, is freeware available at http://atta.labb.usb.ve/Klaus/Programas.htm.

22. Jaffe, K. (2002). An economic analysis of altruism: Who benefits from altruistic acts? *Journal of Artificial Societies and Social Simulations*, 5(3). Available at http://jasss.soc.surrey.ac.uk/5/3/3.html.

23. Jaffe, K. (2004). Altruism, altruistic punishment, and decentralized social investment. *Acta Biotheorica*, 52, 155–172.

24. Jaffe, K. (2006). Simulations show that shame drives social cohesion. In J. S. Sichman et al. (Eds.), *IBERAMIA-SBIA* (pp. 88–97). Berlin: Springer-Verlag.

25. Egas, M., & Riedl, A. (2008). The economics of altruistic punishment and the maintenance of cooperation. *Proceedings of the Royal Society B*, 275, 871–878.

26. Zaballa, L., & Jaffe, K. (submitted). Hobbesian selection: Explaining the evolution of prosocial altruism through co-operative punishment.

27. Stark, R. (2008). The complexities of comparative research. *Interdisciplinary Journal of Research on Religion*, 4, 2–15 [3].

28. Norenzayan, A., & Shariff, A. F. (2008). The origin and evolution of religious prosociality. *Science*, 322, 58–62.

29. Boyer, P. (2008). Being human: Religion: Bound to believe? *Nature*, 455, 1038–1039.

30. Johnson, D. D. P., & Krüger, O. (2004). The good of wrath: Supernatural punishment and the evolution of cooperation. *Political Theology*, 5(2), 159–176.

31. Johnson, D. D. P. (2006). God's punishment and public goods: A test of the supernatural punishment hypothesis in 186 world cultures. *Human Nature*, 16, 410–446.

32. Jaffe, K. (2002). An economic analysis of altruism: Who benefits from altruistic acts? *Journal of Artificial Societies and Social Simulations*, 5(3). Available at http://jasss.soc.surrey.ac.uk/5/3/3.html.

CHAPTER 14

Religious Behavior and Cooperation

Maria Emília Yamamoto, Monique Leitão, Rochele Castelo-Branco, and Fívia de Araújo Lopes

Religion has been studied from a number of different perspectives from the social sciences to evolutionary biology. The methods in which religion can be investigated are also variable. William Grassie,[1] director of the Metanexus Institute on Religion and Science, suggests that religion could be studied from the inside, according to the devotee's view. Using this method, the goal is to understand the meaning of living in a social context with other humans in a universe imbued with power, purpose, and significance. See also Lluis Oviedo's comments on this issue in Chapter 9 in this volume. But religion and religious behavior can also be studied from the outside in an objective and scientific context where one can investigate such questions as the adaptiveness of religious behavior. That is the approach taken in this chapter in terms of the relationship between religiosity and cooperation. By cooperation we mean helping someone else achieve his or her goal rather than just acting in one's own best interest. The opposite of cooperation is selfishness. Cooperative behavior represented a dilemma for the evolutionary explanation: why would natural selection favor self-sacrifice, especially reproductive self-sacrifice, and how could that characteristic be passed on to subsequent generations by nonbreeding individuals? But a careful look at nature shows a large amount of behavior that could be considered all but selfish: alarm calls, grooming, ritual fighting that avoids serious injuries, adoption of infants, and so forth. All these actions are apparently contrary to the idea of natural selection; but they will become perfectly compatible if we understand them as a way for the individual to increase his/her fitness. British evolutionary biologist William D. Hamilton was the first to propose that actions like the ones described above could be explained by an increase in one's fitness as explained by the processes of kin selection and reciprocity.[2]

To understand human cooperation and generosity from an evolutionary perspective, we have to go back to the human origins, not only to the early *Homo sapiens* but even before, when the first great apes and hominids started to cooperate. Many of the human behavioral characteristics were shaped in a much more primitive environment that did not have the technological advances that are part of our lives nowadays.

That primitive environment is known as Environment of Evolutionary Adaptiveness. Many of our present behaviors and physical characteristics were selected in that environment. That means there is a time lag between the modern environment and many of our adaptations, which responded to pressures that are not present anymore. That also means that we have to learn more about the way our ancestors behaved to understand why we behave like we do today.[3]

Hunting and gathering was presumably the only subsistence strategy employed by hominid societies for more than two million years, until the end of the Mesolithic Period. Evidence from modern hunter-gatherers suggests that our ancestors' bands were small, varying between 25 and 50 members, with a median group size of 30. Hunter-gatherers were mostly egalitarians. Reciprocity of favors was not mandatory, except from a moral perspective. Nevertheless, the moral obligation that permeated social life was probably what made human societies possible.[4,5]

Human bands remained small until the onset of agriculture and pastoralism around 10,000 years ago. The growth of human populations favored the emergence of individuals who took advantage of cooperative members of the group to enjoy favors without returning them. These individuals, called free-riders, benefited from formal or informal social contracts, called the common good, but did not contribute by paying for their costs, for which the other group members paid. See Chapter 13 by Klaus Jaffe and Luis Zaballa for more on the common good problem. One example of free-riding in the modern society is the individual who jumps over the subway turnstile and does not pay for the ticket, using freely a service that is paid by all paying passengers.[6,7] Any society can support, and obviously does, a certain number of free-riders. However, when that number is exceeded, the maintenance of the benefit itself is jeopardized. Just imagine what would happen to public transportation if the majority of commuters did not pay for the service.

As suggested by Florida State University anthropologist Frank Marlowe,[8] small scale, face-to-face cooperative societies such as the ones described above were the only ones that could on one hand control free-riders, and on the other hand favor food sharing, the first presumed form of unselfish behavior among early humans. See more on the functions of human food sharing in Chapter 12 by Rick Goldberg. However, social controls could only be maintained as long as the bands remained small and relatively stable during long time spans. The reason for this is that in small groups free-riders are easily identified and punished. In large groups, however, a free-rider could be extremely successful in exploiting one group for a while, unpunished, and then leave to exploit another group.[9]

Throughout our evolutionary history, humans evolved psychological mechanisms to cope with free-riders and with individuals who do not return their generosity; one such mechanism is the assessment of reputation. Reputation can be acquired by a history of good deeds. However, because the individual's history is not always accessed easily, it can sometimes be indicated by a badge. Examples of such badges given in our society are wearing an honor medal or an "I donated blood" pin. The image of an individual's reputation may also be enhanced by his or her affiliation with a group that is selective in its membership criteria, such as religious groups that demand the performance of costly rituals that are difficult to fake.[10] Religious affiliation could, therefore, be a mark for reputation.

There are many ways in which religion can be defined. In his work, Grassie proposed a concept of religion based on Clifford Geertz's writings. In this sense, religion is the following: (a) a system of symbols that acts to (b) establish powerful, pervasive, and long-lasting moods and motivations in people by (c) formulating conceptions of a general order of existence and (d) clothing these conceptions with such an aura of factuality that (e) the moods and motivations seem uniquely realistic. This notion does not prejudge the content of beliefs, practices, and values. It allows one to regard religion as a universal component of human existence.[11] It is this universal component of human existence concept of religion that we will use as a reference in this chapter.

Individuals involved in religious activities identify themselves as part of a group. Theoretically, one would predict that they should preferentially direct their helping and other behaviors to in-group members, related or not, who would be their peers. This prediction is in accordance with the idea of ethnocentrism, which means the tendency to view the world from the perspective of one's own cultural in-group.[12] Sociologist Frans Roes and Michael Raymond,[13] research director at the Centre National de la Research Scientifique (Paris), suggested that with increasing group size, social conflicts, especially between unrelated in-group members, could increase. Increased in-group conflict could cause a lack of biological fitness to the in-group members as well as make the group less competitive in their interactions with other groups.

Religion could act as a mean of controlling such in-group conflict by increasing group cohesion and promoting social order and morality.[14] Religious rituals can provide the feeling of belonging to a group and of being under divine protection. They may also contribute to ideas of solidarity and equality, promoting values and behaviors related to acceptance, tolerance, help, and support to in-group peers.[15] External conflicts between societies, resource rich environments, and the size of societies, all are positively correlated with belief in moralizing gods. Moral rules are more convincing if they have been imposed by impartial gods without material or reproductive interests, in contrast to those imposed by humans, which could generate the suspicion that some members of the group would benefit more from these rules than others. In this way, the moralizing gods could help to maintain a social order.[16]

The social functions of religion, according to evolutionary anthropologist Pascal Boyer, are evident: hold society together, perpetuate a particular social order, and support morality.[17] In this sense the relationship between human evolution and religion is interwoven. How does this interwoven relationship between human evolution and the various social functions of religion help us to understand how religion could have evolved? In fact, we do not know how religion evolved. We only have theories that are supported by evidence of varying degrees of persuasiveness. Let us look at the two main theories on how religion could have evolved.

Joseph Bulbulia,[18] senior lecturer on religious studies at Victoria University, New Zealand, discusses two theoretical evolutionary propositions for religion's evolution: the first one suggests that religion-related behaviors represent a human biological adaptation, growing within the social context of cooperation among groups and allowing the identifications of reliable cooperators. Thus, religions could be considered a kind of "social glue" that supports identity, cohesion, and cooperation within groups. The second theoretical proposition argues that religion is a by-product of something else not related to religion but that was or still is adaptive. In this last theoretical proposition, religion itself would not need to have any adaptiveness or survival value. Rather, religion would have emerged and would currently exist as a consequence of the evolution of something like a hypersensitive agency detection device, called "HADD" in the cognitive theory of mind literature.[19] This type of conceptualization would make religion a *spandrel*, a term proposed by prominent paleontologist and evolutionary biologist Stephen Gould and American geneticist Richard Lewontin.[20] A spandrel is the inverted triangle between two functional architectural arches that only exists as a by-product of the arches. If one makes arches, one will automatically get spandrels as by-products.

Regardless of whether religion is considered an adaptation or a spandrel-like by-product of an adaptation, membership in a religion still signals commitment to the group and strengthening of group identity in accordance with the model of ethnocentric behavior proposed by economist Ross Hammond and political scientist Robert Axelrod, who is the author of some of the most frequently cited publications on human cooperation.[21] Ethnocentrism exists in all cultures. The presumption is that ethnocentric behavior derives from an evolved mechanism.[22,23] If belonging to a specific religion is an example of one of the mechanisms of ethnocentric behavior, we would expect that cooperation would be more frequent between members of a given religion (in-group) than between members of different religions or between religious and nonreligious individuals. We would also expect that the mechanism promoting this in-group cooperation would be the perception of belonging to the group, as suggested by Boyer,[24] evolutionary psychologist Robert Kurzban, and social psychologist Steven Neuberg.[25]

Some studies have investigated the relation between religion and cooperation. Behavioral ecologist and anthropologist Richard Sosis and economist Bradley Ruffle[26] compared Israeli kibbutzim that differed regarding their religious commitment and concluded that the most religious were the most cooperative. Azim Shariff and Ara Norenzayan,[27] scientists from the University of British Columbia, argued that this conclusion does not mean that religious individuals are more cooperative per se. In their study, using an anonymous dictator game, similar results were found when they compared the amount of money donated to strangers by individuals when the authors activated (using the scrambled-sentence paradigm) in the donators God concepts or concepts associated with secular moral institutions.[28] God concepts and the concepts associated with secular moral institutions were considered as moralizing agents that restrained selfishness, even outside of reflective awareness. This suggests that an agency detector, such as the HADD, is activated by both religious and secular stimuli, and that both may trigger the tendency to infer the presence of an intentional watcher and to favor generosity by fear of potential damage to the individual's reputation.

Previous studies on cooperation and religion have been reported on societies that present low religious diversity compared to what is found in contemporary Brazil. This nation is the one with the greatest number of Catholics in the world. On the other hand, it has a surprisingly low proportion of individuals who declare themselves as Catholic and who attend religious services regularly. Another particularity is the large number of religious denominations in Brazil.[29] Also, during the past few decades, the religious panorama in Brazil has been changing. A recent publication[30] compared 1940 and 2000 national population surveys. It shows striking changes in the distribution of declared religions among the population (Table 14.1). During that time interval there was a decrease of more than 20 percent in the number of Catholics, a sixfold increase in the percentage of Evangelicals and an astonishing 36-fold increase in the percentage of individuals who declared that they did not have a religion. This particular arrangement of religious groups presents an interesting framework within which to analyze the modulation of social cooperation among and across religious and nonreligious individuals. A useful aspect of this investigation is its potential application to other countries and/or social contexts.

The aim of the study that we are reporting in this chapter was to test whether religion facilitates in-group cooperation among individuals. As the reader will see, we were able to set up an experimental design in which the relationships between religiosity and cooperation to nonrelated strangers could be studied in a quantitative way. We acknowledge that for this relationship to be fully understood a number of studies need to be done, as no one study can be representative of the actual real-life conditions. If religion does facilitate in-group cooperation, does it do so solely by being an in-group marker or are there other factors peculiar to religious in-groups that would facilitate in-group cooperation?

Table 14.1
Percent distribution of the population according to religion in Brazil in the years 1940 and 2000. (Courtesy of the Brazilian Council for Ethics in Scientific Research.)

	Distribution (%)	
Religion	**1940**	**2000**
Catholic	95.0	76.3
Evangelical	2.6	15.3
Other religions	1.9	3.4
Without religion	0.2	7.4

We tested these ideas through the administration of an online game in which the cooperative token donation behaviors of religious and nonreligious subjects were investigated. We also analyzed the effect of belonging to a particular group (Evangelical or atheist) on cooperative behaviors of the subjects. By looking at a player's profile during the game, it was possible for the subject player to know the past donation history of the other players.

Some important questions were addressed: (a) Should religious-minded individuals, who believe that they were subject to in-group vigilance and God's supervision, be more cooperative in general? (b) Should a consequence of the perception of belonging to a particular group (ethnocentrism) also cause nonreligious subjects to perceive themselves as belonging to an in-group of nonreligious individuals and therefore cause them to be more cooperative among themselves? (c) What is the importance of reputation (past donation history) as compared to membership in a particular in-group in an anonymous game-playing task such as the one presented in this study?

METHOD

SUBJECTS

We assessed two groups of individuals who exhibited the two opposite extremes in terms of involvement with religion. The first group was self-reported Evangelicals, who in Brazil are characterized by active and frequent religious practice. The second group was self-reported atheists. In total, 118 subjects—60 Evangelicals and

58 atheists (48 women and 70 men) with mean age of 29.7 (standard deviation = 2.8 years)—took part in the study.

E-mail invitations were sent to individuals selected from a Brazilian, Portuguese language chat site based on the religion professed on their personal pages (Evangelicals and atheists). In addition, we recruited university undergraduates in classrooms without controlling for their religion.[31] All of the participants were informed that they would be part of a study on cooperation, but nothing was mentioned about the relationship between cooperation and religion. We invited 927 individuals to participate in the study. Of those 927 individuals invited to participate, 320 of them (34.51 percent) agreed. From these 320 individuals we selected 58 atheists and 60 Evangelicals for our study.

THE GAME

To ensure cooperation and to test cooperativeness among the players, we created an online game in which the object was to accumulate the greatest number of tokens at the end. There was not a real gain to accrue from the game, but we took advantage of the fact that young people enjoy playing games on the computer and on the Internet just for the fun of it. Winning or trying to win is a motivation that maintains the behavior of teenagers and young adults for hours. The game that we offered used that motivation. The game was accessed on an Internet site by an individual password sent privately to each of the subjects. This password was deactivated after each subject had played, making it impossible for a particular subject to play more than once. To play, all of the subjects had to sign an informed consent form and fill out a sociodemographic data form, after which the rules of the game were explained to them.[32] From now on, the term *subject* will refer to the individual playing the game who we were studying and the term *players* will refer to all of the individuals playing the game, including the subject and the other players.

The game was always performed by five players, so when viewing the game scenario the subject faced four other players and observed profile cards that contained information about each of the players, which included religion, age, marital state, and schooling level (Figure 14.1). We did not give any information on the sex of the players as we considered that playing against a male or a female opponent could induce the use of different strategies. The subject's own information card was included on screen as one of the five players.

Figure 14.1.   Screen presented to the subjects when playing the online game.

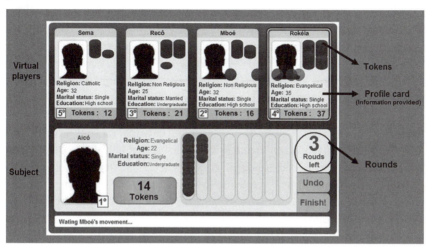

Furthermore, the players were assigned an automatically generated, gender-neutral pseudonym, exhibited on the profile card.[33] During the game, the subjects could interact with the four other players by donating or receiving tokens. The subject could choose the number of tokens to donate and to whom to donate them, or even choose not to donate any tokens at all. All the players started with 20 tokens and five rounds were played. The donations could not occur between the same pair of players in each of the five rounds, which eliminated the possibility of direct reciprocity between any two individuals at the same round. At any one point in time it was possible to visualize the number of tokens each player possessed as well as the movements made by each player. We established those rules because we did not want the game to turn into an exchange of the kind "you give me and I will give you back," but rather to offer opportunities for interaction among all players.

The study subjects, however, were not aware that their opponents were virtual players with donation patterns previously programmed by the system. To assess the effect of the opponents' religion on a subject's playing pattern, the game was set up so that the subject always faced one Evangelical, one Catholic, and two nonreligious opponent players. The other information, such as age and educational level, on the virtual players' profile cards was randomly generated. The study subject was always the first to play in each round, which was established at the onset of the game by a simulated draw that indicated the order of play during the game.

The virtual players' donations were carefully programmed so that we could evaluate if the opponent players' token donation pattern would affect the cooperative behavior of the subjects. Thus, there were always two opponent players who were very generous with their donations, giving away exactly 60 percent of their tokens in each movement. There were also two other opponent players who were less generous, donating only 20 percent of their tokens in each movement. We set up two experimental situations, so that 43 individuals were submitted to a situation in which the religious opponent players were most generous and gave the highest donations and the nonreligious opponent players the lowest donations. Another 43 subjects were tested in the second situation in which the donation patterns were inverted. In this scenario the nonreligious opponent players were the highest donors and the religious opponent players the least.

At the end of the game, the subjects who played the game responded to a questionnaire that investigated the frequency with which they took part in religious activities and how religious they considered themselves. There were also four other distracter questions that were asked. The responses to all the questions were on a 5-point Likert scale.

RESULTS[34]

RELIGION OF THE PARTICIPANTS

Analysis of the sociodemographic data of all 320 participants who played the game online and from whom we chose the 60 Evangelical and 58 atheist subjects for the study reported in this chapter showed a distribution of eight religious options among those provided on the game form (Figure 14.2).

Catholic, Evangelical, and atheist individuals were more represented in our study sample, corresponding to 33.75, 18.75, and 18.12 percent, respectively, of all the 320 participants who played the game. This distribution does not correspond to the natural one found in Brazil, as we directed most of the invitations to play the game to individuals who were in the extremes of religious practice, as mentioned before. This strategy was important for the recruitment of a

Figure 14.2. Distribution of subjects according to their self-proclaimed religion.

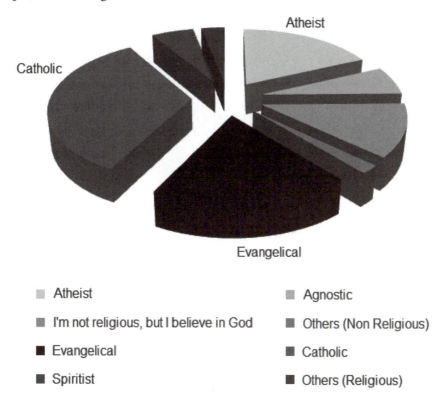

▧ Atheist	▨ Agnostic
■ I'm not religious, but I believe in God	■ Others (Non Religious)
■ Evangelical	■ Catholic
■ Spiritist	■ Others (Religious)

significant number of self-reported atheists, as they are much rarer in the Brazilian population in general.

GENERAL COOPERATION RATES

One of the indicators used in the present study to measure the general cooperative or generous behaviors of the subjects was the total number of tokens they donated to their opponent players during the online game. If we were to assume that religion acts as a promoter of general cooperation or generosity, we would then expect that the Evangelicals would be more cooperative in general than the atheists. However, that is not what we found. Analysis of mean token donation percentages between the two groups showed that general cooperative behavior did not differ. Both the Evangelicals and the atheists donated, on average, around 13 percent of their tokens in each round.[35] This absence of a difference between Evangelicals and atheists can already be seen in the first round of the game.[36] We also observed that both Evangelicals and atheists displayed the same pattern of progressive increase in token donations over the course of the game.[37]

Our data indicate that the religious subjects did not donate more tokens than the nonreligious subjects. These results go against the idea that being religious generates a higher level of general cooperative behavior in individuals.

Choosing with Whom to Play

Given that the Evangelicals and atheists were equally cooperative overall in terms of what percentage of their tokens they donated to other players, a number of other questions were investigated, such as the following: In what way do subjects interact with the other players? Which virtual players do the subjects choose to make their donations to? Was the cooperation rate of the subjects the same when they were playing with players of different religions?

We analyzed the subjects' choice of which other player to donate to and found differences between the Evangelicals and the atheists. The Evangelicals chose to interact more with other Evangelical players rather than the remaining players available[38] (see Figure 14.3). The same occurred with the atheists, who chose more often to play with nonreligious players[39] (see Figure 14.3). This differential selection was observed in the subjects from the moment they started playing, as the data on the choice of opponent players in the first round indicate, for both Evangelicals[40] and atheists.[41]

These analyses produced other interesting results: a comparison of the two groups of subjects (Evangelicals and atheists) studied shows that both groups preferred to *play* with participants with the same religious beliefs or nonbelief as theirs; however, this was significantly more pronounced in the Evangelicals than in the atheists[42] (see dotted line Figure 14.3). Thus, the Evangelicals showed greater group cohesion than atheists in terms of their choice of with whom to interact. However, with whom one preferentially interacts and to whom one preferentially donates tokens are not the same, as we will see below.

Figure 14.3.   Mean and standard deviations of the number of choices of opponent made by atheist and Evangelical subjects.

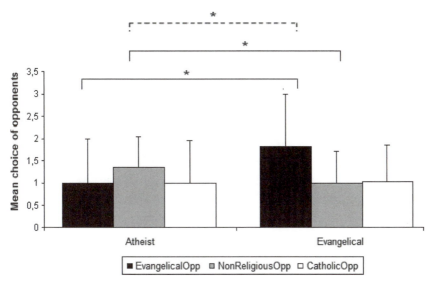

DONATING TO PEERS

Assessment of donation choices revealed that the atheists also exhibit in-group allegiance. A comparison within each group of subjects, considering mean token donation to each different class of players over the course of the game, showed that the atheists donated more tokens to nonreligious players than to the remaining players, a behavior not observed in the Evangelicals, who donated tokens almost evenly across all other classes of players (see Figure 14.4).

These results demonstrate, therefore, that even though both Evangelicals and atheists had a preference for playing with individuals within their own group, the Evangelicals chose to *interact* with, such as play with, other Evangelicals *more so* than the atheists chose to play with other atheists. On the other hand, atheists were preferentially *generous* when interacting with their peers, whereas Evangelicals were equally *generous* to all classes of other players. Thus, the data that we present are consistent in that they support the hypothesis that religion acts as an efficient in-group marker for whom one chooses to associate.

Figure 14.4.   Mean and standard deviations of donations made by atheist and Evangelical subjects to nonreligious, Evangelical, and Catholic opponents. The numbers refer to the percentage of tokens that the subject possessed when making the donation.

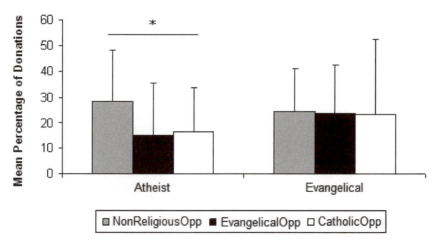

Choice of the Opponent According to the Opponent's Pattern of Donations

The pattern of donations between the subjects submitted to experimental situations showed that both Evangelicals and atheists exhibited a tendency to choose with whom to play according to the donation profile (generous or nongenerous) of the player. Thus, we observed that both Evangelicals (see Figure 14.5A) and atheists (see Figure 14.5B) chose religious players more frequently when they were the most generous donors. They both chose nonreligious players to play with when they donated more. The pattern of donation of the virtual players was the most important variable that influenced the choice of with whom to play.[43] More generous players received more donations, regardless of their religion.

DISCUSSION

Our results support that religion is an in-group marker. Evangelicals showed significantly more preference to play with other Evangelical players than did atheists with other nonreligious players. These findings are in agreement with reports from Shariff and

Figure 14.5.   Mean and standard deviation choice of opponents according to religious orientation by Evangelical (A) and atheists (B) subjects according to game configuration: generous religious player; generous nonreligious player.

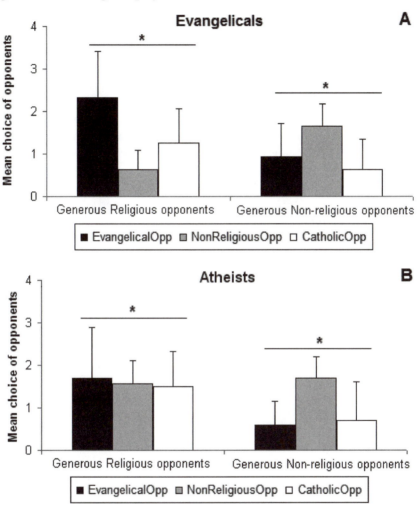

Norenzayan[44] and Sosis and Ruffle[45] that religious groups cooperate more within themselves than nonreligious groups. On the other hand, overall cooperation rates were similar in atheist and Evangelical subjects, suggesting that sharing religious beliefs was not necessary to promote overall cooperation in this virtual game.

The mechanism suggested for cooperation in the case of religious groups is the perception of belonging to the group.[46] This mechanism derives from adaptations that evolved in our hunter-gatherer ancestors as a means for detecting coalitions and other cooperative alliances. They are part of universal predispositions presented by the human mind that are believed to prepare the mind to think in a particular fashion and to react in certain ways.[47] Hammond and Axelrod[48] suggest that ethnocentrism is the result of one of those mechanisms. They suggest that the ability to discriminate between in-group and out-groups favors cooperation even when costs are high and there is no need for reciprocity. Religion clearly marks the boundaries of in-group and out-groups and therefore may favor ethnocentric behavior, cooperation included. However, an unexpected result was that not having a religion was also perceived as a coalition and promoted cooperation. As coalitional dispositions are usually transitory, an alliance tracking program should be designed to use cues that indicate belonging to a group.

In our game religion was readily identifiable. Cooperation was expected. But apparently not having a religion, especially in a country where atheists are regarded suspiciously,[49] may favor the feeling, when facing a fellow nonbeliever, that one has found a partner, someone who shares similar beliefs. That may happen even considering that those who do not have a religion are a much more diverse group, regarding beliefs, than those who share a religious denomination. Therefore, our results suggest that at least in a society where religion is not central to everyday life, it may act as an in-group marker that presents no more impact on cooperation than other strong markers.

One could argue that subjects and virtual players in fact did not belong to the same group, as subjects declared themselves atheists and virtual players were identified only as "nonreligious." Nevertheless, subjects treated nonreligious players differently from religious players (Catholics and Evangelicals), choosing to play with the former preferentially and more generously than with the latter. This suggests that they somehow identified themselves and nonreligious players as belonging to the same group, no matter how loosely defined the group was. Boyer[50] suggests that disbelief is generally the result of a deliberate effort against our natural cognitive dispositions, which predispose us to faith. Maybe the rationality behind the disbelief also favors a rational categorization of the nonbelievers as a group.

One common argument for in-group cooperation among religious groups is that religions are breeding populations, so that people who pray together lay together and raise children together. There are two points that should be addressed regarding this argument. The first is that breeding situations should elicit a great amount of competition, specially directed to same-sexed rivals. Seeing fellow believers or non-believers as part of a breeding population would not, from an evolutionary point of view, favor cooperation or generosity, because at least half of that population is of the same sex and therefore would be considered reproductive rivals. That was the main reason why the sex of the virtual players was not indicated in their profiles or identifiable by their gender-neutral names. The point we make in this chapter is that generosity or cooperation was elicited by the subjects' perception that some of the virtual players belonged to the same group, and, as indicated by Hammond and Axelrod,[51] that kind of perception could promote in-group cooperation as a mechanism that favored social control of free-riders and increased the fitness of in-group members.

The second point regarding this argument refers to the fact that any biological predisposition suffers environmental modulation. In modern industrialized societies, breeding populations are much less strict than they were a few decades ago. Therefore, those who are seen as rivals or as potential partners are not as well defined as they were in the past. That is especially true in Brazil. In an informal survey we asked 136 couples, with ages varying between 18 and 65 years, what was their religion and that of their partners. We found out that 65 percent had partners that shared the same religion or absence of it. However, the high proportion of same religion marriages was due to Catholics, as the proportion decreased to 40 percent when we eliminated all Catholic subjects. Moreover, the high percentage of marriage between Catholics is probably much more an effect of their overwhelming majority in the population than to a strict preference for a partner who has the same religious beliefs. That flexibility represents a major change in breeding patterns regarding both modern populations from two to three decades ago and our hunter-gatherer ancestors from the more distant past. The psychological mechanisms regulating mate choice and breeding competition have probably not changed very much, but the range of potential mates has increased enormously, reflecting an accommodation to a new social situation. All of this is in perfect agreement with evolutionary thinking.

Our results reinforce the idea that religion facilitates identity, cohesion, and cooperation within groups. But do those characteristics explain the origin of religion, justifying its appearance during human

evolution? As previously mentioned, Bulbulia[52] suggests two evolutionary hypotheses to explain the origins of religious behavior. The
first one suggests that religion-related behaviors represent a human
adaptation within the context of social cooperation. This constitutes
an adaptationist hypothesis in that it states that religious behaviors
increased the biological fitness of those presenting them. The second
one regards religion as a by-product of the evolved mind, representing
therefore a nonadaptationist hypothesis (a spandrel hypothesis, *sensu*
Gould and Lewontin[53]).

Evidence so far is not enough to exclude either of these hypotheses.
It would be necessary to show not only that religion promoted cooperation but that religious groups were more successful than nonreligious ones. Sosis[54] compared U.S. religious and secular utopian
communes and concluded that the first were longer-lived than the former. But, as he himself points out, there are significant issues to be
addressed before taking this analysis as supportive of the adaptationist
hypothesis for the origin of religion, such as the causes for dissolution
of the communes, or the fact that religious ideologies may simply
exploit psychological mechanisms that evolved to promote intragroup
cooperation in a classic spandrel-type way.

Of course, our playing conditions were not naturalistic. For example, there were not real face-to-face interactions, which have major
effects on how humans interact with one another. Therefore, our
results are too limited to allow any overall conclusions about the origins of religion. The fact that we did not observe differences between
the overall amount of donations between Evangelicals and atheists
does not mean that their behavior would not diverge in the long term
or in more naturalistic situations, such as in tasks that would involve
their beliefs about religion or human solidarity. That remains to be
tested.

One very interesting result was that Evangelical subjects, more so
than atheists, preferentially chose similar individuals with whom to
play. However, when Evangelicals chose other players who did not
share their religious beliefs, they were equally generous in their donations. That did not happen with atheist subjects who were significantly more generous to nonreligious players than to religious ones.
These results suggest that Evangelical subjects, more so than atheist,
were more inclined to act as good Samaritans, who help other people
without considering their origins or beliefs. It is very tempting to say
that this result is not at all explicable by biological laws and that it
indicates that the lesson "love thy neighbor" promoted by many

religious groups has been well learned by Evangelicals.[55] Even evolutionary-minded thinkers, such as Matt Ridley, acknowledge that when talking about human beings the culture hypothesis can never be entirely rejected.[56] So, are we talking here of a behavior that is the result of pure environmental influences, and that these influences are so strong that they overcome our most basic biological predispositions? We do not believe so. We believe in a human nature that is extremely flexible, and therefore prone to environmental modulation. Certainly the pleadings from the church to the believers to help others has a strong effect on behavior, but that effect may be related, for instance, to the moralizing God effect described previously. Maybe religious people are, in fact, more willing to help their "neighbors" and maybe they are so because of religious education/catechization. That does not mean that religion erased our biological tendencies, but that those tendencies are not so hardwired that they cannot be changed by our experiences and culture. The moralizing God effect is an evolutionary hypothesis and many others could be proposed, but any and all of them have to be tested or they will become a "just-so-story."

Finally, we observed that the best predictor of cooperation was indirect reciprocity. Generous players received more donations by the subjects regardless of their religious affiliation or lack of it. Basically, it is reputation that attracts cooperation from others, as demonstrated by Manfred Milinski, Dirk Semmann, and Hans-Jürgen Krambeck.[57] It could be that religion affiliation worked in the past as a mark for reputation and commitment, attracting cooperation. Sosis[58] suggests that this may be true owing to the need to perform costly rituals. Again, that is something that remains to be tested.

NOTES

1. Grassie, W. (2008). The new sciences of religion. *Journal of Religion and Science, 43*(1), 127–158.

2. Axelrod, R., & Hamilton, W. D. (1981). The evolution of co-operation. *Science, 21*, 1390–1396.

3. Gaulin, S. J. C., & McBurney, D. (2001). *Psychology: An evolutionary approach*. Englewood Cliffs, NJ: Prentice-Hall.

4. Nettle, D. (1999). Language variation and the evolution of societies. In R. I. M. Dunbar, C. K. Night, & C. Power (Eds.), *The evolution of culture* (pp. 215–227). Edinburgh: Edinburgh University Press.

5. Marlowe, F. W. (2005). Hunter-gatherers and human evolution. *Evolutionary Anthropology, 14*, 54–67.

6. Dunbar, R. I. M. (1999). Culture, honesty and the free-rider problem. In R. I. M. Dunbar, C. K. Night, & C. Power (Eds.), *The evolution of culture* (pp. 194–213). Edinburgh: Edinburgh University Press.

7. Cartwright, J. (2000). *Evolution and human behavior*. London: MacMillan Press.

8. Marlowe, Hunter-gatherers and human evolution.

9. Kollok, P. (1998). Social dilemmas: The anatomy of cooperation. *Annual Review of Sociology, 22*, 183–205.

10. Sosis, R. (2000). Religion and intragroup cooperation: Preliminary results of a comparative analysis of utopian communities. *Cross-Cultural Research 34*, 70–87.

11. Grassie, The new sciences of religion.

12. Hammond, R. A., & Axelrod, R. (2006). The evolution of ethnocentrism. *Journal of Conflict Resolution 50*(6), 926–936.

13. Roes, F. L., & Raymond, M. (2003). Belief in moralizing gods. *Evolution and Human Behavior 24*, 126–135.

14. Cruz, E. R. (2004). A Persistência dos Deuses: Religião, Cultura e Natureza. São Paulo: Editora Unesp.

15. Dalgalarrondo, P. (2008). *Religião, Psicopatologia & Saúde Mental*. Porto Alegre: Editora Artmed.

16. Roes & Raymond, Belief in moralizing gods.

17. Boyer, P. (2001). *Religion explained: The evolutionary origins of religious thought*. New York: Basic Books.

18. Bulbulia, J. (2004). The cognitive and evolutionary psychology of religion. *Biology and Philosophy, 19*, 655–688.

19. Boyer, *Religion explained*.

20. Gould, S. J., & Lewontin, R. C. (1979). The spandrels of San Marco and the Panglossian paradigm: A critique of the adaptationist Orogramme. *Proceedings of the Royal Society of London, Series B, 205*(1161), 581–598.

21. Hammond & Axelrod, The evolution of ethnocentrism. See also Axelrod, R. (1984). *The evolution of cooperation*. New York: Basic Books, Inc.

22. Cashdan, E. (2001). Ethnocentrism and xenophobia: A cross-cultural study. *Current Anthropology, 42*, 760–765.

23. Kurzban, R., Tooby, J., & Cosmides, L. (2001). Can race be erased? Coalitional computation and social categorization. *Proceedings of the National Academy of Sciences, 98*, 15387–15392.

24. Boyer, *Religion explained*.

25. Kurzban, R., & Neuberg, S. L. (2005). Managing ingroup and outgroup relationships. In D.M. Buss (Ed.), *Handbook of evolutionary psychology* (pp. 653–675). New York: Wiley.

26. Sosis, R., & Ruffle, B. J. (2004). Ideology, religion, and the evolution of cooperation: Field Experiments on Israeli Kibbutzim. *Research in Economic Anthropology, 23,* 89–117.

27. Shariff, A. F., & Norenzayan, A. (2007). God is watching you. Priming God concepts increases prosocial behavior in an anonymous economic game. *Psychological Science, 18*(9), 803–809.

28. The scramble-sentence paradigm consists of the presentation of five-word sentences, dropping an extraneous word from each to create a grammatical four-word sentence. Shariff and Norenzayan used ten sentences in both situations, among them five that contained the target words "spirit," "divine," "God," "sacred," and "prophet" in the God concepts condition. They used the words "civic," "jury," "court," "police," and "contract" in the secular-prime condition.

29. There are 4,800 different religious denominations in Brazil. Centro Apologético Cristão de Pesquisas. (2003). *Religiões "Mundiais" Diferentes e Seitas Locais.*

30. IBGE. (2007). *Tendências Demográficas.* Rio de Janeiro: IBGE.

31. Internet recruitment did not result in as many subjects as we expected. So we had to recruit students to increase our sample to allow for the necessary statistics.

32. This study is in agreement with the ethical standards for human research of the CONEP (Brazilian Council for Ethics in Scientific Research).

33. The pseudonyms used were verbs in Tupi, an indigenous language spoken by native Brazilians before the Portuguese colonization. For example, *kéra,* which means "to sleep," *sema,* which means "to go out," and *kanhema,* which means "to disappear."

34. Statistical analysis of the general and initial generosity and cooperation rates of the subjects were performed using the univariate General Linear Model (GLM) test. With respect to choice of players, tokens donated to other players, and analysis of game situations, we used the multivariate GLM. In all analyses, we considered $p < 0.05$.

35. GLM; $F = 0.082$; $p = 0.775$.

36. GLM; $F = 0.256$; $p = 0.614$.

37. GLM; $F = 0.605$; $p = 0.438$.

38. GLM; $F = 11.904$; $p = 0.001$.

39. GLM; $F = 5.577$; $p = 0.021$.

40. GLM; $F = 4.328$; $p = 0.041$.

41. GLM; $F = 5.896$; $p = 0.017$.

42. GLM; $F = 4.75$; $p = 0.032$.

43. GLM; Nonreligious Opp—$F = 28,67$; $p = 0.001$; Evangelical Opp—$F = 20,76$; $p = 0.001$; Cath Opp—$F = 6,46$; $p = 0.002$

44. Shariff & Norenzayan, God is watching you.

45. Sosis & Ruffle, Ideology, religion, and the evolution of cooperation.

46. Boyer, *Religion explained.*

47. Kurzban, Tooby, & Cosmides, Can race be erased?

48. Hammond & Axelrod, The evolution of ethnocentrism.

49. Petry, A. (2007). Como a Fé Resiste à Descrença. *Revista Veja, 51*, 68–77.

50. Boyer, P. (2008). Religion: Bound to believe? *Nature, 455*, 1038–1040.

51. Hammond & Axelrod, The evolution of ethnocentrism.

52. Bulbulia, The cognitive and evolutionary psychology of religion.

53. Gould & Lewontin, The spandrels of San Marco and the Panglossian paradigm.

54. Sosis, Religion and intragroup cooperation.

55. Although nowadays the term "neighbor" has most frequently a universal meaning, it originally meant those that belonged to an in-group: a people, religion, or nation.

56. Ridley, M. (1998). *The origins of virtue*. New York: Penguin.

57. Milinski, M., Semmann, D., & Krambeck, H. J. (2002). Reputation helps solve the "Tragedy of the Commons." *Nature, 415*, 424–426.

58. Sosis, Religion and intragroup cooperation.

PART SIX

Conclusion

The preceding five parts of this book have looked at religious behavior from a descriptive, evolutionary, developmental, causal, and adaptiveness perspective. Chapter 15 in this final part summarizes some of the principles presented in the book. The chapter also fills in some of the missing pieces and tries to "whet the appetite" of some readers for further study. The chapter acknowledges the limitations of what has been done so far and offers suggestions for what needs to be done in the future.

CHAPTER 15

Conclusion

Jay R. Feierman

This concluding chapter has several objectives. The first is to cover a few biobehavioral aspects of religious behavior that were not addressed fully in the book. In keeping with the terminology developed in Chapter 2, the term "religious behavior" will mean behavior associated with the communicated acceptance of a supernatural claim.[1] The second objective is to emphasize some of the major "take home points" that have been made in the other chapters. The third objective is to encourage at least some readers to pursue a biobehavioral approach to understanding more about religious behavior. To achieve this third objective, more questions than answers will be presented. The fourth objective is to discuss what needs to be done in the future to understand more about religious behavior from a biobehavioral perspective and to suggest some ways in which this might be done. Throughout the chapter the term "God" is meant to include all deities and supernatural spirits.

In the Preface a number of examples were given of some of the ways in which religion can be good, helpful, and comforting to human beings. A new father asked God to not let his premature child die; a son felt consoled hearing his minister say that his deceased mother is now with her maker; an aged Holocaust survivor said God was all he had at that terrible time in his life; a Navajo woman wanted a traditional Navajo medicine man healing ceremony before she underwent surgery; a young Hindu Balinese man brought a gift to the temporary grave of his father. There is no doubt that these and many other examples that could have been given show how religion can be of great benefit to human beings.

However, the personal-type benefits of religion described above—such as feeling less fearful, comforted, and good—are not the types of benefits that would have allowed religious behavior to have evolved as a *direct* product of Darwinian natural selection. In order for this to have occurred, some of the structural design features that are embedded within or that are contributing causes of religious behavior would have to have conferred direct adaptive benefit to religious individuals.[2] The alternative possibility is that some structural design features that are embedded within or that are contributing causes of religious behavior evolved for something other than religion and were later co-opted (appropriated) to be a contributing cause of religious behavior at some time during human evolution.[3] The term for this type of co-opting in biology is *exaptation*. Let us look at each of these two possibilities separately.

RELIGIOUS BEHAVIOR EVOLVING DIRECTLY BY NATURAL SELECTION

It is important to emphasize that only structural design features can be adaptations,[4] whether they are genetically transmitted across generations in DNA or culturally transmitted across generations by social learning. To review, an adaptation is a structural design feature that, when possessed, improves one's reproductive success (survival value) in a specific environment. Adaptations are direct products of Darwinian natural selection. A *structural design feature* is that which has static or moving architectural mass by which it can be defined. Something, including a behavior, which is definable only by its function, can be neither a structural design feature nor an adaptation. It cannot have evolved as the result of having been a direct product of Darwinian natural selection.[5]

Most and possibly all of the world's religions contain at least one species-universal, behavioral, structural design feature. As was explained in Chapter 5, it is the make-oneself-lower-*or*-smaller-*or*-more-vulnerable behavior (*LSV behavior*)[6] associated with the nonvocal aspect of petitioning prayer. Although LSV behavior has some other functions in humans beside being used in the nonvocal component of petitioning prayer,[7] when LSV behavior is used in the context of petitioning prayer, it has two other characteristics associated with it: (1) it is not done while constantly facing another living person in close proximity (nearness), and (2) under most circumstances it is not associated with a fearful affect or expression on the praying individual's face. Therefore, when the term "LSV behavior" is used in this chapter, these two other characteristics should be presumed to be present. They help to differentiate LSV behavior in religion from its other functions in human social behavior, such as submission and female courtship.

Less culturally specific and less formalized variations of LSV behavior can also be seen in some shamanistic tribal religions.[8] It is not necessarily seen in the behavior of the shaman; rather, it is seen in the behavior of the person who is the recipient of the shaman's healing. LSV behavior can also be seen in less culturally specific and formalized variations in ancestor worship religions as individuals show reverent respect for deceased ancestors at their graves or altars.

APPETITIVE AND CONSUMMATORY BEHAVIORS

There are two related concepts in ethology, the biology of behavior, that need to be reviewed to help the reader understand how certain behaviors could have come to be associated with religion. They are *appetitive* and *consummatory* behaviors.[9] Appetitive behaviors are *proximity*-causing behaviors. When something is proximate, it is near. Proximity can be achieved in two ways: by actively searching or by staying stationary and calling. Almost all appetitive behaviors in religion are calling behaviors.[10] They include such things as the reciting or reading sacred narratives containing the Word of God,[11] congregational singing, the singing of choirs, and the excited incantations of shamans.

Appetitive behavior causes proximity to something structurally identifiable that then "releases" a specific consummatory end act.[12] A consummatory end act is a "fixed action pattern [coordinated motor pattern] that comes at the end of a series of appetitive actions."[13] A consummatory end act does not require that anything be consumed literally.[14]

Some examples of the relationship between appetitive and consummatory behaviors not associated with religion may be helpful. An animal appetitively searches (a proximity-causing behavior) for food until the food is found. Then, the food is ingested (a consummatory end act). A male songbird appetitively sings (a proximity-causing behavior) for a mating partner. Then, when she arrives in his territory and after some preparatory courtship and other behaviors, they eventually mate (a consummatory end act). Young primates, including humans, appetitively make care-eliciting, proximity-causing sounds when they are hurt. When the caregiver arrives, some type of firm bodily contact behavior, the consummatory end act of cuddling, occurs. This consummatory end act of cuddling then terminates the appetitive care-eliciting, sound-producing behavior. In a similar manner the LSV behavior associated with the nonvocal aspect of petitioning prayer is a coordinated motor pattern (Type I Behavior[15]); it is also a consummatory end act. It terminates the appetitive (proximity-causing) calling behaviors to God.[16]

The aware reader may be thinking, "What is *structurally* identifiable that when found, releases the consummatory end act of LSV behavior in the nonvocal act of petitioning prayer?" In the case of the Abrahamic God for whom structural representations are forbidden, the structure would not be found in the extraindividual environment. Could the structure that ends the appetitive search and starts the consummatory prayer be self-contained within the intraindividual environment of the human brain? If so, it would give an entirely different meaning to the words "search" and "when found." One would have to look inward, not outward, for God. The structures would be the brain structures whose functions produce what is called "transcendent consciousness." [17]

In religion, LSV behavior, which is the consummatory end act, utilizes a relatively small amount of time. This is not surprising. Food ingestion, a consummatory end act, also utilizes a relatively small amount of time. Appetitive food acquisition behaviors utilize much more time. Copulation, another consummatory end act, also utilizes a relatively small percentage of total time of sexual behaviors, which also include the appetitive behaviors used in courtship. In humans a cuddling hug, the consummatory end act that terminates the care-eliciting crying when hurt, requires less and less time as toddlers mature into small children. It eventually becomes ritualized into a quick but comforting pat on the back accompanied by some reassuring words, which the child now understands.

There are many different types of human proximity-causing appetitive behaviors. Some are very old, species-universal in form, and therefore are culturally universal. An example would be the ones used in the nonvocal aspect of human female courtship displays. Others that are also very old and species-universal in form include the behaviors that produce hums, grunts, groans, moans, sighs, screams, laughs, and cries. There are also relatively new types of behaviors[18] that are not species-universal in form, such as the ones that create locally acquired, symbolically coded speech with which to recite or read sacred narratives. Interestingly, most of the shamanistic healing ceremony sounds made by the shaman that were heard by the author in Malaysia, which will be subsequently discussed, used pre-symbolic-language, human-universal sounds. As such, the shamanistic calling sounds were more similar to the species-universal calls that are used by birds and other species to call mates, etc. The hums of the Buddhist monks during their prayerful meditations are also pre-symbolic-language, species-universal human sounds. Buddhism predates Christianity in its origin by about six centuries.[19] Could the earliest religious sounds as well as some of the earliest nonvocal religious behaviors have emerged in human evolution prior to the evolution of human language?[20]

AN EXAMPLE OF APPETITIVE AND CONSUMMATORY SHAMINISTIC BEHAVIORS

It has been proposed that the excited incantations of shamans are appetitive, proximity-causing behaviors that are calling God for the individual who is the recipient of the shaman's services. As an illustration of this, the author observed a shamanist *bomohs* performing healing ceremonies on the Malay peninsula in Malaysia. The shaman sat the person to be healed on the ground and put a soot-stained burlap cloth over the person's head. The shaman circled around the person, jumped up and down, yelled at first angrily and then appeared to suddenly cry with very labile affect. He was also perspiring profusely. He shook bones that were tied together with rope into which feathers were woven. He frequently patted the burlap cloth over the person's head. The ritual ended when he broke a chicken's egg on the burlap cloth and then very abruptly removed the cloth. The person then stood up and the next person came and sat down and had a new piece of soot-stained burlap put over his or her head. As the shaman did these various behaviors, the individuals who were the recipients of his services sat quietly on the ground with the burlap cloth over their lowered head in what could easily be described as LSV behavior.

In this religious ritual the appetitive calling behavior of the shaman and what appeared to be consummatory end behavior of the recipient were performed by two different people in close contact with one another at the same time. One person could not have done both behaviors simultaneously. However, this cooperative venture was very efficient as it took only about five minutes for each recipient to receive the shaman's services. There was a line of people patiently waiting. There was also a collection plate on the ground into which some coins were dropped after each person stood up.

EVOLUTION OF NON-LSV RELIGIOUS BEHAVIORS

As a coordinated motor pattern, LSV behavior is a structural design feature that could have evolved as a direct product of Darwinian natural selection.[21] But how could all the other non-LSV behaviors associated with religion that are acquired by social learning and that are not structural design features have evolved initially to be then passed across generations by social learning? They could not have evolved *directly* by Darwinian natural selection. Such behaviors could only have evolved indirectly by Darwinian natural selection by the neural structural design features in the brain whose current functions are the behavior's motivations. Whether the structural design features that produce religious behavior's motivation evolved for religious behavior or whether they evolved for some nonreligious behavioral function and were later co-opted for religious behavior is an open question. Either way, they could now be generating moods and feelings (i.e., emotions) that are associated with a variety of religiously motivated non-LSV behaviors. Examples of such motivations, which would be associated with inclinations to execute religiously motivated behavior, are the so-called positive emotions associated with spirituality. They include the emotions associated with faith, love, hope, joy, forgiveness, compassion, awe, and mystical illumination.[22] Interestingly, spiritually motivated behaviors may not even meet criteria previously given for religious behaviors, as they can also occur in contexts not associated with the communicated acceptance of a supernatural claim. Harvard psychiatrist George E. Valliant believes that this potential dissociation captures the difference between religion and spirituality.[23] They have areas of overlap but are not the same. For the sake of our discussion, however, let us presume that spiritual emotions occur within a religious context.

There is little written about structural design features in the brain whose functions produce religious moods and feelings (i.e., emotions) and that would then be associated with the inclination to execute a variety of non-LSV, functionally defined, religiously motivated behaviors. We are just now learning about such things as mirror neurons, which arguably can facilitate one individual empathetically experiencing the same emotions of another individual. In Chapter 10 it was shown how mirror neurons might underlie the neural basis of animism and spirit. Could they also be the structural design features that underlie the behavior-influencing spiritual emotions that make up a part of many modern religions?

Spiritual-like religious experiences may also be induced by psychoactive drugs, such as the sacramental use of peyote in the Native American Church[24] or methylenedioxymethamphetamine, also known as MDMA or "Ecstasy," which is self-reported by many individuals who use it to make them feel a sense of intimacy with others and a sense of reduced fear in nonreligious contexts.[25] There have also been human studies on the effects of the hormone and neurotransmitter oxytocin on bonding and trust behavior.[26] The importance of oxytocin's relationship to trust is, as Vaillant believes, that trust is the basis of faith.[27] In addition, neuroscientists are now measuring what the brain does when people pray or engage in spiritual meditation as measured by single photon emission computed tomography. These types of studies are just the beginning of what has been called "neurotheology,"[28] which is the study of the relationship between such things as functional brain imaging with religious experiences and their expressions. It is not to be confused with neuroethology,[29] which is the neural basis of naturally occurring behavior.

It was proposed in Chapters 13 and 14 that at least modern religion may function to promote interpersonal as well as group harmony through facilitating emotions related to prosocial altruism, cooperation, and generosity. This function of modern religion has been used to support the argument that religion evolved as the result of natural selection acting primarily at the group level where religion would have facilitated in-group cooperation. In-group cooperation would make groups that had religion more competitive with groups that did not.[30] However, the facilitation of in-group cooperation may be a function that has been taken over by modern religions rather than having been passed on from ancient religions, given that "the gods of Sumer, Egypt, Greece, and Rome ... had no interest in how humans treated one another."[31] This historical perspective supports

that religion's initial function was not to create human morality
de novo, which may appear counterintuitive to some readers. Instead,
more recent religions appear to have become its current purveyor
and enforcer.[32] In support of this perspective is the observation that
many rudiments of human morality can be found as far back as nonhuman primates.[33] Religion, as a human social institution, appears to
have culturally evolved in function as well as in form throughout
human evolution.

As previously explained, non-LSV religious behaviors could have
evolved by natural selection by co-opting structures in the brain that
evolved for other functions.[34] This is the previously explained process
of exaptation. The two most common examples of co-opted brain
structures now used for religion in the literature have to do with the
so-called hypersensitive agency detection "device" (HADD)[35] as well
as the attachment system.[36] The proponents of the HADD argue that
it evolved to detect predators, other nonpredator species (such as dangerous hoofed animals), and dangerous other humans. The attachment system evolved independently in birds and mammals to
facilitate parental-child and parental-parental affectual bonds.
According to these theories, religious individuals perceive God's presence through the HADD and have a need for God as a result of the
attachment system.

All of the co-opted theories of non-LSV religious behaviors' evolution presume that the motivations to execute these behaviors are generated by yet-to-be-discovered, structural design features (i.e., neural
tissues) in the brain. Yet, to date the objects of study, such as the
HADD "device," are only identifiable by their function. As a result,
the list of *presumed* structural adaptations in the brain whose functions
could be the objects of interest is potentially very large.[37] More
importantly, it is difficult to study presumptions or to set up ways in
which to disprove hypotheses generated by these theories, which is
usually how science advances.[38]

IMPLICATIONS OF BEING AN ADAPTATION
OR A CO-OPTED ADAPTATION FOR NON-LSV
RELIGIOUS BEHAVIOR'S EVOLUTION

There are theological implications beyond the scope of this book if
the structural design features by which non-LSV religious behaviors
could have evolved by natural selection are adaptations for non-LSV

religious behavior or just co-opted adaptations now used for non-LSV religious behavior. If non-LSV religious behaviors evolved by co-opting structural design features in the brain that evolved initially for nonreligious functions, their current functions could simply be to be good, helpful, and comforting to human beings. These could now be their primary functions even if executing religious behaviors was not beneficial to the reproductive success and survival of human beings. This possibility was discussed in Chapter 9 in terms of various religious behaviors evolving to meet "inner needs" that may have freed themselves to some degree from natural selection. However, even more interesting is the following. If the structural design features in the brain by which non-LSV religious behaviors evolved are adaptations specifically for non-LSV religious behaviors, whether natural selection pressures acted at the level of the individual or the group, then this is evidence that these structural design features are adaptations to something. What could that something be?

It is helpful to think of an adaptation as living organisms' structural response to the environment over time, which through Darwinian natural selection maximizes the organisms' reproductive success and survival in a specific environment. The Nobel Prize winning ethologist Konrad Lorenz was fond of saying that the horse's hoof (an adaptation) tells as much about the steppe (ground) upon which the horse evolved as it tells about the horse.[39] If structural design features in the brain that motivate non-LSV religious behaviors are primary and not just co-opted from a previous, nonreligious function, do they tell us something about that to which they are adapted? Can the horse's hoof's relationship to the steppe be a model for these structural design features' relationship to something, whatever that something might be?[40] These are intriguing, albeit highly speculative questions that hopefully will pique the imagination of some readers.

WHERE IS NATURAL SELECTION ACTING?

Another related and important question in the biobehavioral study of religious behavior is the level at which natural selection is acting.[41] Is it acting at the level of the individual, the social group, or both?[42] This question is important irrespective of where the structural design features associated with religious behavior are located: either embedded in LSV religious behavior itself or as neural structural design features in the brain that produce the motivation for non-

LSV religious behaviors. This is an unanswered question with evidence slowly accruing on each side of the argument. There are social policy implications for the level at which natural selection acts in terms of some of religion's historical functions in society. What would the long-term consequences be for societies without religion?[43]

RELIGIOUS BEHAVIORS AS IN-GROUP MARKERS FOR BREEDING POPULATIONS

An often overlooked aspect of religious behaviors is the degree to which they serve as in-group markers for what in biology are called "breeding populations." As was stated in the Preface, in many parts of the world individuals who pray together tend to lay together. They then have children together. This fact alone makes religious behaviors of interest biologically, as they are associated with what in biology and genetics are called positive "assortative matings." This term means that individuals with certain recognizable *phenotypes* are preferentially attracted to one another and have children together more so than by chance alone. A phenotype is the interaction of a genotype (one's genetic makeup) with the environment. All biobehavioral aspects of religion that are manifested by human beings are phenotypes.

Behavioral phenotypes are one of the main factors that differentiate one religion from the other as well as differentiating the religious community of believers from secular nonbelievers. A variety of studies that have been done on identical twins suggest that the predisposition to engage in religious behavior has culturally acquired as well as genetic determinants.[44] Behavioral geneticists have stated that "the tendency for assortative mating seems stronger for behavioral traits than for physical traits,"[45] which is why religious behaviors are good in-group markers for assortative mating for religiosity. In many but not all modern, pluralistic Western societies language, dress, and adornments are more or less the same across many religious groups.[46] Yet, individuals of the same religious affiliation tend to mate with one another preferentially. They find each other on the basis of similar behaviors and behavioral biasing beliefs and values. When they do this, they are also mating assortatively for the general trait of religiosity. They marry and have babies with other co-religious individuals more so than by chance alone.[47] When they assortatively mate for religiosity, they also are increasing the probability that their offspring, versus the offspring of two nonbelievers, will be born with a predisposition to religiosity in general. They obviously would not be born with a predisposition to a specific religion.

Assortative mating, such as religious people tending to marry and have children with other religious people, by itself cannot change gene frequencies in the larger population over time. Such marriages will not make more people religious in the larger population. It is not a mechanism by which religious behavior could have evolved directly or even indirectly by Darwinian natural selection. Assortative mating does reduce what is called *heterogyzosity* for recessive traits, where individuals in the population contain recessive genes that are carried but not expressed. Assortative mating for engaging or not engaging in religious behavior would cause the larger population to be more divided genetically. It is presumed that there are multiple genes either at different genetic loci (polygenic inheritance) or at the same genetic locus (polymorphic alleles) that predispose individuals to engage in religious behavior.[48] Assortative mating for religious behavior versus nonreligious behavior would produce a bimodal distribution of two subpopulations rather than a single normal distribution for the tendency to engage in religious behavior within the larger population. What is the significance of a bimodal distribution of, for example, the frequency of engaging in religious behavior per year in the larger population? Let us see.

Today, a wave of secularization is sweeping across parts of the Western industrialized democracies. In many parts of Western Europe individuals engaging in religious behavior are outnumbered by secularists. If people of faith, who engage in religious behavior, preferentially (i.e., assortatively) marry and have children with other people who engage in religious behavior, and if people who do not engage in religious behavior preferentially marry and have children with other similar people, then two phenotypically distinct breeding subpopulations could emerge. The genes predisposing for religiosity and nonreligiosity could become segregated bimodally within each of the two subpopulations. This scenario may be the opportunity to truly determine the adaptiveness and survival value of engaging in religious behavior, at least in a modern, pluralistic society. Is secularism the last phase in the cultural evolution of religious behavior? Or, is secularism the beginning of the end of human society as we have known it? There are many opportunities for interested individuals to study and answer these questions, which could have profound implications for humankind.

It needs to be said that the above naturalistic "experiment" has one major methodological problem. It has been widely supposed (although the evidence for the supposition is meager)[49] that religious behavior, like language, has some type of critical or sensitive period in which it must be exhibited in childhood for it to be expressed phenotypically in adulthood.[50] This would be something like the hypothetical situation of someone carrying the genes for exhibiting human symbolic language not talking in adulthood because he or she did not speak any language as a prepubertal child. There are opportunities to study these and other similar questions in the former Eastern block countries in Europe where public exhibition of religious behavior was suppressed by governments for several generations.

It is also important to appreciate that in many parts of the world people's identity comes as much or more from the types of religious behaviors they express (as well as the beliefs and values that motivate these behaviors) as from their national identity. That should not be surprising. Many of the specific religious behaviors of the world are several millennia to many centuries old. Some of the nations in which individuals who exhibit these religious behaviors reside are only a fraction that old. People also have ethnic and tribal identities that often transcend their newer national identities.[51] The ethnic and tribal identities often overlap with their religious identities. All of these factors must be considered in understanding the biobehavioral aspects of religious behavior.

THE DARWINISTIC AND ETHOLOGICAL APPROACH TO RELIGION

The contributors were aware that writing a book about religious behavior from a biobehavioral perspective was not going to easy, as many readers who are interested in religious behavior may not have a biobehavioral science background and vice versa. We were aware that some of the vocabulary and concepts that were developed in the book would be new and challenging for some readers to understand. We hope that we succeeded in explaining some rather complex concepts in ways that were understandable to the nonspecialist reader. For the specialist reader, either in religion or in the biobehavioral sciences, we provided opportunities for more in-depth study by references in the endnotes. We also hope that we succeeded in being sensitive to the issue of using Darwinism in a religious context because of the preconceived negative views of Darwinism that many religious readers may have had. We also are aware that there is room for reconciliation.[52]

THE EMERGENCE, SPREAD, AND EXTINCTION OF DIFFERENT RELIGIOUS BEHAVIORS IN SPACE AND TIME

Just as most species[53] and most languages[54] that once existed no longer exist, the same can be said for most religious behaviors.[55] Can the emergence, spread, and extinction of religious behaviors be studied like the emergence, spread, and extinction of species[56] or languages?[57] Religious behavior, like language, contains innate[58] as well as culturally acquired components. Most of the innate components of religious behavior are the structural design features in the brain that are contributing, motivational causes of the behavior. However, as reviewed in Chapter 1, we also know that religious behavior has culturally evolved and differentiated throughout human evolution. As a result of the differences in religious behaviors throughout both space and time, it is difficult to make generalizations about religious behaviors that do not have exceptions. This posed a constant challenge for the contributors. I am sure that there are some exceptions that we have failed to acknowledge.

Religious behavior and the religions to which they belong have some characteristics that currently are being studied and modeled by economists using rational choice theory. Economists study the "religious marketplace."[59] They compare the declining religious monopolies in parts of Europe with the vibrant "emerging religious marketplace" found in the United States. Whereas many industries in the world are consolidating through mergers and acquisitions, this is not the case with religion. Religions are continuing to differentiate and create new religions through New Religious Movements. Yet, at the same time, a few major religions are "gaining in market share" and are now the religions of most of the earth's inhabitants. Some appear to be spreading and growing like successful franchises in the business world. In parts of the world, such as Latin America, Evangelical and Pentecostal Christian denominations are slowly taking "market share" away from Catholicism. How does one understand such changes? Are these changes in the world's religions just an example of the human species' general propensity to grow, split, culturally differentiate, and then compete?[60]

What is the understanding of why some religious behaviors, such as seen in Judaism, do not spread to non-Jews? Yet, other religions' behaviors, such as those seen in Christianity and Islam, do spread? Think of how the Muslim prayer behavior on the knees with the forehead on the ground spreads through a population as the result of religious conversion. Just as in biology where one can see a common structure in closely related species due to a common ancestor, one can also see a common religious behavior in Jews and Muslims. A good example is the culturally influenced back and forth bowing behavior[61] as they both read sacred narratives.

What is the significance in how different religious behaviors spread? For example, it has been said that the religious behaviors associated with Christianity spread like aspen trees that send pollen in the air from one mountaintop to the other in the form of missionaries. By contrast, religious behaviors associated with Islam spread like a pine forest in which pine cones dropped from the parental generation produce a new generation of pine trees very near the parental tree.[62] These topics are very applicable for biobehavioral-type studies and analysis.

SOME TAKE-HOME POINTS FROM THE BOOK

Religious behavior was the object of our undertaking primarily because it is observable. Being observable made it easier to be that which we were trying to understand. Questions about its cultural evolution as well as what it is and how it can be recognized and distinguished from nonreligious behaviors were addressed. Whereas most religious behavior involves the body as a whole, we also learned that the eyes are an object of interest for understanding the type of relationship the religious practitioner has with God. We also were shown how religious behaviors contain patterns that are governed by mechanisms similar to the mechanisms that govern other patterns found in nature.

It was shown that when religious behavior is conceptualized as the movement of individuals, it can be defined either by its form and function (e.g., LSV religious behavior) or only by its function (e.g., non-LSV religious behavior). This distinction was used to show how non-LSV religious behavior, which is most religious behavior, could, if it increased the reproductive success of its bearers, have led to the evolution of brain structures whose functions make up what are called many parts of the human mind.[63]

A usual way of thinking about childhood and religious behavior is that religious behavior—as well as the emotions, beliefs, and values that are its contributing causes—influence childhood. However, counterintuitively, it also was shown that at least in Christianity psychological trauma may play a role in determining religious behavior. It was also shown how and why adolescence, as a stage in human development, is an important time for acquiring particular religious behaviors along with the beliefs and values that motivate them.

Mechanisms were discussed by which adaptations in the brain associated with behavioral biasing religious beliefs could "soothe the brain." It was also shown how religious behavior could be guided by "inner factors" not under the direct influence of natural selection. It was shown how some recent findings in cognitive neuroscience regarding mirror neurons can be used to understand how the emotional attribution of spirit, which influences religious behavior, could have evolved. It was proposed that new, behavioral-biasing religious beliefs and the formation of new religious movements could be mechanisms by which human groups split. The adaptive uses of fasting and feasting behaviors in religion were presented as were models and data on religion's ability to foster prosocial altruistic and cooperative behavior.

These are some of the take-home points for the reader. In some ways they resemble what we found as the result of a series of test wells that we drilled in various locations over a vast plateau. There may be much more of what is to be found in between the wells than what we found where we drilled. Keeping with the metaphor, the interested reader is offered the opportunity to continue this undertaking by drilling more wells!

WHAT MORE NEEDS TO BE DONE

We hope that the reader has learned some new things about religion in general and religious behavior in particular from the biobehavioral perspective in this book. If at least some readers are persuaded by the perspective's usefulness to pursue the understanding of religious behavior further, then we would have achieved at least one of our goals. The perspective used in the book has been narrow in one respect. We concentrated on religious behavior. However, it has been a broad perspective in another respect. We stepped back and looked at religious behavior in general rather than any specific religion's behavior in particular. This perspective is quite different from the religion-specific perspective with which most people who are religious see their own religious behavior. We hope that this broader perspective was helpful, especially in allowing the reader to put particular religious behaviors with which they are familiar into a more general context. In the future, subject-matter experts on particular religious behaviors need to deductively test the degree to which some of the generalities created in the book at the broad level fit or do not fit the behaviors associated with particular religions.[64]

The Biology of Religious Behavior has only been able to present a fragmentary overview of some of the many potential applications of the biobehavioral sciences to the understanding of religious behavior. One of the goals of this application was to advance our knowledge of religious behavior so that we can better appreciate what different religions have in common. Hopefully, this appreciation will help to bridge the religious divide, which is so dangerously dividing the world. We sincerely hope that we have had some success in this endeavor.

NOTES

1. This is the definition of religious behavior that was developed in Chapter 2.

2. Feierman, J. R. (2009). How some major components of religion *could* have evolved by natural selection. In E. Voland and W. Schiefenhövel (Eds.), *The biological evolution of religious mind and behavior*. New York: Springer-Verlag. Also, beyond the scope of this chapter are such concepts as self-organization in relation to natural selection. See Batten, D., Salthe, S., & Boschetti, F. (2008). Visions of evolution: Self-organization proposes what natural selection disposes. *Biological Theory, 3*(1), 17–29.

3. Feierman, How some major components of religion *could* have evolved by natural selection.

4. Williams, G. C. (1966). *Adaptation and natural selection: A critique of some current evolutionary thought*. Princeton, NJ: Princeton University Press.

5. A behavioral characteristic that can be defined only by its function can "have adaptiveness" if, when executed, there is an increase in the reproductive success or survival of the individual that executes the behavior. Natural selection would not be selecting for the specific behavior per se. Rather, natural selection would be acting on a structural result or outcome of the behavior as well as the nonmovement structural design features in the brain that are motivational causes of the behavior.

6. Note the conjunction "or" is used, rather than the conjunction "and." An individual has to exhibit only one of these three possibilities to be exhibiting LSV behavior.

7. These other functions for LSV behavior are submission and what is called proceptive courtship behavior in women when they flirt.

8. This is the personal observation of the behavior of a shaman in Malaysia by the author.

9. Eibl-Eibesfeldt, I. (1970). *Ethology: The biology of behavior*. New York: Holt, Rinehart and Winston.

10. The exceptions to religious appetitive behaviors being proximity-causing calling behaviors are long religious pilgrimages and shorter religious processions, sometimes done on one's knees, which bring one into close proximity to a sacred place.

11. Repeating the Word of God has the effect of calling God with familiar words.

12. Eibl-Eibesfeldt, *Ethology: The biology of behavior*.

13. Immelmann, K., & Beer, C. (1989). *A dictionary of ethology* (p. 86). Cambridge, MA: Harvard University Press. The synonym is "end act." Nothing has to be "consumed" literally in a consummatory act.

14. Even though "consummatory" derives from the Latin *summa*, which means a total or sum, in classical ethological theory of motivation, the consummatory end act "consumed" the energy propelling the appetitive actions.

15. A Type I Behavior is a behavior that is definable by form and function in a natural environment and is species-universal in form. Examples include such things as smiling and walking. More was said about Type I and Type II Behaviors in Chapter 5. Synonyms of Type I Behaviors are coordinated motor patterns, fixed action patterns, and modal action patterns.

16. As explained in more detail in Chapter 5, the consummatory end act of petitioning prayer relieves fear and anxiety, which are physiological states of the praying individual. The dissipation of fear and anxiety can be one of the motivations for the consummatory end act associated with the nonvocal aspect of petitioning prayer. The mechanism by which LSV behavior could reduce fear and anxiety also is discussed in Chapter 5. There can also be other functions of LSV behavior.

17. See Mandell, A. J. (1980). Toward a psychobiology of transcendence: God in the brain. In R. J. Davidson & J. M Davidson (Eds.), *The psychobiology of consciousness* (pp. 379-464). New York: Plenum Publishing. Also, see Canton, H. (1986–1987). Psychobiology as self-transcendence. *Krisis* (5–6), 136–147, in which he states, " 'God' is an affect of the drive-arrest-release sequence actioned by psychotropic neurotransmitters in the temporal lobe limbic structures" (p. 143). It would be those structures that, when accessed, result in the search-ending consummatory act. See also Newberg, A., d'Aquili, E., & Rause, V. (2001). *Why God won't go away. Brain science and the biology of belief*. New York: Ballantine Books. These neuroscientists

have shown by single photon emission computed tomography that when people meditate they have decreased blood flow to the posterior superior parietal lobe, an area of the brain that keeps track of the you/not-you dichotomy. As a result, "the brain would have no choice but to perceive that the self is endless and intimately interwoven with everyone and everything else the mind senses" (p. 6). This may be what allows one the sense of communion with God.

18. As explained in Chapter 5, behaviors that produce spoken (as well as written) symbolic human language are Type II Behaviors (describable by form and definable by function in a natural environment and not species-universal in form).

19. Interestingly, Buddhists display LSV behavior to statues of the Buddha when they pray for enlightenment.

20. The "talking in tongues" in some Pentecostal Christian religions may be a vestigial remnant of such pre-symbolic-language sounds.

21. Feierman, How some major components of religion *could* have evolved by natural selection.

22. Vaillant, G. E. (2008). *Spiritual evolution: A scientific defense of faith*. New York: Broadway Books.

23. Ibid.

24. Steward, O. C. (1987). *Peyote religion: A history*. Normal, OK: University of Oklahoma Press.

25. Greer, G., & Tolbert, R. (1986). Subjective reports of the effects of MDMA in a clinical setting. *Journal of Psychoactive Drugs, 18*(4), 319–327. Note that this study was done before MDMA was made a controlled substance. The health risks of MDMA are not known.

26. Kosfeld, M., et al. (2005). Oxytocin increases trust in humans. *Nature, 435*, 673–676.

27. Valliant, *Spiritual evolution: A scientific defense of faith*.

28. Newberg, d'Aquili, & Rause, *Why God won't go away*. See also Runehov, A. L. C. (2007). *Sacred or neural: The potential of science to explain religious experience*. Göttingen: Vandenhoeck & Ruprecht; Seybold, K. S. (2007). *Explorations in neurosciences, psychology, and religion*. Burlington, VT: Ashgate, Aldershot; Beauregard, M., & O'Leary, D. (2007). *The spiritual brain: A neuroscientist's case for the existence of the soul*. New York: Harper One.

29. Camhi, J. M. (1984). *Neuroethology: Nerve cells and the natural behavior of animals*. Sunderland, MA: Sinauer.

30. Wilson, D. S. (2002). *Darwin's cathedral: Evolution, religion, and the nature of society*. Chicago: The University of Chicago Press.

31. Stark, R. (2008). The complexities of comparative research. *Interdisciplinary Journal of Research on Religion, 4*, 2–15 [3].

32. See the computer simulation in Chapter 13 that supports this function for religion.

33. De Waal, F. B. M. (1996). *Good natured: The origins of right and wrong in humans and other animals.* Cambridge, MA: Harvard University Press.

34. Another way of conceptualizing a brain structure being co-opted for another function at a more general level is that "Religion is not an evolutionary adaptation per se, but a recurring cultural by-product of the complex evolutionary landscape that sets cognitive, emotional, and material conditions for ordinary human interactions." Atran, S., & Norenzayan, A. (2006). Religion's evolutionary landscape: Counterintuition, commitment, compassion, communion. *Behavioral and Brain Sciences, 27*(6), 713–730 [713].

35. Barrett, J. L. (2004). *Why would anyone believe in God.* Walnut Creek, CA: AltaMira Press.

36. Kirkpatrick, L. A. (2005). *Attachment, evolution, and the psychology of religion.* New York: Guilford.

37. In evolutionary psychology this is called "massive modularity." See Tooby, J., & Cosmides, L. (1992). The psychological foundations of culture. In J. Barkow, L. Cosmides, and J. Tooby (Eds.), *The adapted mind.* New York: Oxford University Press. Massive modularity, which is essentially a "theory about mind," also has its critics. See Samuels, R. (1998). Evolutionary psychology and the massive modularity hypothesis. *The British Journal for the Philosophy of Science, 49*(4), 575–602.

38. See, for example, the review by Oviedo, L. (2008). Steps towards a cognitive science of religion. *Zygon, 43*(2), 385–393.

39. Lorenz, K. (1977). *Behind the mirror: A search for a natural history of human knowledge.* New York: Harcourt Brace Jovanovich.

40. This could be a yet-to-be-developed argument for God's existence. However, the argument is predicated upon the structural design features associated with religion having evolved directly for religion and not just having been co-opted by religion after having evolved for some other function.

41. Wilson, *Darwin's cathedral: Evolution, religion, and the nature of society.*

42. The level of selection issue relates to whether there is more variance in the extinction rates in individual humans, who are members of groups, or in the groups themselves over time. In social mammals under most circumstances there is more variance in the extinction rates in individuals than in the groups to which they belong. Yet, selection may still be operating at the group level at the same time as it is acting at the individual level but just to a lesser degree.

43. The relationship of religion to prosocial group altruism and to co-operation and generosity was discussed in Chapters 13 and 14.

44. Bouchard, T. J., Jr., McGue, M., Lykken, D., & Telegren, A. (1999). Intrinsic and extrinsic religiousness: Genetic and environmental influences. *Twin Research, 2*, 88–99. See also Bradshaw, M., & Christopher, G. E. (2008). Do genetic factors influence religious life: Findings from a behavior genetic analysis of twin siblings. *Journal for the Scientific Study of Religion, 47*(4), 529–544.

45. Ehrman, L., & Parsons, P. A. (1976). *The genetics of behavior* (p. 158). Sunderland, MD: Sinauer Associates, Inc.

46. Some religious groups, such as Muslims, often have clothing styles, especially for women, which serve as obvious in-group markers in pluralistic societies. However, there are other more subtle articles of clothing, such as head coverings for Muslim and orthodox Jewish men. Even more subtle is jewelry, such as wearing a small cross around the neck for Christian women. In many modern pluralistic societies one's religion is not obvious by one's day-to-day public behavior, clothing, or adornments.

47. Marrying someone of the same religion, who is therefore religious, is an example of assortative mating (preferential mating based on the phenotype of religiosity in general) as well endogamy (preferential marrying someone of the same religious in-group in particular). Assortative mating for religiosity in general but not endogamy for marrying someone of the same religion is what can segregate genes in a larger population into two subpopulations. In this case the genes being assorted into two subpopulations would be the genes that underlie general aspects of religiosity.

48. Reviewed in Saler, B., & Ziegler, C. A. (2006). Atheism and the apotheosis of agency. *Temenos, 42*(2), 7–41.

49. See Gera, D. L. (2003). *Ancient Greek ideas on speech, language, and civilization.* Oxford, U.K.: Oxford University Press, for a discussion of King Frederick II of Hohenstaufen, who in the eighteenth century is alleged to have had a child raised without exposure to language, as previously mentioned in Chapter 7.

50. There is a folklore that says Sigmund Freud, Margaret Mead, and the Jesuits all knew that things learned in early life have a lasting impression on one throughout life. We do know that when a language is learned after puberty, one always speaks this new language with an accent from one's mother tongue. Yet, any language learned prior to puberty can be spoken as a native.

51. Eibl-Eibesfeldt, I., & Salter, F. K. (1998). *Ethnic conflict and indoctrination: Altruism and identity in evolutionary perspective.* New York: Berghahn Books.

52. See Barbour, I. G. (1966). *Issues in science and religion.* New York: Prentice-Hall; Ruse, M. (2005). *The evolution-creation struggle.* Cambridge, MA: Harvard University Press; Dowd, M. (2007). *Thank God for evolution: How the marriage of science and religion will transform your life and our world.* New York: Viking/Plume.

53. Ehrlich, P. R. (1985). *Extinction: The causes and consequences of the disappearance of species.* New York: Ballantine Books.

54. Harrison, K. D. (2007). *When languages die: The extinction of the world's languages and the erosion of human knowledge.* New York: Oxford University Press.

55. Channa, S. M. (Ed.). (2002). *International encyclopedia of tribal religions*. New Delhi: Cosmo Publications.

56. Eisenberg, J. F. (1981). *The mammalian radiations: An analysis of trends in evolution, adaptation, and behavior*. Chicago: The University of Chicago Press. Also see Rolston, H., III. (1999). *Genes, Genesis, and God*. Cambridge: Cambridge University Press.

57. Ruhlen, M. (1996). *The origin of language: Tracing the evolution of the mother tongue*. New York: Wiley.

58. Bouchard, McGue, Lykken, & Telegren, Intrinsic and extrinsic religiousness.

59. Young, L. A. (1997). *Rational choice theory and religion: Summary and assessment*. New York: Routledge.

60. Alexander, R. (1979). *Darwinism and human affairs*. Seattle: University of Washington Press.

61. The bowing behavior that Jews and Muslims engage in as they read sacred narratives is an LSV behavior, as by bowing they are making themselves lower.

62. This simile of how Islam spreads differently from Christianity was told to me by Wulf Schiefenhövel, a human ethologist/anthropologist who has worked in the highlands of western New Guinea (Irian Jaya, Indonesia) with the Eipo people for many decades. Another simile is that Islam spreads like lava flow as it moves through a geographical area. The classic example of this is how Islam spread from north to south through the large island of Java in Indonesia between the thirteenth and sixteenth centuries by assimilating the previously Buddhist and Hindu inhabitants. However, Muslim immigrants are also now moving into pluralistic but predominantly Christian Western societies.

63. Religion may have increased the brain's symbolic capacity. This is a counterintuitive proposition that is an alternative to the more intuitive proposition of Steven Pinker, who in writing about the evolutionary psychology of religion suggested that "religious psychology [may be] a by-product of many parts of the mind." See Pinker, S. (2006). The evolutionary psychology of religion. In P. McNamara (Ed.), *Where God and science meet: How brain and evolutionary studies alter our understanding of religion. Volume 1, Evolution and the religious brain* (p. 8). Westport, CT: Praeger. For the counterintuitive proposition to be correct, the structural design features whose functions make up many parts of the human mind would have had to have been direct products of natural selection for religion and not co-opted for religious use from some other function for which they would have evolved. The originator of the by-product theory of religion is Boyer, P. (2001). *Religion explained: The evolutionary origins of religious thought*. New York: Basic Books.

64. Subject-matter experts on particular religions might find this book helpful in the following ways: (1) testing exceptions to different religions' adapting to socioecological contexts, (2) testing the universality of

acceptance of a supernatural claim as a defining feature of religious behavior, (3) testing exceptions to eye behaviors in particular religions, (4) finding no religious-specific pattern of behavior, (5) finding religions in which no LSV behaviors are executed, (6) finding religions where sacred narratives are not influenced by childhood experiences, (7) finding religions not acquired in adolescence, (8) finding religions with no behavioral biasing beliefs, (9) finding religions not internally guided by religious feelings, (10) finding religion in autistic persons whose mirror neuron functions are impaired, (11) finding new religious movements started without new beliefs, (12) finding religions that do not include fasting or feasting rituals, (13) finding no correlation between religion and in-group prosocial altruism, and (14) finding no correlation between religion and out-group generosity.

About the Editor and Contributors

THE EDITOR

Jay R. Feierman received a B.S. in Zoology from Pennsylvania State University and an M.D. from the University of Pennsylvania. He did post-doctoral psychiatric residency training at Washington University in Saint Louis and the University of California at San Diego. He now is retired as Clinical Professor of Psychiatry at the University of New Mexico, where he was on the faculty for 30 years. He is a past Fellow of the American Psychiatric Association and former President of the Psychiatric Medical Association of New Mexico. For many years he was a consultant for personnel security to the United States National Nuclear Security Administration and Adjunct Instructor at the Non-Proliferation and National Security Institute. He was a medical consultant for behavioral health issues for Roman Catholic priests for close to 20 years and has been the psychiatric medical director of two hospitals in New Mexico as well as the New Mexico Department of Corrections. He has authored a number of scientific articles as well as two other edited volumes on the application of behavioral biology to issues of social concern: *The Ethology of Psychiatric Populations* (Supplement 3, 1987, Ethology & Sociobiology) and *Pedophilia: Biosocial Dimensions* (1990). He lives in a small village in New Mexico with his wife, two children, their spouses, and five grandchildren—life's dessert.

THE CONTRIBUTORS

Benjamin J. Abelow is an independent scholar of religion. He holds a B.A. in History from the University of Pennsylvania and an M.D. from Yale Medical School, where he also taught on faculty. He has presented his work at academic conferences in the United States and Europe. benjamin.abelow@gmail.com; www.benjaminabelow.com.

Candace S. Alcorta is an evolutionary anthropologist specializing in the behavioral ecology and neurophysiology of religion. Dr. Alcorta has conducted ethnographic fieldwork in Thailand and the United States on adolescent religious involvement and resilience. She is currently a Research Scientist in the Department of Anthropology at the University of Connecticut.

Rochele Castelo-Branco is a biologist and a Ph.D. student at the Psychobiology Graduate Program, Universidade Federal do Rio Grande do Norte, Brazil. She studies Primate Cognition and, more recently, Evolutionary Psychology.

Thomas B. Ellis (Ph.D., University of Pennsylvania) is Assistant Professor of Religion in the Department of Philosophy and Religion at Appalachian State University in Boone, North Carolina. He specializes in the religious and philosophical traditions of South Asia, employing primarily psychology and biology in his research.

Ryan M. Ellsworth is a graduate student in the department of anthropology at the University of Missouri–Columbia. His current research focuses on the application of evolutionary biological theory to religious behavior as well as the testing of alternative definitions and evolutionary explanations of religion.

Rick Goldberg, an independent scholar, is the founder of Binah Yitzrit Foundation. B.Y.F. develops scholarly work exploring religion, especially Judaism, from an evolutionary perspective. Goldberg is the editor of a new book, *Judaism in Biological Perspective* (2008), that interprets biblical lore and Judaic practices from the perspective of extant biological theory.

Klaus Jaffe graduated in Chemistry from the Universidad Simón Bolívar, studied Biochemistry at the Instituto Venezolano de Investigaciones Científicas, and obtained a Ph.D. from the University of Southampton. He studies the evolution of societies using methods from chemistry, biology, physics, sociology, anthropology, and computer sciences. At present he coordinates the Doctoral Program of Interdisciplinary Science at USB.

Monique Leitão has graduated in Psychology and is a Ph.D. student at the Psychobiology Graduate Program, Universidade Federal do Rio Grande do Norte, Brazil. She investigates human cognition, future discounting, and religious behavior from an evolutionary perspective.

Fívia de Araújo Lopes graduated in Psychology from Universidade Federal do Rio Grande do Norte, Brazil. She obtained a Psychobiology Ph.D. from the same university. At present she is assistant professor of Evolutionary Psychology and the vice-coordinator of the Psychobiology Graduate Program, Universidade Federal do Rio Grande do Norte, Brazil.

Magnus S. Magnusson received Copenhagen University's Silver Medal and Ph.D. in Psychology, 1983. His professional experiences include Deputy Director, Anthropology Laboratory, Museum of Natural History, Paris, 1984–1988, and Invited Professor in Psychology and Ethology, University of Paris and the Sorbonne. Since 1991, he has been Research Professor, founder & director, Human Behavior Laboratory, University of Iceland; DNA analysis project co-director, 2002–2004; and the Co-editor of *The Hidden Structure of Interaction: From Neurons to Culture Patterns* (2005).

Michael T. McGuire graduated from the University of California at Berkeley with a B.S. and from the University of Rochester with an M.D. Postdoctoral training was done at Harvard. Subsequently he matriculated to the University of California at Los Angeles (UCLA) where he spent his career investigating the behavior and brain chemistry of nonhuman primates.

Lluis Oviedo was born in Ontinyent (Spain) in 1958. He completed studies in Philosophy and Theology in Valencia and Rome. He has a doctorate from Gregoriana University (Rome) with a thesis on secularization. He is full professor of Theological Anthropology and Interdisciplinary Issues in Religion, Society and Science at Antonianum and Gregoriana Universities in Rome.

Craig T. Palmer earned a Ph.D. in Cultural Anthropology from Arizona State University in 1988. He is currently Associate Professor of Anthropology at the University of Missouri. His primary fieldwork site is in Newfoundland, Canada. His research focuses on incorporating cultural traditions into evolutionary explanations of human social behavior.

John S. Price is retired from psychiatric practice in the U.K. National Health Service. Previously he worked for the Medical Research Council, in the Psychiatric Genetics Research Unit and in the Clinical Research Centre. For many years he was European Editor of the ASCAP (Across Species Comparisons and Psychopathology) Newsletter. Visit www.johnprice.me.uk.

Stephen K. Sanderson is a sociologist at the University of California, Riverside. He is the author or editor of ten books, the most recent of which is *Evolutionism and Its Critics: Deconstructing and Reconstructing an Evolutionary Interpretation of Human Society* (2007). His major research focus is currently the long-term evolution of religion.

Lyle B. Steadman earned a Ph.D. from the Australian National University in 1972. He is currently Professor Emeritus of the School of Human Evolution and Social Change at Arizona State University. His primary fieldwork site has been with the Hewa of Papua New Guinea. His main interests are kinship, religion, and the evolution of traditions.

Lionel Tiger is the Charles Darwin Professor of Anthropology at Rutgers University. He has been co-research director of the Harry Frank Guggenheim Foundation and has lectured widely in many universities. Among his books are *Men in Groups; The Imperial Animal* (with Robin Fox); *Optimism: The Biology of Hope; The Manufacture of Evil; Ethics, Evolution and The Industrial System; The Pursuit of Pleasure; and The Decline of Males.* He lives in New York City.

Burgess C. Wilson holds a B.A. in Art History from Stanford University, and an M.D. from Northwestern University Medical School. He is a psychiatrist on the clinical faculty at Rush University and is in private practice. He has presented at a number of academic conferences regarding the relationship between inanimate objects and religion.

Maria Emília Yamamoto is a full professor at Universidade Federal do Rio Grande do Norte, Brazil. She is an evolutionary psychologist investigating cooperation and group coalition and currently coordinates a research network, the Millenium Project, that involves scientists from various Brazilian universities.

Luis Zaballa is a law graduate and career diplomat, currently posted as Scientific and Cultural Attaché to the Spanish Embassy in Venezuela. He is a member of the International Society of Human Ethology and President of the Spanish Society of Biosocial Studies. He has authored several articles on the evolutionary basis of human society, as well as the book *Polis: A Natural History of Society* (2003).

Index